INNOVATIONS AND CHALLENGES IN LANGUAGE LEARNING MOTIVATION

Innovations and Challenges in Language Learning Motivation provides a cutting-edge perspective on the latest challenges and innovations in language learning motivation, incorporating numerous examples and cases in mainstream psychology and in the field of second language acquisition. Drawing on over three decades of research experience as well as an extensive review of the latest psychological and SLA literature, Dörnyei provides an accessible overview of these cutting-edge areas and covers novel topics that have not yet been addressed in L2 motivation research, such as:

- fundamental theoretical questions such as mental time travel, ego depletion, psychological momentum and passion, and how the temporal dimension of motivation can be made consistent with a learner attribute;
- key challenges concerning the notion of L2 motivation, ranging from issues about the nature of motivation (e.g. trait, state or a process?) and questions surrounding unconscious versus conscious motivation, the motivational capacity of vision, and long-term motivation and persistence;
- highly practical classroom-specific challenges such as how technological advances could be better integrated in teachers' repertoires of motivational strategies.

This distinctive book from one of the key voices in the field will be essential reading for students in the field of TESOL and Applied Linguistics, as well as language teachers and teacher educators.

Zoltán Dörnyei is Professor of Psycholinguistics at the School of English, University of Nottingham, UK. He has published extensively on various aspects of language learner characteristics and second language acquisition, and he is the (co-)author of over 90 academic papers and 25 books.

INNOVATIONS AND CHALLENGES IN APPLIED LINGUISTICS

Series Editor:

Ken Hyland is Professor of Applied Linguistics in Education at the University of East Anglia and Visiting Professor in the School of Foreign Language Education, Jilin University, China.

Innovations and Challenges in Applied Linguistics offers readers an understanding of some of the core areas of Applied Linguistics. Each book in the series is written by a specially commissioned expert who discusses a current and controversial issue surrounding contemporary language use. The books offer a cutting-edge focus that carries the authority of an expert in the field, blending a clearly written and accessible outline of what we know about a topic and the direction in which it should be moving.

The books in this series are essential reading for those researching, teaching, and studying in Applied Linguistics.

Titles in the series:

Innovations and Challenges in Applied Linguistics from the Global South
Alastair Pennycook and Sinfree Makoni

Innovations and Challenges in Language Learning Motivation
Zoltán Dörnyei

Innovations and Challenges: Women, Language and Sexism
Carmen Rosa Caldas-Coulthard

www.routledge.com/Innovations-and-Challenges-in-Applied-Linguistics/book-series/ICAL

INNOVATIONS AND CHALLENGES IN LANGUAGE LEARNING MOTIVATION

Zoltán Dörnyei

Routledge
Taylor & Francis Group

LONDON AND NEW YORK

First published 2020
by Routledge
2 Park Square, Milton Park, Abingdon, Oxon OX14 4RN

and by Routledge
52 Vanderbilt Avenue, New York, NY 10017

Routledge is an imprint of the Taylor & Francis Group, an informa business

© 2020 Zoltán Dörnyei

The right of Zoltán Dörnyei to be identified as author of this work has been asserted by him in accordance with sections 77 and 78 of the Copyright, Designs and Patents Act 1988.

All rights reserved. No part of this book may be reprinted or reproduced or utilised in any form or by any electronic, mechanical, or other means, now known or hereafter invented, including photocopying and recording, or in any information storage or retrieval system, without permission in writing from the publishers.

Trademark notice: Product or corporate names may be trademarks or registered trademarks, and are used only for identification and explanation without intent to infringe.

British Library Cataloguing-in-Publication Data
A catalogue record for this book is available from the British Library

Library of Congress Cataloging-in-Publication Data
A catalog record has been requested for this book

ISBN: 978-1-138-59914-7 (hbk)
ISBN: 978-1-138-59916-1 (pbk)
ISBN: 978-0-429-48589-3 (ebk)

Typeset in Bembo
by Newgen Publishing UK

CONTENTS

Series editor's preface   *vii*

    Introduction: The ever-changing landscape of language learning motivation research   1

1   Fundamental challenges I: The conceptualisation of 'motivation'   4
    Challenge 1: What is motivation: a trait, a state or a process? 4
    Challenge 2: How can we conceptualise motivation in a process-oriented manner? 9
    Challenge 3: Is it possible to distinguish motivation from affect and cognition? 14
    Challenge 4: Conscious versus unconscious motivation 15

2   Fundamental challenges II: Motivational dynamics   21
    Challenge 5: How to account for the context of motivation 21
    Challenge 6: The issue of different timescales 32
    Challenge 7: The interference of multiple parallel goals 36
    Challenge 8: How to handle the dynamic complexity of motivation 41

3   Fundamental challenges III: Motivation applied   50
    Challenge 9: Motivation and SLA 50
    Challenge 10: How to enhance motivation meaningfully, without carrots and sticks 53
    Challenge 11: How can we measure a dynamic concept such as motivation? 65

4　Research frontiers I: Unconscious motivation　　　　　　　　　　76
　　Human agency and its unconscious limits 77
　　Unconscious goal setting and goal pursuit 84
　　Dual-process theories and the interaction of the conscious and the
　　　　unconscious mind 87
　　Researching unconscious motivation 88
　　Summary 96

5　Research frontiers II: Vision　　　　　　　　　　　　　　　　　100
　　What is vision? 101
　　Applications of vision in the social sciences 109
　　How does vision motivate? 115
　　Vision and L2 motivation 123
　　Summary 128

6　Research frontiers III: Long-term motivation and persistence　　136
　　High-octane motivational fuel: 'Self-concordant vision' 137
　　Limiting energy depletion through energy saving 139
　　Regenerating energy 1: Lessons from 'directed motivational currents' 142
　　Regenerating energy 2: Lessons from 'psychological momentum' 145
　　Augmenting energy with positive emotionality 151
　　Motivational breakdown cover: Persistence and self-control 153
　　Summary 161

　　Conclusion　　　　　　　　　　　　　　　　　　　　　　　　166

Author index　　　　　　　　　　　　　　　　　　　　　　　　*169*
Subject index　　　　　　　　　　　　　　　　　　　　　　　　*176*

SERIES EDITOR'S PREFACE

Applied Linguistics investigates real-world problems involving language. As such it involves both academic study and lived experience, mediating between theory and practice and attempting to reconcile opposed interests and perspectives. Encompassing issues as diverse as speech pathologies, language teaching and critical literacy, this is a socially accountable discipline which seeks to better understand and intervene in practical issues. It is a field central to understanding society and human responses to it.

The *Routledge Innovations and Challenges in Applied Linguistics Series*, as its name suggests, seeks to tap into the large and growing interest in this area through a number of topic-based books focusing on key aspects of applied linguistics. Unlike many series, however, it does not set out to provide another overview of the field or detailed analysis of a single study. Instead, each book offers a strong personal view by a recognised expert of where the field is heading in a specific area. Volumes in the series give an accessible and structured overview of each area as a context for the topic, while the main part of the book takes up and develops this topic with a personal and cutting-edge perspective which points the way forward. Where necessary, to capture the diversity of a current and controversial issue, topics will be addressed by several authors in an edited collection. In every case, though, books in the series discuss a current and controversial issue surrounding contemporary language use and are authored/edited by leading authorities.

There are, in sum, five main goals guiding this series:

1. The series will address issues of contemporary concern in applied linguistics and related areas and offer *cutting-edge* theories, approaches, methodologies and understandings to those issues.
2. Authors in the series will bring their *own perspectives* to issues rather than simply offering a general overview of the topic.

3. The series will be *comprehensive*. Each issue will be treated thoroughly and critically, taking account of various approaches, issues and problems but always looking forward.
4. Each book will be *reader-friendly* with numerous examples and described cases and these will be closely related to research and theory.
5. All the books in the series will emphasise *connectivity*, helping readers understand the relationships between theory, research and how language works in the real world.

The books, then, blend a clearly written and accessible outline with an appreciation of an expert's take on the field. Each is written for those keen to learn more and delve more deeply into a topic by understanding what we know of a field, where it is heading, and the challenges involved. We hope that the titles will generate discussion and debate within the academic community and will be read by teachers and researchers as well as by postgraduate students.

Ken Hyland
University of East Anglia

INTRODUCTION

The ever-changing landscape of language learning motivation research

'Motivation' as a technical term has been introduced in the social sciences to refer to the psychological foundation of any human behaviour or thought, subsuming all the factors that shape what we do or think. The notion is a prime candidate for a discussion within the current series on *Innovations and Challenges*, because, as will be shown in the following chapters, challenges in the domain abound, resulting in an ongoing succession of creative innovations both in mainstream psychology and in the field of second language acquisition (SLA). The most fundamental of the challenges concerns the conceptualisation of motivation itself, questioning whether the notion is meaningful at all: because human behaviour is influenced by a very wide range of factors – from external motives, such as rewards and punishments (the 'carrot' and the 'stick'), to various types of internal needs, beliefs, interests and desires – one may rightly wonder whether the term has too many meanings and is therefore not very useful in a scientific sense; in fact, according to Walker and Symons (1997), there was indeed a point when the American Psychological Association considered replacing the word as a search term in its main psychological database, *Psychological Abstracts*, for this very reason.

We can easily see the psychologists' dilemma: does it make sense to have a single notion associated with as disparate targets as one's love of food, money, work, family, freedom or faith, to mention only a few? And can indeed a single notion explain acts that we do out of fear, out of duty, out of joy or out of conviction? One wonders. Yet, there is something compelling about the concept of motivation, and we can mention at least three reasons why it was never abandoned in psychology: (a) it has definite *intuitive appeal*: people use it widely in a variety of everyday and professional contexts without the slightest hint that there should be a problem with its meaning; (b) it is not an abstract notion but a *tangible* and *discernible phenomenon*: people simply know and feel when they are motivated and also when they are not (a topic that will be discussed further in Chapter 1); (c) when we observe people, the *difference* between the motivated and the unmotivated is *obvious*. Thus, motivation appears to have profound relevance to human experiences and affairs, and as Richard Ryan (2012) explains, it is also a distinguishing feature of research conducted in the social sciences in contrast to investigations in the natural sciences:

> Motivation is a problem unique to life scientists. Indeed it is the organized nature of actions that separates the life sciences from the physical sciences, where organized, purposive, behaviour does not occur, and where entropy is the dominant force. Instead, in the life sciences, and in the understanding of human behaviour, the core interest is in discovering the bases of the neg-entropic, coherent, and integrated efforts of individuals as they pursue specific goals and outcomes.
>
> *p. 5*

Within the social sciences, motivation has specific relevance for educators, because an area where the impact of motivation – or the lack of it – is particularly salient is *student learning*. In fact, according to Danziger (1997), it was the expansion and rationalisation of educational systems in Europe and the US at the beginning of the twentieth century that gave a large push to interest in motivational matters. At that time, in order to understand individual differences between more and less successful students, scholars first turned to the notion of intelligence – producing as a result the first instrument in this area, the Binet-Simon Intelligence Scale, as early as 1905 – but it was soon realised that student underachievement cannot always be blamed on cognitive abilities, as some of its antecedents are related to the learners' lack of commitment. In accordance with this observation, as Danziger explains, the first book to have 'motivation' in its title was Wilson and Wilson's (1916) *The Motivation of School Work*, and in the Preface of this volume the authors stated:

> The most difficult phase of teaching is not acquiring the necessary information nor controlling the class, but it is discovering problems and motives for the work that will make it appeal to and interest the pupils. This book is designed to furnish concrete help of a fundamental kind in solving this daily problem of every teacher.
>
> *p. iv*

Thus, over the past century the notion of motivation has proved to be indispensable and it is therefore here to stay. This, however, raises the question of how such a multi-faceted notion should be conceptualised to meet scientific criteria. The first three chapters of the current book ("Fundamental challenges 1–3") address this issue by presenting 11 basic challenges concerning the notion of motivation, accompanied by 'innovations', that is, attempts in the field to respond to these challenges. Then, the second half of the book will zoom in on three specific areas that I believe are particularly topical at the current stage of development of our field – unconscious versus conscious motivation; long-term motivation and perseverance; and vision – with a chapter devoted to each ("Research frontiers 1–3"). The discussion of most of the topics is relatively self-contained (and possible links and cross-references are marked), which allows for selective reading, skipping some less relevant parts when time is at a premium (as it so often is).

References

Danziger, K. (1997). *Naming the mind: How psychology found its language*. London: Sage.
Ryan, R. M. (2012). Motivation and the organisation of human behavior: Three reasons for the reemergence of a field. In R. M. Ryan (Ed.), *The Oxford handbook of human motivation* (pp. 3–10). New York: Oxford University Press.
Walker, C. J., & Symons, C. (1997). The meaning of human motivation. In J. L. Bess (Ed.), *Teaching well and liking it: Motivating faculty to teach effectively* (pp. 3–18). Baltimore, MD: Johns Hopkins University Press.
Wilson, H. B., & Wilson, G. M. (1916). *The motivation of school work*. Boston, MA: Houghton Mifflin.

1

FUNDAMENTAL CHALLENGES I

The conceptualisation of 'motivation'

The first set of fundamental challenges to be discussed concerns the very nature of motivation. It was said in the Introduction that the notion has intuitive appeal, and its frequent use in day-to-day communication does not seem to cause any misunderstandings. However, in contrast to this problem-free situation in everyday parlance, when it comes to describing precisely what the term signifies in scholarly discourse, opinions diversify at an alarming rate. Indeed, the meaning of the concept can span such a wide spectrum that one sometimes wonders whether people are talking about the same thing at all. For example,

- motivation has been seen as a stable individual difference variable – that is, a *trait* – but also as a transient *state* characteristic;
- it has been described as a *personal attribute* but also as a *process* that is in constant flux, going through ebbs and flows;
- it has been referred to both as *affect* (emotion) and *cognition*;
- it has traditionally been treated as a *conscious* variable – that is, something we are aware of – yet there has been increasing evidence of the impact of *unconscious* motives on human behaviour.

This chapter addresses these challenging issues one by one. Some of the discussion will be followed up in the next chapter focusing on the dynamic nature of motivation, and the topic of unconscious motives will be analysed in detail in Chapter 4.

Challenge 1: What is motivation: a trait, a state or a process?

When people refer to someone in everyday communication as 'motivated,' they usually mean a relatively stable characteristic; that is, a sentence such as *"Geraldine is a motivated student"* implies a steady, ongoing and general commitment, rather than a transient, temporary state. Yet, if we look at our fictitious Geraldine more closely, we shall find that she is unlikely to display her motivation evenly across all the subject matter at school; instead, she will be keen in certain areas but far less committed in others, and there might even be aspects of her learning that she neglects. This being the case, we can view motivation in two different ways: as a relatively enduring disposition (i.e. 'trait') that is largely task-independent (after all, Geraldine *is* a more motivated learner than Jim, full stop) and as a more task-dependent, situation-specific 'state' that is transitory and temporary (e.g. a new job opportunity has recently increased Jim's flagging motivation no end). The trait–state distinction has been a well-rehearsed understanding in psychology, applied to many aspects of human personality, from emotions (e.g. state vs. trait anxiety) to motivation. Yet if we look more closely at this dichotomy, it does not really *explain* what a personal characteristic such as motivation is, but merely gives descriptive labels to two different and in fact somewhat contradictory aspects of it. So, the challenge is to decide which one is true of L2 motivation.

In addition to the trait–state dilemma, if we consider the situational dependence of motivation (e.g. the emerging new job opportunity in Jim's case), we cannot but take the logical step and recognise that similar to how situations can rapidly evolve, so can motivation. Even our reliable Geraldine might lose some of her commitment after, say, she has received some disappointing test results, and she may also be less keen on school on a Friday afternoon than earlier in the week. Such insights have led scholars to the conclusion that it may be more profitable to conceive of motivation as an ever-changing 'process' with regular ebbs and flows than as an attribute. This, however, raises again the question of what motivation really is: a trait, a state or a process?

Innovation 1: McAdams's 'New Big Five' theory of personality

The dominant approach of describing human attributes in psychology has been centred around 'individual differences' (IDs), that is, features that mark a person as a distinct and unique human being. IDs have been conceptualised as broad dimensions that are applicable to everyone and that are *stable* in that they exhibit continuity over time. Thus, they have been understood as *trait-like characteristics*. In accordance with this approach, as described by Dörnyei and Ryan (2015; see also Dörnyei, 2017), around the end of the twentieth century a consensus emerged in the field of personality psychology with regard to the main dimensions of human personality, resulting in the 'Big Five' model, which was made up of five broad personality traits: Openness, Conscientiousness, Extraversion-Introversion, Agreeableness and Neuroticism-Emotional Stability (e.g. Costa & McCrae, 1985, 2008; Goldberg, 1992). This construct has stood the test of time both from a theoretical and a measurement perspective, and it also has general, intuitive appeal: as Sheldon (2004) rightly points out, humans have an inherent propensity to describe people in trait terms and to produce personality profiles of others in this manner (e.g. *"Roderick is a hardworking, reliable and sociable person"*).

6 The conceptualisation of 'motivation'

While the Big Five construct has proved its usefulness in many areas, it did not offer any real explanation for the widely observed within-subject variation (i.e. when the same person displays different characteristics in different situations), and it was thus mostly silent about the trait–state dichotomy. A major innovation in this respect was presented by Dan McAdams's 'New Big Five' model (e.g. McAdams & Pals, 2006), which includes five layers, of which the three middle levels are of particular interest for our current purpose. These constitute, in effect, a three-tier framework of personality:

(a) *Dispositional Traits*, referring to relatively stable and decontextualised broad dimensions of individual differences.
(b) *Characteristic Adaptations*, referring to constructs that are highly contextualised in time, place and/or social role, and which include "motives, goals, plans, strivings, strategies, values, virtues, schemas, self-images, mental representations of significant others, developmental tasks, and many other aspects of human individuality" (p. 208).
(c) *Integrative Life Narratives*, referring to "internalized and evolving life stories that reconstruct the past and imagine the future to provide a person's life with identity (unity, purpose, meaning)" (p. 212).

Looking at the three tiers, it becomes immediately obvious that the model was not intended to replace but to complement the 'old' Big Five construct, as it does *not* reject the classic notion of personality traits but rather suggests that individual differences occur at different levels of situatedness. Indeed, Dispositional Traits involve stable personality dispositions that explain consistencies perceived in behaviour across situations and over time, and thus include the main components of the Big Five model. The next tier of the framework, Characteristic Adaptations, concerns more situated propensities, that is, contextualised aspects of individuality that interact with specific environmental conditions (e.g. when someone is more anxious in certain situations than in others, as in stage fright). We may place many of the variables investigated in classic ID paradigms on this level of personality, and this separation of traits and more situated characteristics has been a strength of the New Big Five model. The real innovation of the model, however, has been the addition of its third tier, Integrative Life Narratives. This refers to a highly personal organisational framework – broadly speaking, a personal story or account – that people develop for themselves on the basis of their unique idiosyncratic experiences in order to help them to make sense of their lives. In many ways, therefore, this component of the New Big Five model can be understood to constitute a person's *narrative identity*. As Dörnyei and Ryan (2015) explain,

> the addition of the novel narrative dimension accounts for a so far overlooked level of the self, whereby people organize and understand their experiences and memories in the form of autobiographical stories and thus, we may say, they *narrate themselves into the person they become*. The quality of personal life

stories, therefore, is seen to constitute a crucial aspect of why and how people differ from each other.

pp. 12–13; emphasis in the original

McAdams et al. (2004) have expressively summarised the essence of the interrelationship of the three tiers as follows: "If dispositional traits sketch an outline and characteristic adaptations fill in some of the details of human individuality, then internalized life stories speak to what a person's life may mean in the overall" (p. 762). Accordingly, the three tiers can be seen as three layers of description, and this implies that learner characteristics do not have to be assigned exclusively to one level or the other, but can be relevant to all the three spheres of the model at the same time; for example, Şimşek and Dörnyei (2017) have shown that anxiety has meaningful manifestations at the trait, the state and also at the narrative levels. We should note here that McAdams's model enriches not only the understanding of personality in this way but also the measurement procedures associated with it: while trait researchers have traditionally employed quantitative surveys with large respondent samples, narrative psychologists have typically relied on in-depth qualitative, idiographic studies.

In sum, the New Big Five model offers some novel theoretical guidance on the age-old trait–state distinction in psychology. It, however, has less explanatory power regarding the *process-oriented nature* of motivation; while the notion of narrative identity is to some extent relevant to change in that a person can re-narrate his/her disposition (see below), this is not a comprehensive account for the ever-changing nature of motivation. Further explanation on that matter will be offered when we discuss Challenge 2 below concerning time, but let us first look at the motivational implications of the model.

Innovation 2: Motivational implications of the New Big Five model

A useful way of demonstrating the relevance of McAdams's three-tier conceptualisation of personality is through identifying its motivational implications. Let us consider each layer of the New Big Five model one by one.

Dispositional Motivational Traits

At the genesis of modern psychological research on motivation in the 1950s, the pioneers of the classic notion of achievement motivation, John Atkinson and David McClelland, presumed the existence of trait-like motivational dispositions (for an intriguing personal account by Atkinson's most famous doctoral student, Bernard Weiner, see Weiner, 2019). The construct Atkinson studied most, 'need for achievement,' was conceptualised in this vein, and was assumed to display itself across all areas of life. However, such a trait-like conception became problematic when researchers increasingly recognised that need for achievement does not impact every achievement-related situation equally (McClelland, Koestner &

Weinberger, 1989). Yet, while a similar conclusion can be drawn about most trait-like qualities, it still remains the case that some attributes do appear to be more consistent than others. Sheldon (2004) explains, for example, that some dispositions have biological/genetic underpinning – that is, "physiological and biological regularities built into the person's brain and nervous system" (p. 68) – and he also points out that enduring ways of thinking, feeling and being motivated often emerge in people in response to formative experiences and reinforcements in their childhood as part of their developmental history. Accordingly, Sheldon notes, stable motivational tendencies of this kind – sometimes referred to as 'chronic motives' – should be included amongst the personality traits.

The main point for the current discussion is that assuming a somewhat 'flexible' notion of a trait is in accordance with McAdams's multi-layered understanding of personality. A 'trait-like' disposition can be seen in this sense as the source of a tendency for a repeated impulse to do something, and the nature of the specific situation and the person's other life concerns will determine the extent to which this impulse will express itself (see e.g. McClelland et al., 1989). Besides need for achievement, two further examples of such a 'trait-like' disposition that have been discussed recently both in the psychological and the SLA literature are *mindsets* (e.g. Dweck & Yeager, 2018; Lou & Noels, 2017; Ryan & Mercer, 2012; Waller & Papi, 2017) – a topic we shall return to later (CHALLENGE$_{10}$/INNOVATION$_4$) – and motivational inclinations related to *approach–avoid* tendencies and the related *promotion versus prevention-specific regulatory focus* (e.g. Browman, Destin & Molden, 2017; Han & McDonough, 2018; Heggestad & Kanfer, 2000; Papi, 2018).

Characteristic Motivational Adaptations

Student motivation in instructional settings has typically concerned motives that can be linked to the Characteristic Adaptations layer of McAdams' model, because many of the learners' thoughts and actions are guided by motivational stimuli associated with their immediate learning environments: educational situations and conditions can incentivise learning in many ways, giving rise to motivational demands and surges, which in turn will interact with people's more enduring domain-general motivational orientations discussed above (see e.g. Browman et al., 2017). Indeed, as already cited, the notion of motivation has been specifically highlighted by McAdams and his colleagues when describing this personality dimension: "Included at this level are constructs such as current concerns and strivings, goals and motives, defensive and strategic operations, conditional patterns, and other constructs that are contextualized in time, place, or social role" (2004, p. 762).

Integrative Motivational Life Narratives

One strength of the third layer of the New Big Five model is that *Integrative Life Narratives* can be seen as a mediating link between the first two levels, offering an explanation of how people navigate the various situational demands in relation to their more established motivational dispositions. The personal narratives that people form for themselves can offer a coherent framework to organise and manage the multiple pulls and pushes that they encounter in their daily lives. Browman et al. (2017) argue that the self-knowledge that people develop to categorise and process the critical psychological features of various situations can be understood as sets of distinct identities, and this is in full accordance with McAdams' proposal of a *narrative identity*, that is, "a person's internalized and evolving life story, integrating the reconstructed past and imagined future to provide life with some degree of unity and purpose" (McAdams & McLean, 2013, p. 233). It has been found that the clarity and coherence of a personal narrative is closely associated with the pursuit of self-relevant goals (Wong & Vallacher, 2018), which implies that by improving their self-narratives, people can enhance their motivation.

Motivational narratives have not been subject to much research either in mainstream psychology or SLA yet, but the extensive study of *attributions* is directly relevant to them; motivational attributions are, in effect, personal narratives explaining past successes and failures. Humans have an almost unstoppable proclivity to analyse themselves and to understand why something has happened, and attribution theory (e.g. Weiner, 2019) stipulates that future action will depend on the quality of these explanations: for example, past failure that is ascribed to stable and uncontrollable factors such as low ability (e.g. *"I failed because I am too stupid"*) hinders future achievement behaviour more than failure that is ascribed to unstable and controllable factors (i.e. ones that the learner can change, such as effort; e.g. *"I didn't pass the test because I hadn't prepared enough for it"*).

Challenge 2: How can we conceptualise motivation in a process-oriented manner?

As seen above, McAdams's New Big Five model offers a useful theoretical framework to understand the trait–state distinction observed in learner characteristics, but it has only limited explanatory power regarding motivational *change, evolution* and *fluctuation*. This is not a unique shortcoming limited to this particular model but is typical of psychology's handling of time in general; as Dörnyei, Henry and Muir (2016) have argued, psychological theories have traditionally displayed a certain amount of *unease* about relating motivation to time, as a result of which *temporal aspects* of motivation have been rather overlooked in theorising. The curious aspect of this neglect is that it has not been due to a lack of recognition of the significance of the issue. To the contrary: in their classic volume on *Motivation and Education*, Pintrich and Schunk (1996) defined motivation as "the process whereby goal-directed activity is instigated and sustained" (p. 4). This emphasis on the process aspect of motivation could not have been any clearer, yet the field as a whole (including Pintrich and Schunk themselves) has by and large ignored its implications for actual research. This happened despite the fact that people in applied contexts, such as workplaces or classrooms, know all too well that motivation is not constant

10 The conceptualisation of 'motivation'

but displays continuous ebbs and flows as people go through good and bad patches, with a wide range of circumstances and events having the potential to impact their motivation both in positive and negative ways. In SLA, one of the first scholars to highlight the issue of motivational change was Ema Ushioda (1996) when she argued that even within the duration of a single L2 course, most learners would experience a fluctuation of their enthusiasm/commitment, sometimes on a day-to-day basis; as she concluded, "within the context of institutionalised learning especially, the common experience would seem to be motivational flux rather than stability" (p. 240).

One reason why a static perspective on motivation has been so prevalent is undoubtedly the issue mentioned already with regard to the trait–state distinction (CHALLENGE$_1$), namely that humans have an inherent propensity to describe people in terms of more static attributes and to produce personality profiles of others without usually acknowledging any transience in this respect. Psychology, however, has gone against folk wisdom in several areas in the past, so why not here? Why have theories been so ineffective at accounting for temporal processes in human motivation? The answer is partly related to the traditional view of motivation as the *antecedent* of action. As we have seen earlier, the concept of motivation was originally introduced in psychology to represent the initial disposition and force that creates direction and energy for the behaviour that is to follow. According to this understanding, then, the time element is not part of the core motivation concept but concerns only the behavioural outworking of motivation: to put it broadly, first there is motivation proper and what happens after is its behavioural consequence.

A second factor contributing to the time challenge is the fact that 'change,' by definition, concerns ongoing variability, and the potentially wide-ranging variability related to change in time is difficult to capture in a rigorous scientific manner. This challenge has deterred many scholars in the past, but the current impasse is slowly being broken: Innovation 1 below concerns process models of motivation which started to appear as early as the 1980s, and Innovations 2 and 3 present some further theoretical attempts in motivational psychology to 'capture time.' The next chapter, then, will address a major ongoing shift in the social sciences – the introduction of a dynamic systems perspective – that has explicitly foregrounded the understanding of time scales and change patterns. Finally, the concluding chapter of this book (Chapter 6) will address recent efforts in different strands of psychology to offer a better account of *long-term motivation* and *persistence* in behaviour.

Innovation 1: Process models of motivation

The first serious theoretical attempt to account for the temporal development of motivation was Heinz Heckhausen's 'Rubicon Model' (for an English summary, see Heckhausen, 1991), which was extended into a more detailed 'Theory of Action Control' by Heckhausen and Kuhl (1985) and then into the 'Mindset Theory of

The conceptualisation of 'motivation' 11

Action Phases' by Gollwitzer (1990) (for an overview, see Achtziger & Gollwitzer, 2008). The theory is in effect a step-by-step description of how action develops from initial planning through a number of transitional phases. Heckhausen and Kuhl divided up the action sequence into three main stages, *preactional*, *actional* and *postactional*, which are associated with processes of deliberation/planning, action and evaluation, respectively. An important element of this division is that each phase is associated with a unique *mindset* that activates different motives. This aspect was further developed for the purpose of understanding SLA by Dörnyei and Ottó (1998), who followed Heckhausen and Kuhl's principles and proposed a three-phase process model:

- *Preactional Stage.* Motivation needs to be generated and the motivational dimension related to this initial phase can be referred to as *choice motivation*, because it involves the selection of the goal/task to be pursued.
- *Actional Stage.* The generated motivation needs to be actively maintained and protected while the particular action lasts. This motivational dimension has been referred to as *executive motivation*, and it is particularly relevant to learning in classroom settings, where students are exposed to a great number of distracting influences, such as off-task thoughts, irrelevant distractions from others, anxiety about the tasks or physical conditions that make it difficult to complete the task.
- *Postactional Stage.* The final phase, *motivational retrospection*, follows the completion of the task and concerns the learners' retrospective evaluation of how things went. The way students process their past experiences in this retrospective phase will determine the kind of activities they will be motivated to pursue in the future.

Our model offered an elaborate description of the main motivational functions and influences associated with each phase, thereby producing a kind of flow chart of motivational evolution. It received indirect validation by the fact that Dörnyei (2001) provided a comprehensive set of motivational strategies divided up into clusters according to the three phases of the model; however, the model was never empirically tested, and while it successfully integrated a wide range of motivational factors that affect the student's learning behaviour in classroom settings, its theoretical foundation soon raised questions. These will be addressed in the next chapter (CHALLENGE$_7$/INNOVATION$_1$).

Innovation 2: Other theoretical attempts to 'capture time'

Process models attempted to offer a comprehensive account of motivational evolution through time, but they did not represent the only paradigm available to capture the time element in relation to motivation. The common feature of the following time-related theories is that rather than modelling the temporal development of motivation as a whole, they focus only on certain key principles. Three such 'partial' theories will be discussed here, *contingent path theory*, *time perspective* and the study of *velocity in goal pursuit*. The first specifies how the steps of a sequence of motivated behaviour (e.g. advancement along a career path) build on each other to best effect; the second describes individual differences in how people relate to the future; the third addresses the motivational impact of 'velocity,' that is, how fast one is approaching the motivational target.

Contingent path theory

Contingent path theory (also called 'step-path theory') (Raynor, 1974; Raynor & Entin, 1983; Raynor & Roeder, 1987) grew out of classic achievement motivation theory (e.g. Atkinson & Raynor, 1974) and is based on the principle that a series of tasks can be linked together in a chain by the fact that successful achievement in one task is necessary to earn the opportunity to perform the next (i.e. to continue along the pathway). Thus, a *contingent path* is made up of consecutive steps – for example, someone takes an exam to be able to carry on studying towards further exams and eventually a degree – with each successful step leading to the next. The principal idea behind this theory is that a properly constructed contingent pathway can intensify an individual's success orientation for the future. It was potentially an important, forward-pointing theoretical initiative to add such a temporal axis to an ongoing course of action, yet the approach never really took off the ground and it is fair to conclude in retrospect that it failed to produce any noteworthy results.

This is a curious case, though, because the main components of the theory – which Raynor and Entin (1983) call 'path characteristics' – all make perfect sense: the number of steps in a path; the time to complete a step; the difficulty of attaining the outcome of a step; the value of the outcome of a step; the sequence of steps in terms of their difficulty; the linkages between steps in terms of earning the opportunity to move from step to step; the number of steps taken relative to the number to be taken; and whether the final step is fixed or changing. The reason why this paradigm has not had a more salient impact on the field is likely to be the way in which these variables have been treated: Raynor and his colleagues followed the standard approach of classic achievement motivation theory by assigning simple numerical values to the various path characteristics and then including these into mathematical equations. This allowed them to prove some basic principles, for example that the number of steps in a contingent path increase the amount of aroused achievement motivation, or that the increase of the anticipated time spent on the path has a negative effect. However, in the absence of more creative ideas, the approach was never picked up by other scholars, even though the principle of path contingency had further mileage in it. Indeed, action sequences linked together in a coherent chain by their *interdependence* has re-emerged again recently under the rubrics of 'psychological momentum' and 'directed motivational currents,' both of which will be discussed in detail in Chapter 6 when describing long-term motivation.

Time perspective

The notion of *time perspective* is a theoretical approach that has been around in mainstream psychology since the 1980s (e.g. DeVolder & Lens, 1982) but gained momentum only over the past 15 years. It concerns individuals' general disposition and personal understanding regarding the future, based on the observation that people tend to differ in this respect: some people seem to be more concerned with the past, some with the present, while some others attach increased importance to the future (e.g. Zimbardo & Boyd, 1999). The reason for the popularity of this theory is that the relatively stable orientation at its centre affects people's present actions and has discernible practical implications: it has been repeatedly shown (e.g. Kauffman & Husman, 2004) that *future-oriented* students tend to be more persistent and obtain better overall academic results in the present. This is because learners who are able to link their current behaviour with its future implications are more willing and resolute when engaging in non-interesting yet essential activities than their present-oriented peers (who are guided by factors related to the here and now). Moreover, people with a longer or deeper 'future time perspective' tend to formulate longer-term goals and can be motivated by anticipated but rather distant events (Lens & Seginer, 2015).

While future time perspective is clearly an important individual difference factor regarding motivation to reach future targets, Lens and Seginer (2015) are right in pointing out that it is a relatively simple construct, concerning only the question of how far into the future people project their goals and aspirations. This basic formula has recently been extended by also taking into account the characteristics of the *content* of future-oriented thinking (e.g. degree of realism and clarity of the objectives) as well as the *emotional valence* one has about the future (e.g. looking at the future in an optimistic or confident way) (Janeiro et al., 2017). Perhaps even more importantly, future time perspective has been increasingly used as an independent variable in research designs that aim at understanding factors related to long-term perseverance such as grit (e.g. Fong & Kim, in press) and resilience (e.g. Göllner et al., 2018) (to be discussed in Chapter 6).

Motivational velocity

Velocity has been used in connection with goal pursuit to indicate the *rate* at which people approach their goals, and thereby the rate they reduce their distance from them. Thus, the notion reflects the speed of a person's movement towards (or away from) a salient goal. Carver and Scheier (1990, 2013) have suggested that how one perceives this movement determines the person's emotional response; while insufficient progress causes negative affect (e.g. anxiety or frustration), rapid progress causes positive emotions (e.g. satisfaction). In this way, as Lawrence, Carver and Scheier (2002, p. 799) conclude, "affect ties the goal-related aspect of motivation to the dimension of time." In support of the velocity–emotion link, Chang, Johnson and Lord (2010) present evidence that relates employee satisfaction to velocity in real workplaces, and in a longitudinal educational study, Elicker et al.

(2010) have demonstrated that velocity uniquely contributes to the prediction of students' performance satisfaction. One important consequence of this capacity is that velocity – that is, the rate of reducing the discrepancy between where someone is and where the person would want to end up – can *compensate* for the size of the discrepancy: even when the target seems to be more distant, a sufficiently high progress rate can maintain a positive, expectant stance in the individual. Just like future time perspective, velocity is also a relatively simple measure, but it has been used as a building block for the conceptualisation of the notion of 'psychological momentum,' which will be discussed in Chapter 6.

Challenge 3: Is it possible to distinguish motivation from affect and cognition?

While motivation has traditionally been treated as an 'affective' variable, almost all influential contemporary motivation theories in psychology are in fact cognitive in nature (e.g. by including as a key component the appraisal of a task or a situation, which is a primary cognitive function); as we shall see in Chapter 5 (under the rubric of 'Vision and emotions'), affective (i.e. emotional) issues rarely feature on motivation research agendas. When I explored the psychological foundation of SLA in a book-length overview (Dörnyei, 2009), one of the surprises was the lack of any clarity in the literature on this issue. A closer scrutiny revealed that motivation, like most higher-order mental functions, involves a *blended* operation of cognitive, affective and motivational components. Mayer, Chabot and Carlsmith (1997) claimed over 20 years ago that "the differences among motivation, affect, and cognition become paper thin" (p. 32), and this observation has gained further support in neuropsychological research; for example, Crocker et al. (2013, p. 2) conclude that "Cognitive, emotional, and motivational processes are implemented by overlapping networks of regions that play various roles depending on the task/context." In other words, from a neurobiological point of view motivation is hardly distinguishable from cognition or affect, and Buck (2005, p. 198) has accordingly famously concluded that "In their fully articulated forms, emotions imply cognitions imply motives imply emotions, and so on." This, however, poses a serious challenge: if cognition, emotion and motivation are so intricately intertwined, is it still possible to determine where to draw the line between them? In other words, does it still make any theoretical sense to distinguish motivation from cognition and affect?

Innovation: A phenomenological account

It was mentioned in the Introduction that even though it may be difficult to define motivation precisely or to distinguish it scientifically from other mental dimensions in an abstract sense, it remains a personally *discernible* phenomenon: people simply know and feel when they are motivated or when they are not. This kind of account is *phenomenological* in nature, as it relies on *experiencing*, and this phenomenological approach can be extended to distinguishing motivation from affect and cognition: although a neuropsychological view of the networked neural architectures of the brain supports an integrated approach to conceptualising higher-order mental functions, on a phenomenological basis it *is* possible to separate 'wanting' (motivation) from 'feeling' (affect) and 'thinking' (cognition). In fact, from an everyday human perspective this issue seems to be totally arbitrary: although thoughts and feelings can lead to motivation, people simply 'know' which one is which. And taking the phenomenological approach further, the three notions – motivation, cognition and affect – are associated with different consequences: the 'wanting' aspect of motivation is linked to goal associations, the 'feeling' aspect of affect to well-recognisable emotional states, whereas thoughts (cognition) are not gradable in terms of their intensity – as are motivational and emotional states in the sense that you can be slightly motivated/happy or incredibly motivated/happy – which is why they have sometimes been referred to as the 'cold intellect.' Thus, there is something fundamental about the tripartite division of human mental functioning according to motivation, cognition and affect, and indeed, this division can be traced back in history as far as Plato (see e.g. Matthews & Zeidner, 2004; Mayer et al., 1997; Scherer, 1995).

Interestingly, cutting-edge neurobiological research seems to have produced findings that support the distinction between motivation and affect. The renowned neuroscientist, Kent Berridge, has for example argued that although the established view at the end of the last century was that 'wanting' and 'liking' – his way of referring to motivation and some aspects of affect – were merely "two semantic sides of the same psychological coin" (2018, p. 5), both animal and human studies now suggest a definite neurobiological distinction. Apparently, a lot rests in this argument on a chemical neurotransmitter, dopamine, which conveys the signals between nerve cells: laboratory studies showed that dopamine mediated 'wanting' but not 'liking' food, because, as Berridge summarises, blockading dopamine in various ways (e.g. by antagonist drugs or dietary-induced reductions) reduced people's subjective wanting to consume more food, but it did not reduce their subjective liking ratings for food pleasure. This points to the conclusion that hedonic and motivational mechanisms are distinct in the brain.

Challenge 4: Conscious versus unconscious motivation

The issue of unconscious motivation will be addressed in detail in Chapter 4, so here the discussion will be limited to providing a brief history of this area and outlining some of its inherent challenges. As we shall see, the subject of conscious versus unconscious motivation is such a cutting-edge development in mainstream psychology that no established strategies or solutions have emerged yet, and within the field of SLA fewer than a handful of papers have touched upon this subject. The reason for the paucity of research is not that people have had doubts about the existence of at least some unconscious motives. While most humans would probably maintain that they are more or less aware of the reasons for their behaviours – an assertion whose validity we shall examine in Chapter 4 – few would disagree with the claim that sometimes our unconscious mind directs us to do things in a way that we cannot fully explain. Whether we ascribe such less-than-rational episodes to intuitions, habits, long-forgotten but (perhaps unexpectedly) resurfacing memories or deep-seated desires does not change the fact that they do occur sometimes and take us by surprise. Also, subconscious motives constituted a central issue back at the genesis of motivation research at the beginning of the twentieth century, as illustrated for example by the work of Sigmund Freud on the role of dreams and instincts.

So, what happened? Why did unconscious motivation disappear from the research scene and why did it then re-appear a hundred years later? As Baumeister and Bargh (2014) explain, although Freud and his followers made a persuasive case that people are not fully aware of all the causes of their actions, and thus made the 'subconscious' metaphor part of everyday parlance, the onset of behaviourism in psychology (starting in the 1910s) relegated this line of enquiry from academic psychology to the clinical psychological domain as something that is only relevant to psychotherapy. As a result, early theories of motivation that had been influenced by Freud's emphasis on deep, pervasive drives and instincts went out of fashion.

The cognitive revolution that eclipsed behaviourism around the 1960s did not provide fertile ground for the study of non-cognitive, unconscious motives either, and therefore it was only after the heyday of cognitive psychology, in the 1990s, that voices arguing for the inclusion of unconscious motivation into research paradigms started to gain volume. In 1986, Weiner still wrote that "for the typical and prevalent aspects of being – that is, considering how life is spent and what is reflected upon – direct access to the determinants of motivation and emotion is quite possible" (p. 285), and accordingly, he concluded, "For most of us at most times, a royal road to the unconscious is less valuable to the motivation researcher than the dirt road to consciousness" (ibid). However, ten years later we find a transformed zeitgeist, as evidenced, for example, by Sorrentino's (1996, p. 635) conclusion: "We have an incomplete picture of what determines information processing and performance if we do not look at both conscious and nonconscious forces as they interact with each other." This position was affirmed by Eccles, Wigfield and Schiefele's (1998, p. 1074) summary of the field in the *Handbook of Child Psychology* – "As we approach the 21st century, the role of ... less conscious processes is re-emerging as a central theme" – and add another 15 years and in the concluding chapter of the *Oxford Handbook of Human Motivation*, Ryan and Legate (2012) assigned unconscious issues top priority in research:

> Perhaps the most widely cited future direction that emerged was, at least for us, a somewhat surprising one. Mentioned more than any other area for future research was investigations of dual-process [i.e. conscious vs. unconscious] models or more study of the distinctions and relations between automatic, or implicit, and deliberative, or explicit, goals. The fact that this interest emerged in so many papers reflects motivation researchers' *renewed interest in nonconscious processes* and the motivated behaviour they can organize. We

would add to this the strong interest in the dynamic nature of motivation, as implicit and explicit processes can operate congruently or be in conflict.

p. 563; emphasis added

The current climate is highly favourable for researching unconscious motivation: one of the main proponents of the approach, John Bargh, is now senior professor at Yale University, and the fact that in 2014 he co-authored a substantial review article on "Conscious and unconscious: Toward an integrative understanding of human mental life and action" with Roy Baumeister, one of the most ardent champions of conscious self-regulation (e.g. Baumeister & Vohs, 2007; Vohs & Baumeister, 2011), indicates that the study of unconscious motivation has reached the psychological mainstream. Indeed, as the two scholars state,

> We, the authors of this chapter, have found ourselves on opposite sides of debates about several important questions, including the efficacy of conscious thought and the scientific viability of free will ... Whatever we may have thought and seemed to say in the past, at present we both think that most human behaviour comes from a blend of conscious and unconscious processes working together to meet the person's critical needs and facilitate important goal pursuits.
>
> *Baumeister and Bargh, 2014, pp. 35, 46*

Such an emerging agreement concerning the joint operation of conscious and unconscious processes does not mean, however, that the challenges posed by unconscious motives have been eliminated. Far from it. Questions abound about the collaboration between the conscious and the unconscious mind in general, and about what roles the two processes play in guiding human behaviour in particular. There are, for example, sharp disagreements in the scholarly community about which is ultimately in charge of human action: the conscious or the unconscious? Researchers also face considerable challenges concerning how unconscious attitudes, goals and motives can be identified and investigated, given that the particular person who beholds them is actually unaware of them. These and other matters will be further discussed in Chapter 4.

References

Achtziger, A., & Gollwitzer, P. M. (2008). Motivation and volition in the course of action. In J. Heckhausen & H. Heckhausen (Eds.), *Motivation and action* (2nd ed., pp. 272–295). Cambridge: Cambridge University Press.

Atkinson, J. W., & Raynor, J. O. (Eds.). (1974). *Motivation and achievement.* Washington, DC: Winston & Sons.

Baumeister, R. F., & Bargh, J. A. (2014). Conscious and unconscious: Toward an integrative understanding of human mental life and action. In J. W. Sherman, B. Gawronski & Y. Trope (Eds.), *Dual-process theories of the social mind* (pp. 35–49). New York: Guilford Press.

Baumeister, R. F., & Vohs, K. D. (2004). *Handbook of self-regulation: Research, theory, and applications*. New York: Guilford Press.

Berridge, K. C. (2018). Evolving concepts of emotion and motivation. *Frontiers in Psychology*, 9(1647), 1–20.

Browman, A. S., Destin, M., & Molden, D. C. (2017). Identity-specific motivation: How distinct identities direct self-regulation across distinct situations. *Journal of Personality and Social Psychology*, 113(6), 835–857.

Buck, R. (2005). Adding ingredients to the self-organizing dynamic system stew: Motivation, communication, and higher-level emotions – and don't forget the genes! *Behavioral and Brain Science*, 28(2), 197–198.

Carver, C. C., & Scheier, M. F. (1990). Origins and functions of positive and negative affect: A control-process view. *Psychological Review*, 97(1), 19–35.

Carver, C. C., & Scheier, M. F. (2013). Self-regulatory perspectives on personality. In I. B. Weiner, N. W. Schmitt & S. Highhouse (Eds.), *Handbook of psychology* (2nd ed., Vol. 5, pp. 119–139). Hoboken, NJ: Wiley.

Chang, C.-H. D., Johnson, R. E., & Lord, R. G. (2010). Moving beyond discrepancies: The importance of velocity as a predictor of satisfaction and motivation. *Human Performance*, 23, 58–80.

Costa, P. T. Jr., & McCrae, R. R. (1985). *The NEO personality inventory manual*. Odessa, FL: Psychological Assessment Resources.

Costa, P. T. Jr., & McCrae, R. R. (2008). The revised NEO Personality Inventory (NEO-PI-R). In G. Boyle, G. Matthews, & D. Saklofske (Eds.), *The SAGE handbook of personality theory and assessment. Volume 2, Personality measurement and testing* (pp. 179–199). London: Sage.

Crocker, L. D., Heller, W., Warren, S. L., O'Hare, A. J., Infantolino, Z. P., & Miller, G. A. (2013). Relationships among cognition, emotion, and motivation: Implications for intervention and neuroplasticity in psychopathology. *Frontiers in Human Neuroscience*, 7(261), 1–19.

De Volder, M. L., & Lens, W. (1982). Academic achievement and future time perspective as a cognitive–motivational concept. *Journal of Personality and Social Psychology*, 42(3), 566–571.

Dörnyei, Z. (2001). *Motivational strategies in the language classroom*. Cambridge: Cambridge University Press.

Dörnyei, Z. (2009). *The psychology of second language acquisition*. Oxford: Oxford University Press.

Dörnyei, Z. (2017). Conceptualizing L2 learner characteristics in a complex, dynamic world. In L. Ortega & Z. Han (Eds.), *Complexity theory and language development: In celebration of Diane Larsen-Freeman* (pp. 79–96). Amsterdam: John Benjamins.

Dörnyei, Z., & Ottó, I. (1998). Motivation in action: A process model of L2 motivation. *Working Papers in Applied Linguistics (Thames Valley University, London)*, 4, 43–69.

Dörnyei, Z., & Ryan, S. (2015). *The psychology of the language learner revisited*. New York: Routledge.

Dörnyei, Z., Henry, A., & Muir, C. (2016). *Motivational currents in language learning: Frameworks for focused interventions*. New York: Routledge.

Dweck, C. S., & Yeager, D. S. (2018). Mindsets change the imagined and actual future. In G. Oettingen, A. T. Sevincer & P. M. Gollwitzer (Eds.), *The psychology of thinking about the future* (pp. 362–376). New York: Guilford Press.

Eccles, J. S., Wigfield, A., & Schiefele, A. (1998). Motivation to succeed. In W. Damon & N. Eisenberg (Eds.), *Handbook of child psychology 5th edition, Vol. 3: Social, emotional, and personality development*. (pp. 1017–1095). New York: John Wiley and Sons.

Elicker, J. D., Lord, R. G., Ash, S. R., Kohari, N. E., Hruska, B. J., McConnell, N. L., & Medvedeff, M. E. (2010). Velocity as a predictor of performance satisfaction, mental focus, and goal revision. *Applied Psychology: An International Review*, 59(3), 495–514.

Fong, C. J., & Kim, Y. W. (in press). A clash of constructs? Re-examining grit in light of academic buoyancy and future time perspective. *Current Psychology*, 1–14.

Goldberg, L. R. (1992). The development of markers for the Big-Five factor structure. *Psychological Assessment*, 4(1), 26–42.

Göllner, L. M., Ballhausen, N., Kliegel, M., & Forstmeier, S. (2018). Delay of gratification, delay discounting and their associations with age, episodic future thinking, and future time perspective. *Frontiers in Psychology*, 8(2304), 1–15.

Gollwitzer, P. M. (1990). Action phases and mind-sets. In E. T. Higgins & R. M. Sorrentino (Eds.), *Handbook of motivation and cognition: Foundations of social behaviour* (Vol. 2, pp. 53–92). New York: Guilford Press.

Han, Y., & McDonough, K. (2018). Korean L2 speakers' regulatory focus and oral task performance. *International Review of Applied Linguistics*, 56(2), 181–203.

Heckhausen, H. (1991). *Motivation and action*. New York: Springer.

Heckhausen, H., & Kuhl, J. (1985). From wishes to action: The dead ends and short cuts on the long way to action. In M. Frese & J. Sabini (Eds.), *Goal-directed behaviour: The concept of action in psychology* (pp. 134–160). Hillsdale, NJ: Lawrence Erlbaum.

Heggestad, E. D., & Kanfer, R. (2000). Individual differences in trait motivation: Development of the Motivational Trait Questionnaire. *International Journal of Educational Research*, 33, 751–776.

Janeiro, I. N., Duarte, A. M., Araújo, A. M., & Gomes, A. I. (2017). Time perspective, approaches to learning, and academic achievement in secondary students. *Learning and Individual Differences*, 55, 61–68.

Kauffman, D. F., & Husman, J. (2004). Effects of time perspective on student motivation: Introduction to a special issue. *Educational Psychology Review*, 16(1), 1–7.

Lawrence, J. W., Carver, C. C., & Scheier, M. F. (2002). Velocity toward goal attainment in immediate experience as a determinant of affect. *Journal of Applied Social Psychology*, 32(4), 788–802.

Lens, W., & Seginer, R. (2015). Future time perspective and motivation. In J. D. Wright (Ed.), *International encyclopedia of the social & behavioral sciences* (2nd ed., Vol. 9, pp. 561–566). Amsterdam: Elsevier.

Lou, N. M., & Noels, K. (2017). Measuring language mindsets and modeling their relations with goal orientations and emotional and behavioral responses in failure situations. *Modern Language Journal*, 101(1), 214–243.

Matthews, G., & Zeidner, M. (2004). Traits, states, and the trilogy of the mind: An adaptive perspective on intellectual functioning. In D. Y. Dai & R. J. Sternberg (Eds.), *Motivation, emotion, and cognition: Integrative perspectives on intellectual functioning and development* (pp. 143–174). Mahwah, NJ: Lawrence Erlbaum.

Mayer, J. D., Chabot, H. F., & Carlsmith, K. M. (1997). Conation, affect, and cognition in personality. In G. Matthews (Ed.), *Cognitive science perspectives on personality and emotion* (pp. 31–63). Amsterdam: Elsevier.

McAdams, D. P., & McLean, K. C. (2013). Narrative identity. *Current Directions in Psychological Science*, 22(3), 233–238.

McAdams, D. P., & Pals, J. L. (2006). A new Big Five: Fundamental principles for an integrative science of personality. *American Psychologist*, 61(3), 204–217.

McAdams, D. P., Anyidoho, N. A., Brown, C., Huang, Y. T., Kaplan, B., & Machado, M. A. (2004). Traits and stories: Links between dispositional and narrative features of personality. *Journal of Personality*, 72(4), 761–784.

McClelland, D. C., Koestner, R., & Weinberger, J. (1989). How do self-attributed and implicit motives differ? *Psychological Review*, 96(4), 690–702.

Papi, M. (2018). Motivation as quality: Regulatory fit effects on incidental vocabulary learning. *Studies in Second Language Acquisition, 40*(4), 707–730.

Pintrich, P. R., & Schunk, D. H. (1996). *Motivation in education: Theory, research, and applications.* Englewood Cliffs, NJ: Merrill.

Raynor, J. O. (1974). Motivation and career striving. In J. W. Atkinson & J. O. Raynor (Eds.), *Motivation and achievement* (pp. 369–387). Washington, DC: Winston & Sons.

Raynor, J. O., & Entin, E. E. (1983). The function of future orientation as a determinant of human behaviour in step-path theory of action. *International Journal of Psychology, 18*, 464–487.

Raynor, J. O., & Roeder, G. P. (1987). Motivation and future orientation: Task and time effects for achievement motivation. In F. Halisch & J. Kuhl (Eds.), *Motivation, intention, and volition* (pp. 61–71). Berlin: Springer.

Ryan, R. M., & Legate, N. (2012). Through a fly's eye: Multiple yet overlapping perspectives on future directions for human motivation research. In R. M. Ryan (Ed.), *The Oxford handbook of human motivation* (pp. 554–564). New York: Oxford University Press.

Ryan, S., & Mercer, S. (2012). Implicit theories: Language learning mindsets. In S. Mercer, S. Ryan & M. Williams (Eds.), *Psychology for language learning* (pp. 74–89). Basingstoke: Palgrave Macmillan.

Scherer, K. R. (1995). Plato's legacy: Relationships between cognition, emotion, and motivation. *Geneva Studies in Emotion and Communication, 9*(1), 1–7 (https://archive-ouverte.unige.ch/unige:102030).

Sheldon, K. (2004). *Optimal human being: An integrated multi-level perspective.* Mahwah, NJ: Lawrence Erlbaum.

Şimşek, E., & Dörnyei, Z. (2017). Anxiety and L2 self-images: The 'anxious self'. In C. Gkonou, M. Daubney & J.-M. Dewaele (Eds.), *New insights into language anxiety: Theory, research and educational implications* (pp. 51–69). Bristol: Multilingual Matters.

Sorrentino, R. M. (1996). The role of conscious thought in a theory of motivation and cognition: The uncertainty orientation paradigm. In P. M. Gollwitzer & J. A. Bargh (Eds.), *The psychology of action: Linking cognition and motivation to behaviour* (pp. 619–644). New York: Guilford Press.

Ushioda, E. (1996). Developing a dynamic concept of motivation. In T. J. Hickey & J. Williams (Ed.), *Language, education and society in a changing world* (pp. 239–245). Clevedon: Multilingual Matters.

Vohs, K. D., & Baumeister, R. F. (Eds.). (2011). *Handbook of self-regulation: Research, theory, and applications* (2nd ed.). New York: Guilford Press.

Waller, L., & Papi, M. (2017). Motivation and feedback: How implicit theories of intelligence predict L2 writers' motivation and feedback orientation. *Journal of Second Language Writing, 35*, 54–65.

Weiner, B. (1986). Attribution, emotion and action. In R. M. Sorrentino & E. T. Higgins (Eds.), *Handbook of motivation and cognition: Foundations of social behaviour* (pp. 281–312). New York: The Guilford Press.

Weiner, B. (2019). My journey to the attribution fields. In A. J. Elliot (Ed.), *Advances in motivation science* (Vol. 6, pp. 185–211). Cambridge, MA: Academic Press.

Wong, A. E., & Vallacher, R. R. (2018). Reciprocal feedback between self-concept and goal pursuit in daily life. *Journal of Personality, 86*, 543–554.

Zimbardo, P. G., & Boyd, J. N. (1999). Putting time in perspective: A valid, reliable individual-differences metric. *Journal of Personality and Social Psychology, 77*(6), 1271–1288.

2

FUNDAMENTAL CHALLENGES II

Motivational dynamics

In everyday speech the word 'motivation' usually refers to something solid and stable about a person – as mentioned earlier, a sentence like *"Geraldine is a motivated student"* would suggest to most people that motivation is a relatively enduring feature of Geraldine. However, we saw in the previous chapter that this non-technical meaning of the word is at odds with a more scientific definition of motivation, which includes a temporal, process-oriented element. In this chapter we further elaborate on the non-static, dynamic nature of motivation by first investigating the role of the motivational context, that is, the fact that some aspects of motivation are not internal to the learner but are externally determined by the sociocultural set-up of the learner's environment (e.g. language attitudes are influenced by the interethnic relationships within language communities). The picture is further complicated when we also take into account different timescales and multiple parallel goals. The chapter will conclude with a discussion of how all this variability can be handled within the framework of complex dynamic systems theory.

Challenge 5: How to account for the context of motivation

Traditionally, motivation was conceptualised as a function of an individual's internal needs, goals, attitudes, beliefs, interests, desires, values, etc. Such an approach was an example of an *individualistic perspective*, whereby the social or cultural environment surrounding (and affecting) a person is considered through the individual's eyes and is thus seen to play a marginal role. The other extreme would be a *societal perspective*, according to which the individual's behaviour is seen to be determined by powerful contextual forces at large such as sociocultural norms, intergroup relations, acculturation/assimilation processes. According to this latter perspective, therefore, an individual's personal identity is overridden by their social identity, and social constraints limit one's motivational choices. The theoretical dilemma that context poses further increases when we also consider the impact of the broad notion of 'culture' on motivation. Markus (2016, p. 161) outlines the scope of this issue as follows:

> Motivation is shaped by the multiple intersecting cultures, those of national origin but also those of gender, race, ethnicity, class, religion, workplace, sexual orientation, etc. that people engage each day and across their lives. Cultures are systems of ideas, interactions, institutions that guide the actions of individuals. The first contribution of a culturally comparative approach to motivation is that the answers to the question of 'why a particular action' depend on the cultural context in which they are asked.

To illustrate the power of cultural influences, let us consider a study reported by King and McInerney (2014), in which Anglophone children were found to become more motivated in a problem-solving task when they were allowed to make personal choices, whereas with Asian children, motivation increased when trusted authority figures or peers made the choice for them. In this latter case, therefore, cultural factors overrode the power of the 'need for autonomy,' which is a pillar of self-determination theory. On the basis of this and similar examples, the authors conclude:

> Culture plays an important role in students' motivation in school but prominent motivation theories have relegated it to the sidelines. Few of the existing studies examine or challenge the essential components or meaning of motivation as articulated in particular theoretical models within different cultural contexts.
>
> *p. 194*

Rauthmann et al.'s (2015) observation about context in general echoes the same point:

> The person and the situation at any given moment are inextricably interwoven. Almost all psychological theories have acknowledged this truism. Yet, psychologists have not made much progress in describing, explaining and predicting person–situation transactions: how people construe, maintain, select, evoke, change and create situations in their daily lives. Why is this the case? Although most psychological theories incorporate situational influences, these influences are rarely couched within a set of guiding principles of what situations are and how they can operate.
>
> *p. 363*

Thus, while the notion of context has emerged as an unavoidable issue in psychology over the past two decades, serious challenges remain concerning the appropriate theoretical handling of contextual factors in relation to individual characteristics.

Innovations 1–3 will present three promising responses to these challenges. If we turn to the field of SLA, we also find tensions between various cognitive and social agendas with regard to integrating contextual issues in theoretical and research paradigms (see e.g. Lafford, 2007; Larsen-Freeman, 2007; Zuengler & Miller, 2006). Recently, however, a group of eminent scholars – the 'Douglas Fir Group' – have gone on record emphasising the central aspect of contextual factors in applied linguistics; note that the term 'context' is used as many as five times in the following passage:

> Language learning begins at the micro level of social activity through L2 learners' repeated experiences in regularly occurring and recurring contexts of use, often characterized by interpersonal (oral, signed, or written) interaction with other social actors. From these situated, local iterative contexts, language use and language learning can emerge—though they do not always do so. The scope of these contexts can be wide-ranging and includes everyday, informal contexts of interaction, such as ad hoc conversations, text messaging, online game-playing, as well as more formal contexts such as those comprising L2 classrooms...
>
> *Douglas Fir Group, 2016, p. 27*

Consistent with this stance, one of the main conclusions of my 2005 overview of individual differences in SLA (Dörnyei, 2005) was that the most salient aspect of nearly all the ID literature reviewed concerned the emerging theme of context; it appeared that cutting-edge research on virtually every L2 learner characteristic had been addressing the situated nature of ID factors in one way or another. When a decade later Stephen Ryan and I revisited the subject (Dörnyei & Ryan, 2015), we found that the earlier calls for a greater awareness of context had been borne out by concrete developments, and grappling with the challenges posed by the situated and context-bound nature of human dispositions has become an ongoing aspect of the agenda in most strands of SLA. As we shall see in Innovations 4 and 5, L2 motivation research has been attempting to respond to the contextual challenge since its genesis. Also, because the question of context is part of the broader discourse related to the relevance of complex dynamic systems theory, aspects of this issue will be revisited in the discussion of Challenge 8.

Innovation 1: The systematic characterisations of context

With contexts – or as they are also referred to in the psychological literature, 'situations' – receiving increasing attention, one logical response to this issue has been to try and define the notion more precisely. Let us look at three ambitious attempts to do so, two from mainstream psychology (Rauthmann et al., 2015; Wosnitza & Beltman, 2012) and one from the SLA literature (Douglas Fir Group, 2016). They all propose multi-layered specifications for context, and while the following accounts cannot provide a full description, they will illustrate the approaches by describing the main constituents of the underlying frameworks.

Wosnitza and Beltman's (2012) three-tier framework of context

Wosnitza and Beltman (2012) set out to present the development of a heuristic framework that integrates three aspects of context which they termed 'Perspective,' 'Content' and 'Level.' Each dimension of this three-tiered framework is further broken down into sub-dimensions:

- *Perspectives*. Wosnitza and Beltman distinguish two perspectives, *subjective* and *objective*, which is consistent with the age-old dilemma in psychology (already discussed briefly under the individualistic–societal dichotomy) as to whether the main thrust of an analysis should focus on the objective features of the ecological environment (i.e. objectively 'out there') or rather on how people subjectively perceive and process these features (i.e. 'in the head').
- *Contents*. In a synthesis of past research, Wosnitza and Beltman offer an elegant and parsimonious division of a potentially very long list of context-specific elements into three components: *physical elements* (e.g. books, buildings), *social elements* (e.g. friends, colleagues) and *formal elements* (e.g. rules, regulations, curriculum).
- *Levels*. Wosnitza and Beltman's framework draws on Bronfenbrenner's (1979) influential division of context into a *microsystem* (i.e. the immediate environment), a *mesosystem* (the interaction of several microsystems), an *exosystem* (settings that do not involve the individual but which have a bearing on the microsystem) and a *macrosystem* (i.e. the overall combination of all the lower-order systems into the subculture/culture as a whole). This comprehensive division has also been adopted by other proposals; for example, Gurtner, Monnard and Genoud (2001) applied Bronfenbrenner's system to educational settings, linking the microlevel to task motivation, the mesolevel to the classroom situation, the exolevel to school factors and the macrolevel to all outside influences. Within SLA, Yashima and Arano (2015) successfully employed a similar three-level model of human development by Valsiner (2007) for the purpose of analysing the dynamics of L2 motivation, comprising a microgenetic, a mesogenetic and an ontogenetic domain (the latter roughly corresponding to the macrosystem).

In sum, Wosnitza and Beltman's division follows broad principles of common sense and tradition, but one cannot help wondering how useful a 24-component matrix (which is the total permutation of the various sub-dimensions) might be for discussing specific situational characteristic surrounding an agent and their behaviour.

Rauthmann, Sherman and Funder's (2015) principles of 'psychological situations'

While Wosnitza and Beltman (2012) pursued a common-sense, generic and heuristic approach, Rauthmann and his co-authors (2015) – who include David

Funder, one of the best-known specialists in the area – have focused more closely on person–situation transactions in 'psychological situations.' They aimed to integrate six main theoretical approaches (environmental-ecological, behavioural, trait-psychological, cognitive-attributional, social-interactional and transactional-dynamic) by offering three broad principles of situation research (further clarified by a number of corollaries):

- *The Processing Principle* stipulates that situations will only have consequences if they are processed and psychologically experienced by the people concerned.
- *The Reality Principle* states that any perception of a situation is grounded in three types of 'reality': "physico-biological cues ('objective' physical reality), canonico-consensual aspects (normative, quasi-objective social reality) and subjective-functional aspects (distinctive, idiosyncratic personal reality)" (p. 368).
- *The Circular Principle* concerns the empirical measurement of situational information. It states that situation variables, when defined only by 'person variables' (e.g. participant's perceptions or behaviours), run the risk of blurring the distinctions amongst persons, situations and behaviours. As we shall see below in Innovation 5 (concerning person-in-context approaches), contemporary research on context revolves around the very question of whether it is legitimate to separate persons from the situations in which they operate, so it might be useful to present here the three corollaries of this principle:
  (a) *The State Corollary* states that if people's subjective and behavioural states in a situation are regarded as actual descriptors of the situation, then the person and the situation become in effect indistinguishable.
  (b) *The Consequences Corollary* states that circularity is introduced by *post hoc* explanations/definitions of a situation in terms of its consequences.
  (c) *The Approximation Corollary* states that a psychological situation is best assessed using at least two rating sources (by focal participants, observers/bystanders and/or lab raters).

The Douglas Fir Group's (2016) three-tier framework of contextual influences

Within SLA contexts, one of the most ambitious conceptualisations of contextual influences has been provided by the Douglas Fir Group (2016) as part of a systematic analysis of multilingualism. In order to accommodate and organise a number of language-related theories and processes, they propose a broad, three-tier framework based on Bronfenbrenner's (1979) theory (described above): *microlevel* of social activity; *mesolevel* of sociocultural institutions and communities; and *macrolevel* of ideological structures. They see L2 learning as an ongoing process that begins at the microlevel through the learner's engagement in varied social interactions, which in turn are situated within, and shaped at, the mesolevel by sociocultural institutions and communities (e.g. family, school, places of work and worship, clubs and online forums of various kinds). The authors emphasise that the institutions and communities at the mesolevel represent powerful social conditions (e.g. economic, cultural, religious, political), which create social identities and determine the degree of access to particular types of social experiences. The macrolevel involves society-wide ideological structures with particular orientations towards L2 learning and use, which display a two-way interaction with the institutions and communities of the mesolevel and the agency of the individual people in the microlevel. This is thus a robust division whose aim is, similar to the other two frameworks above, to process the multi-layered complexity of contextual influences in a systematic manner and to elaborate on the linguistic impact of each level.

Innovation 2: The rise of 'social motivation'

We have seen earlier that motivation research in psychology has traditionally adopted an individualistic perspective and focused largely on personal factors (e.g. needs, beliefs, desires, goals) as the primary determinants of human behaviour. This emphasis does not mean, however, that social concerns and influences were completely ignored, as some motivational factors did concern interpersonal factors. To offer a few high-profile examples, the 'need for affiliation' (i.e. a need to feel a sense of involvement and belonging within a social group) was linked to classic achievement motivation theory as a central motive in people's lives as early as the 1960s (e.g. McClelland, 1961), and a similar construct, the 'need to belong,' was included in Maslow's (1970) famous needs hierarchy. More recently, self-determination theory has posited that the 'need for relatedness' (i.e. the need to have close, affectionate relationships with others) is one of the basic human needs (Deci & Ryan, 1985). Finally, a considerable body of research in educational psychology has focused on the motivational impact of 'classroom reward structures' concerning the cooperative versus competitive relational systems amongst peers (e.g. Ames & Ames, 1984). Thus, as Graham (1996) has summarised, the historically dominant theories of motivation did recognise to some extent the importance of interpersonal relationships as determinants of human behaviour; yet, she argued, these social concerns did *not* affect the core trajectory of motivation research, which had been dominated by the study of "intrapsychic processes and individual achievement strivings" (p. 349).

This general trajectory underwent a profound change in the 1990s. The growing awareness of the unaccounted influence of social issues reached a tipping point in motivation research, resulting in the introduction of the concept of 'social motivation' in mainstream psychology. An influential manifestation of the changing climate was a paper written by one of the leading motivation experts of the time, Bernard Weiner (1994), entitled "Integrating social and personal theories of achievement motivation." What is particularly noteworthy from our perspective is that the main emphasis within this new approach was on student motivation, as reflected for example in Weiner's explanation:

A fuzzy yet useful and conceptually reasonable distinction can be drawn between social and personal motivation. For example, how others react to the shy or the handicapped in school – with help, flight, aggression, etc. – illustrates what I mean by social motivation.

p. 557

The concept of social motivation was embraced by the research community, and two years later Cambridge University Press published an edited volume entitled *Social Motivation: Understanding Children's School Adjustment* (Juvonen & Wentzel, 1996), with contributions by some of the most established scholars in the field, from Dale Schunk and Barry Zimmerman to Carol Dweck and Sandra Graham. Wentzel's (1996) statement in the introduction could not have been any more explicit concerning the new agenda: "We hope ... that the work presented in this volume will provide inspiration and a challenge to continue research and theory development on social motivational perspectives" (p. 2).

Although the labelling of the new motive 'social motivation' was ambitious, the initial theorising concerning its content was far more tentative. Weiner (1994) originally used the term exclusively to refer to interpersonal influences: "Social motivation requires the psychological presence of another, and determines reactions to that person, dyad, or group" (p. 557), and in a similar vein, Wentzel (1996) highlighted 'social relationships' as providing school-aged children with "motivational contexts for development" (p. 3). Accordingly, key issues in the emerging new perspective included the motivational impact of friendships, teacher–student relationships and the learner's peer group, but it was stressed that "further exploration of social-cognitive and other social psychological factors, and identification of variables that capture the quality of relationships and social contexts, must take place before the nature of 'social' motivation can be understood fully" (p. 5).

Once the floodgate had been opened, a continuous stream of publications related to social motivation emerged (e.g. Pintrich & Maehr, 1995; Urdan, 1999; Volet & Järvelä, 2001; Wentzel, 1999), and it is interesting to see how much the field matured in only a few years, as reflected by the fact that the title of another anthology on the topic – featuring yet another sterling cast of contributors – specifically included the terms 'context and culture': *Student Motivation: The Culture and Context of Learning* (Salili, Chiu & Hong, 2001). Thus, by the beginning of the new millennium, social motivation had clearly passed its infancy, and Urdan's (2001) summary of the subject expressed the new confidence:

> In achievement goal theory, as in the broader discipline of psychology, a false dichotomy has obfuscated our understanding of the influences of contextual and personality features on behaviour. Thankfully, this problem is being addressed by many scholars. Just as the nature versus nurture debate has waned among psychologists, the person versus environment divide in motivation research ... is currently being bridged.

p. 171

Innovation 3: The rise of qualitative research

Traditional psychological research has used *variable-centred* research paradigms and analysed the data though *quantitative, statistical* procedures. Having human participants as the main units of analysis, this approach kept contextual variables separated from the individual even when the aim of a study was to investigate the relationship between personal and contextual variables (e.g. by means of computing correlations between them). However, some scholars such as Nolen, Horn and Ward (2015) have argued that capturing the essence of a context through a list of variables *cannot* work, because the notion is so intricately assembled of diverse elements at different levels of abstraction that it will defy all attempts to describe it by compiling lists of variables:

> Context ... cannot adequately be characterized through analyses of individual variables. The layers of context that influence individual identity and learning are not simply nested like Russian dolls; instead, they are interwoven like a cloth, with threads that may strain more or less in different situations, which begs attention to individuals' meaning making and thick descriptions of the different settings in which individuals participate.
>
> *p. 241*

In order to achieve such a thick description, a growing number of scholars started to advocate replacing quantitative research with a qualitative methodology. Although this may sound like a major shift away from tradition, if we look at the issue more closely, it does not constitute such a dramatic deviation. As Ushioda (2020a) explains, because motivation is not directly observable (only its consequences), motivation research has typically relied on *self-report measures* to tap into what is in the individual's mind. Such self-report can be solicited both quantitatively (through questionnaires) and qualitatively (through asking the individual directly in interviews), and thus the proposed alteration only concerned in effect the medium of inquiry. Yet, this change offered marked advantages in exploring the role of motivational contexts; as Ushioda explains,

> qualitative research on L2 motivation thus facilitates a holistic perspective on the lived experience of language learners as people located in specific socio-historical as well as cultural and physical contexts, who have complex social and personal histories contributing to their current motivations and aspirations for the future ... [It] allows for the possibility of understanding people's motivations and behaviours as these emerge in dynamic interaction with local social and contextual processes, and (importantly) as people engage with and shape these evolving contextual and relational processes through their own reflexivity and agency.
>
> *pp. 11–13*

A study conducted by Boo, Dörnyei and Ryan (2015) to survey a ten-year period in the history of L2 motivation research (from 2005–2014) shows that there was a consistent increase of qualitative methods of inquiry during this time, whether used independently or in combination with a quantitative component within mixed methods research designs. For example, in 2005/6 there were 2.5 times more quantitative studies than qualitative/mixed methods ones, whereas in 2013/4 the same ratio was .91 (i.e. pure quantitative studies were in the minority). The desire to offer a more nuanced account of the motivational context definitely played a key role in this paradigm shift, but we should note that the increased application of qualitative research was also motivated by other factors. As Ushioda (2020a) points out, the notable growth coincided with a period of significant theoretical reframing of L2 motivation in relation to concepts of self and identity, as well as to complex dynamic systems theory. We shall address these points under Challenge 5.

A clear sign of the growing maturity of the new qualitative research practice was that mainstream psychological research on motivation has also started to acknowledge the advantages of qualitative inquiries. In the second edition of their seminal work on motivation in education, Pintrich and Schunk (2002, pp. 11–12) for example submitted that "Qualitative/interpretive research yields rich sources of data that are much more intensive and thorough than those typically obtained in correlational or experimental research." They then argued that because this research paradigm has "the potential of raising new questions and new slants on old questions that often are missed by traditional methods ... its influence will continue to grow." We shall come back to this question in the next chapter when discussing measurement issues (CHALLENGE[11]).

Innovation 4: Gardner's fusion of personality and social psychology

One of the most original insights in the history of L2 motivation research has been directly related to the impact of contextual factors, and this insight, made by Robert Gardner, was in fact at the heart of the genesis of the field. In 1959, Gardner and Lambert proposed (see also Gardner, 1985a) that success in L2 learning was a function of the learner's attitude to the linguistic-cultural community of the target language, thus adding a social dimension to the motivation to learn an L2. Living in bilingual Montreal at that time, where the often tense relationship between the Anglophone and Francophone communities was a salient issue, Gardner was sensitive to the social aspects of L2 motivation, and he argued accordingly that the mastery of an L2 is not merely an educational matter but also a deeply social event that requires the incorporation of a wide range of elements of the L2 culture:

> The words, sounds, grammatical principles and the like that the language teacher tries to present are more than aspects of some linguistic code; they are integral parts of another culture. As a result, students' attitudes toward the specific language group are bound to influence how successful they will be

in incorporating aspects of that language ... As long as language programmes require students to make the other language part of their behavioural repertoire, it seems reasonable to hypothesize that such attitudes will influence the relative degree of success with which this can be achieved.

pp. 6–7

This position resonated with the field and soon became a 'given' in L2 motivation research, as reflected, for example, by Williams's (1994, p. 77) summary a decade later:

There is no question that learning a foreign language is different to learning other subjects. This is mainly because of the social nature of such a venture. Language, after all, belongs to a person's whole social being: it is part of one's identity, and is used to convey this identity to other people. The learning of a foreign language involves far more than simply learning skills, or a system of rules, or a grammar; it involves an alteration in self-image, the adoption of new social and cultural behaviours and ways of being, and therefore has a significant impact on the social nature of the learner.

Nowadays, we tend to take this social aspect of language learning for granted, but Gardner's original act of incorporating a social dimension in a motivation theory was a radical and, quite frankly, unprecedented, move that preceded similar developments in mainstream psychological research by decades (as seen in Innovation 2 earlier regarding the emergence of social motivation). In developing the details of his paradigm, Gardner (1985a) drew upon Ajzen and Fishbein's (1980) social psychological theory of reasoned action, in which one of the chief determinants of a person's intention to perform a particular act was the *attitude* towards the behaviour in question, with the rationale being that one's attitude towards a target influences the overall pattern of one's responses to that target. However, when Gardner applied this theory to language learning, he extended it by first splitting the 'attitude' component into three – attitudes towards the L2 community, attitudes towards the learning situation and attitudes towards learning the L2 – and then by adding to the mix a few variables that one would have expected to see in a comprehensive motivation construct: a goal (integrative orientation), two personal factors related to languages (one's interest in foreign languages in general and in learning the specific L2 in question in particular), as well as an index of the estimated intensity of one's intended learning effort. Thus, in the resulting construct, termed the 'integrative motive,' Gardner merged in effect an individualistic motivation paradigm with a social psychological one, thereby succeeding in covering both learner-internal factors and social attitudes towards the sociocultural context of L2 learning.

Gardner was a specialist on psychometrics (e.g. he has written a statistical text for using the software SPSS; Gardner, 2001), and he applied the established procedures for assessing attitudes in social psychology to the measurement of L2 motivation. The result was a standardised questionnaire, the Attitude/Motivation Test Battery (Gardner, 1985b), which offered scholars interested in studying L2 motivation a professional survey instrument for the first time, an act that contributed greatly to the increase of research on L2 motivation. Furthermore, by creating a novel motivational–social interface, Gardner also initiated a process of exploring other context-related factors that play a decisive role in motivating people (for recent reviews, see Rubenfeld & Clément, 2020; Yim, Clément & MacIntyre, 2020). Without being able to go into detail here, we should note that the most prominent of these developments was Richard Clément's (1980, 1986) socio-contextual model describing the influence of the macro-social context on SLA as well as the study of a situated language identity by Clément, Noels and their associates (e.g. Clément & Noels, 1992; Noels, Pon & Clément, 1996).

Innovation 5: Person-in-context approaches

Ushioda (2015) submits that separating the individual from the context may be problematic because learners are "inherently part of, act upon and contribute to shaping the social, cultural and physical environments with which they interact" (p. 48). Indeed, learner and context mutually shape each other, and therefore treating them as distinct entities is as meaningless as separating the dancer and the dance (as Ushioda cites Claire Kramsch's Yeats-inspired metaphor). This is in accordance with Paris and Turner's (1994) seminal work which stated that conceptualisations of motivation should consider the characteristics of individuals in specific situations because a "person's motivational beliefs and behaviour are derived from contextual transactions" (p. 214). In a position paper that projected the development of educational psychology for the new millennium, Pintrich (2000) argued similarly: future models "must help us conceptualize and understand how the individual and context work together to facilitate or constrain learning ... highlighting the 'individual in context'" (p. 223). According to this position, therefore, an appropriate unit of analysis for motivation research should be some kind of combination of the person and the context, and, for example, Rueda and Dembo (1995) referred to this unit as "individual-in-action within specific contexts," Volet (2001) as "person-in-context" and Nolen et al. (2015) as "learners-in-context."

Looking back, Ushioda (2020b) makes an interesting point when she explains that the changing perspective has partly been due to the increasing use of qualitative research, as it was the sensitive magnifying glass of qualitative inquiry that has uncovered, amplified and thus foregrounded L2 learners' "context-bound histories, social relationships and lived experience as well as individuality" (p. 203). Building on these foundations, she developed a situated analytical approach (Ushioda, 2009) that she termed the 'Person-in-Context Relational View of Motivation,' which highlights the agency of L2 learners, conceived as real people who are located in particular sociocultural and historical contexts and whose motivation and identities are in a relational (rather than linear) association with these contexts. As she explains:

> Real language learners are not generalized theoretical abstractions or idealized bundles of variables, but uniquely individual complex human beings situated in complex social realities. We run the risk of forgetting that language learners are 'people,' and people for whom learning a language is just one very small part of their lives and certainly not a prominent or defining feature of their identity ... In my arguments to date for this 'person-in-context' perspective on motivation, I have usually highlighted the research value of focusing on the rich individuality of language learners as 'people,' and of attending to the social-contextual and relational dynamics through which their motivational processes evolve. I have also usually highlighted the pedagogical importance of understanding and motivating the 'person,' in preference to using generalized techniques to motivate the generalized L2 learner.
>
> Ushioda, in press

The approach therefore posits a dynamic interaction between a person's agency and his/her background, history, identity, goals and motives, as well as the social relations, activities and contexts in which the individual is embedded. This conceptualisation makes Ushioda's theory compatible with a complex dynamic systems approach, which also blurs the distinction between the agent and its context, and we shall therefore return to this matter when discussing Challenge 8 below. However, it is worth noting here Ushioda's (in press) caution about the propensity of dynamic systems approaches to shift into abstraction, leaving the 'person-in-context' behind:

> when we read theoretical accounts of L2 motivation that take a complex dynamic systems approach, we find that the discourse often tends to move into a rather abstract plane where the focus is on self-organizing 'systems' and their components and processes, and where we seem to lose sight of the individual agency and reflexivity of the person whose motivation is under focus.

Challenge 6: The issue of different timescales

Once we accept that motivation often behaves like a process that unfolds in time and which displays ebbs and flows during its course (see CHALLENGE₂), we encounter a perhaps unexpected challenge: what *timescale* shall we use? That is, how global should our perspective be: should we measure motivational change according to hours, days, months or years? And what should be the span of the *time window* in question? That is, how long should be the period to be studied? These are essential questions, because as de Bot (2015) argues in his intriguing discussion of timescales, we will get different results depending on the length of the time window and the granularity of the timescale used: "While on timescales of fine granularity the data may suggest slight decline, that change may actually be part of a pattern of growth on a scale that has a lower granularity and a longer time window" (p. 32). Indeed, different types of change require different timescales to document them; for example, as de Bot points out, research on language attrition tends to be done on larger timescales than research on language acquisition, simply because researchers feel that in order to obtain measurable results for attrition, one needs to have less frequent data points (often years or even decades); therefore, to take an extreme example, if a study were to examine attrition over a period of one day with one-hour intervals, the results will indicate that language attrition does not exist!

Once we start exploring the issue of timescales, we encounter further surprises. MacIntyre (2012), for example, points out that if we reduce the granularity of the scales, contextual issues become increasingly prominent:

> If we put a microscope on the ways in which communication traits work, it is astonishing to consider how quickly characteristics of the individual converge with features of the situation to create communication behaviour. The affective and cognitive context that envelopes communication is simultaneously created and recreated on-the-fly, as it is being enacted, moving relentlessly forward in time.
>
> *p. 362*

This recognition has led MacIntyre (2012) to develop the *idiodynamic method* of analysis, which will be described in Innovation 1. Another curious aspect of timescales is that while on a finer scale we might observe more fluctuation, a larger timescale perspective of the same phenomenon might attest to overall stability. This raises the question of how different timescales interact with each other: while it stands to reason that what happens on, say, the minutes scale has an impact on what happens on higher time scales and the other way around, what determines the overall dynamics and trajectory of the process? There is growing evidence that *perceptually interconnected timescales* – for example, when short-term trajectories result in a psychological state that affects longer-term trajectories, as is the case in sport when a few victories can lead to a winning streak – can build up 'psychological momentum,' and we shall revisit this question in Chapter 6 when discussing long-term motivation.

Finally, Milyavskaya and Werner (2018) are right to point out that one aspect of goal pursuit that has often been overlooked in the past is the idea that goals can unfold over many different timescales, with some goals accomplished within a day or so, while others may take weeks or months. Do goals have optimal timescales in terms of their motivational force? We shall explore this question further in Innovation 3 below concerning 'proximal subgoals.'

Innovation 1: The idiodynamic method

The *idiodynamic method* is not so much a theory as an innovative research approach with an explicit focus on capturing the temporal dimension of the affective or cognitive states that accompany human communication. It was developed by Peter MacIntyre (2012) in order to examine the interplay of various variables affecting a speaker in real time. The challenge that MacIntyre addressed was this: given the fluctuations in affect – and as we have also seen, in motivation – from one moment to the next, how can we track this moving target in order to understand its influences on various criterion measures? The term 'idiodynamic' refers to "the dynamic changes within an individual as an event unfolds" (p. 362), and the method consists of five steps (see e.g. Boudreau, MacIntyre & Dewaele, 2018; MacIntyre, 2012):

(a) A communication task is video recorded.
(b) The research participant watches the recording and, using specially designed software, provides moment-by-moment ratings of the variable under investigation (e.g. the level of anxiety or willingness to communicate experienced when originally producing the text).
(c) The ratings are recorded at a rate of approximately one per 1–5 seconds, and the software produces a corresponding continuous graph that displays the fluctuations in the variable.
(d) The graph is printed out immediately and is used as input for conducting a retrospective interview (stimulated recall) with the participants to find out the reasons for changes in the variable of interest.
(e) The interview is transcribed and analysed.

As cited earlier, MacIntyre (2012) argues that the idiodynamic method can be understood as a metaphorical microscope with which to examine familiar learner characteristics from a new angle, using a timescale that has not typically been investigated in the past. Since its introduction, the method has been employed in several studies in SLA, and has produced unique results that would not have been obtained using a larger timescale; for example, MacIntyre and Serroul (2015) used the procedure to look at approach–avoidance motivation in an L2 communication task and documented rapid fluctuation of anxiety, avoidance motivation, perceived competence and willingness to communicate – which they called "the four horsemen" – due to factors related to task demands, content difficulties and available communication/coping strategies (see also Yim, Clément & MacIntyre, 2020).

Innovation 2: Appropriate time window and timescale

Although timescales are a novel research concept in SLA (and also in the social sciences), there is ample anecdotal evidence that one can be locked in a counterproductive timescale or time window, both as a researcher and as a language learner.

Regarding research, the extreme example is a cross-sectional survey, which imposes a snapshot view of the respondents' motivation state, without accounting for any time element, and yet most quantitative research in the field still relies on this convenient method. Interestingly, even longitudinal studies can be of an inadequate length for documenting real changes (e.g. a two-week investigation of a language class is unlikely to identify any substantial developments in the students' L2 proficiency). Thus, an inappropriate timescale can simply block the researcher's view of the larger picture or of phenomena on different timescales. Because currently we have little concrete empirical data concerning the conscious manipulation of timescales, let us consider two studies, Sampson (2016) and Waninge, Dörnyei and de Bot (2014), as illustrations of the application of multiple timescales.

Richard Sampson (2016) presents an autoethnographic case study of his own L2 teaching motivation through the analysis of rich data from his research journal and student learning diaries, collected over a period of one academic year. He provides a fine-grained analysis of certain classroom episodes from different perspective (i.e. those of the teacher and the students) and different temporal contexts (i.e. short-term impact and long-term impact), thereby making the point powerfully that events have different implications on different timescales. For example, an occasion when he had to chastise the class for being non-cooperative appeared to him at the timescale of the lesson a complete "mess" and had a "crushing effect" on his ideas of future lessons with that class. Yet, contrary to expectations, the episode had a positive impact in the long run as it made students reflect on what went on and how they would like things to proceed. In fact, experiences of an event having different meanings in the short and the long run are not uncommon, and one way of making sense of the seeming contradiction is by investigating them on different timescales.

Waninge et al. (2014) used a fine-grained analysis of the motivational dynamics of four language learners during their language lessons over a period of two weeks, using real-time student feedback data taken at five-minute intervals in class, combined with classroom observations and a general questionnaire on motivation and attitude. This resulted in progress diagrams of the four students' motivational disposition during the observed classes, in which the main motivational states, including the rises and falls, were accompanied by classroom observational data and student comments. One of the main lessons emerging from the study was the fact that the evolution of the motivation to learn an L2 may be influenced by different types of motivation on different timescales; for example, long-term motivation was more closely associated with career plans, shorter-term motivational states with the characteristics of the tasks that the students were involved in, and minute-by-minute variation with various classroom episodes (e.g. pre-lesson events and peer conflicts). The various timescales interacted with each other, which was indicated by the fact that the fluctuation observed within classes was affected by the students' longer-term motivation, as manifested by the differences amongst the four students. Reflecting on this study, de Bot (2015) concluded that in order to obtain a full picture of the motivational disposition of a person in a particular setting, data from different timescales have to be gathered and combined. Hiver and Al-Hoorie (2016) add that, realistically, researchers will rarely be able to claim comprehensiveness of all the considerations that might bear on a phenomenon, but these authors suggest a simple strategy that may help to set the appropriate level of granularity, namely to add two adjacent timescales to the timescale of primary interest and thus generate complementary data at these corresponding timescales.

Innovation 3: 'Proximal subgoals'

As mentioned earlier, different personal goals tend to be associated with different timescales, ranging from very short to very long term, which raises the question as to whether variation in the timescales affects the goal's motivational capacity. Although goal pursuit is subject to a great deal of fluctuation due to a host of goal-relevant factors, a classic finding in psychology, discovered over 50 years ago, was the detection of a robust tendency regarding timescales, namely that shorter timescales tend to exert significantly more power than longer ones. In a seminal paper, Bandura and Simon (1977) examined the weight-loss efforts of dieters under two different timescale conditions: one group adopted distal goals defined in terms of weekly goal limits, and the other set proximal goals specifying the goal limits for four time periods during each day. The results showed that within the distal goal-setting condition, people achieved only a relatively small weight loss, whereas those who set short-term subgoals for themselves attained substantial reductions in their weight. This finding has been replicated widely in various contexts (for a recent review, see e.g. Ballard, Vancouver & Neal, 2018), and there is a consensus amongst motivation scholars that goals with shorter deadlines are generally more motivating than goals with longer deadlines: distal goals are too far off – or too general – to motivate specific actions in immediate situations; for this to happen, people have to create for themselves 'proximal subgoals' to guide a detailed course of action which leads to the distal outcome. Not only is the proximal value of the subgoals more salient and therefore more motivational, but the shorter deadline also means that less time is available to complete the task, which generates greater time pressure and thus a stronger need to act on the goal (Ballard et al., 2018). This is thus a textbook example of how two different timescales with different motivational properties interact and shape each other: a long-term vision might lead to the setting of subgoals with shorter timescales that, in turn, energise behaviour to sustain behaviour on the longer timescale. In Chapter 6, we shall return to examining the role played by proximal subgoals in sustaining long-term motivation.

Challenge 7: The interference of multiple parallel goals

People usually have to juggle several personal goals that they are simultaneously motivated to attain in every area of their lives, all of which compete for the individual's limited supply of energy and time, and some may even be in conflict with the others. This means that these multiple parallel goals inevitably interfere with each other in that focusing on one particular goal will limit the ability to make progress on other goals. In our current multi-tasking world, therefore, people constantly have to make choices about which goals to select or prioritise in order to manage their limited resources effectively (Ballard et al., 2018). This being the case, we cannot fully understand the motivational disposition associated with a particular course of action without considering the potential impact of competing options and preferences. For example, in the typical L2 classroom, students' engagement in learning will interact with a complex variety of other competing attentional demands, activities, goals and pressures. This has been clearly highlighted by Ushioda (1998) concerning language education when she argued over two decades ago that

> the flesh-and-blood language student is often at the same time a student of mathematics or science or history, or has been a student of other disciplines in the past ... [and is] unlikely to perceive the motivation for language learning to be wholly independent of the motivation (or lack of motivation) for other areas of learning. This relative perspective may be instrumental in helping to define or modify the developing goal structure of students' language learning motivation, as they weigh the potential pros and cons of making particular choices and pursuing different vocational directions.
>
> p. 83

Understanding student motivation is further complicated by the interplay of the learners' simultaneous focus on the subject matter and on the social features of the classroom; indeed, for an average pupil, 'school' represents just as much a social arena as the scene of academic work. The curious fact is, however, that while most scholars would agree with these considerations, most motivation theories focus on explaining and predicting specific types of behaviours in relative isolation, without accounting for any interaction with other ongoing behaviours in which the actor is engaged. This is partly due to the fact that research on how people deal with multiple parallel goals has been rather scarce relative to other facets of motivation, and thus little is known about the complex processes whereby individuals manage competing goals. In a recent overview of the dynamic self-regulation of multiple-goal pursuit, Neal, Ballard and Vancouver (2017, p. 402) describe numerous challenges people face in connection with having multiple interfering goals:

> we have to choose where to spend our time, how much effort to exert, and what strategies to employ, given the deadlines that we are under. Despite efforts to focus on tasks that enable rapid progress toward our core goals, we can be distracted or interrupted by other tasks. Some goals may be relatively easy to achieve whereas others may be difficult. Perhaps most critically, the environment may change rapidly and unpredictably, making it difficult to assess whether a goal can be achieved, whether a strategy for achieving a goal

is still effective, or whether other goals need attention. As a result, we may need to abandon a goal that may not be attainable in the time available, postpone it, or change our strategy for achieving it.

The good news is that scholars over the past decade have increasingly recognised the fact that "managing multiple goals is the norm rather than the exception" (Unsworth, Yeo & Beck, 2014, p. 1064), and consequently, the growing body of research in this area allows us to formulate some initial, tentative principles about how multiple goals are prioritised and structured. The emerging interest in complex dynamic systems (to be discussed under Challenge 8) has also provided an alternative to single-goal studies. We begin addressing existing innovations in this area by considering how process models have been found wanting from a dynamic systems perspective.

Innovation 1: From process models to a dynamic conception

Chapter 1 (CHALLENGE$_2$/INNOVATION$_1$) presented Dörnyei and Ottó's (1998) process model of L2 motivation, which described the initiation and enactment of motivation from the setting to the accomplishment of a goal. Although the model comprises several actional phases and various types of motivational influences, it concerns the attainment of a single goal only. This was consistent with Heckhausen and Kuhl's (1985) Theory of Action Control, which also considered the motivational process underlying a course of action in isolation, without any interference from other ongoing behaviours in which the actor was engaged. Unsworth et al. (2014) argue that in view of the complexities involved in the pursuit of multiple goals, findings from single-goal research are unlikely to be useful in informing multiple-goal contexts, and while this may perhaps be too extreme a position, the decline of scholarly interest in process models is certainly in line with this claim. The model by Dörnyei and Ottó (1998) did not account for any interactions with alternative behavioural intentions, which was coupled, as I summarised elsewhere (Dörnyei, 2000, 2009), with the fact that in complex behavioural sequences within real-life situations it may not be straightforward to distinguish different actional phases. For example, with regard to a first-year college student, where would the borderline be between pre-action and action? At the point when she decides to study in higher education? Or enrols in a particular university? Or selects her specific courses? Or attends a particular class? Or engages in a particular activity within this class? It seems logical that the consecutive steps will result in increasingly action-oriented mindsets, but this would also mean that the 'choice' phase of one actional step might happen simultaneously to the 'executive' phase of another, resulting in complex interferences.

Looking back, we may also query the linear nature of the motivational flow diagram presented by process models. As discussed in Dörnyei (2009), constructs such as the Dörnyei–Ottó model have multiple, parallel and interacting cause–effect relationships, accompanied by several circular feedback loops, which blur the claims about a uniform underlying motivational sequence and which raise the question as to whether it would be more profitable to replace the linear links with two-way, dynamic interactions. It was therefore a matter of time before I had to realise that such a patchwork of interwoven cause–effect relationships would not do the complexity of the motivation system justice and that a more radical reformulation was therefore needed. Such a radical change required the adoption of a dynamic systems approach to the understanding of the composition and collaboration of various motivational elements,

Interestingly, the thinking of a leading emotion researcher, Klaus Scherer, has gone through a similar transformation, arriving at the same conclusion regarding the modelling of emotions. Originally interested in the componential structure of emotions (for a review, see Scherer 2001), he became acutely aware of the changing nature of these components over time. Therefore, he called for the abandoning of "static state concepts" (Scherer, 1995, p. 5) and suggested instead that scholars "move from a domain-oriented approach to a process-oriented approach" (ibid). However, the recognition of the interlinking nature of different functional cognitive, affective and motivational aspects soon pushed his conceptualisation one step further, in the direction of a dynamic systems approach:

> Unfortunately, neither our conceptual nor our methodological tool kits are adapted to dealing with systems of the degree of complexity exhibited by emotion processes. There is little hope of 'repairing' our concepts and methods in a piecemeal fashion in order to do justice to the phenomenon under study. Rather, we need a complete revolution in our thinking about the nature of emotion, comparable to other paradigm shifts in the history of science. In particular, we need to move from thinking in terms of discrete boxes, labels, or even neural programs to a nonlinear dynamic systems perspective of emotion.
>
> *Scherer, 2000, pp. 77–80*

In summary, the main lesson from considering the history of process models is that while they responded to the challenge of treating learner characteristics in a process-oriented manner by adopting a genuine time and change perspective, they only played a transitional role. Their decline offered evidence that in order to capture the true dynamism of the interplay of various relevant motivational factors, scholars need to follow some of the principles of complex dynamic systems theory. However, as we shall see in Challenge 8, this is sometimes easier said than done.

Innovation 2: Goal configurations and temporal structuring

The prominence of multiple-goal interferences in shaping motivation has raised the question of how such interferences can best be accounted for. Hofer (2010) highlights the notion of 'goal configuration' as a useful organisational principle in this respect: "Given the concept of multiple goals as an adequate description of a person's life space, not a single goal but the goal configuration triggers behaviour" (p. 159). He distinguishes four main types of interrelationship between goals: (a) *goal convergence*, when different goals can be reached simultaneously (e.g. taking an extracurricular course partly to acquire knowledge and partly to meet new people); (b) *goal competition*, when resources are drawn away from one goal when another is chosen and vice versa; (c) *goal compensation*, when "a high preference for one goal might compensate for not pursuing another goal" (p. 159); and (d) *unrelated goals*, when pursuing one goal has no beneficial or detrimental relationship with realising another.

A useful notion related to the first type, 'goal convergence,' is *goal alliance*, which occurs through merging or nesting goals in an activity (Unsworth et al., 2014). We can make a learning task particularly attractive to students if it is shown that the required action can fulfil multiple goals of a different nature. Another way of coordinating multiple goals is through *temporarily structuring* them, which is, for example, the standard way of dealing with diverse demands and preferences in family life (see Hofer, 2010) through setting fixed times for various activities (e.g. leisure time, homework, household chores). Hofer argues that the essence of perceived goal conflict is "the feeling of uncertainty as to whether one should be doing something else rather than the activity that is currently being pursued" (p. 163), and fixed daily routines can reduce this tension. Such recurring time slots can also lead to the formation of *habits*, which will be an important issue when discussing long-term motivation and perseverance in Chapter 6.

Innovation 3: Principles of goal prioritisation

If goals cannot be aligned, some kind of goal prioritisation is needed, and the importance of this process is indicated by the fact that most of the recent literature on multiple goals in psychology concerns the reasons for directing resources to one activated goal and not another. Research has identified a number of factors playing a role in this selective practice (Neal, Ballard & Vancouver, 2017; see also Ballard et al., 2018; Unsworth et al., 2014):

- *Expectations* about what it will take to achieve a goal in terms of effort and time. Some people will focus first on the goal that has the best chance of achievement, while others may choose first the most demanding one or the one with the nearest deadline. When people expect that all the goals are achievable, they tend to prioritise the most distant goal, but shift to the nearest goal when not all the goals appear achievable. Shortening a deadline for a goal increases the tendency to prioritise it, unless the goal becomes too difficult to achieve.
- *Incentives* for goal achievement. People tend to rank goals according to their incentive value, but if two parallel goals have a positive and a negative incentive, they would usually allocate more resources to the goal for which failure is penalised (i.e. negative incentive).

- *Environmental certainty/uncertainty*. People tend to give preference to goals that are associated with unpredictable environments in which the amount of resources required to realise the goal could increase, whereas in predictable environments they would plan sequentially according to the feasibility of the goals.
- *Type of goal.* With 'avoidance goals' (i.e. goals which have an undesired outcome that one wants to prevent) the preference is for the goal for which the undesired state is closest, but people would also take risks to try and avoid all the negative outcomes; with 'approach goals' people tend to be more risk-averse in the spirit of a bird in the hand being worth two in the bush.

This list suffices to indicate that there are no simple principles when it comes to negotiating multiple competing roles. The outcome of the prioritisation will be dependent on a dynamic process of deliberation, which again highlights the relevance of dynamic systems principles (to be discussed below). Goal prioritisation becomes particularly relevant in student motivation when it comes to 'temptations,' that is, distracting goals that offer some immediate reward (e.g. playing a video game instead of preparing for an exam). We shall come back to this important issue in Chapter 6 when we discuss the role of self-control in perseverance, but it should be noted here that, as Hofer (2010) explains, the presence of a temptation may actually strengthen the commitment to the primary goal, because it brings its importance to the fore.

Challenge 8: How to handle the dynamic complexity of motivation

In the initial chapter of the *Oxford Handbook of Human Motivation*, Ryan (2012) cautions readers about the complexity of the subject:

> it is clear that when it comes to motivation there is rarely if ever a singular cause at work. Rather, actions can be depicted best as outcomes of a set of determinative processes that can be described through various levels of analysis and theoretical models.
>
> *p. 5*

The overview in this book so far has confirmed the truth of Ryan's claim. We have surveyed a series of fundamental challenges regarding the conceptualisation and understanding of motivation, ranging from the trait/state dichotomy and the existence of unconscious motives to contextual issues and various time-related factors. The emerging picture has been complex and multi-faceted but, quite frankly, should we realistically expect anything else? What complicates things further is that the confounding factors exert their influence simultaneously, thereby causing intricate interactions. This has led several scholars to the conclusion that the study of L2 motivation should draw on the principles of complex dynamic systems theory, which we shall discuss in Innovation 1. A fundamental question in applying this theory to human motivation is to decide what a 'complex dynamic system' consists of in our case, particularly in the light of the arguments we have reviewed earlier concerning context (CHALLENGE$_5$/INNOVATION$_5$), namely that in situated motivation research the most appropriate unit of analysis should be the 'person-in-context.' The challenge of identifying system boundaries in such a blended construct will be addressed in Innovation 2.

Innovation 1: Applying the principles of complex dynamic systems theory

The current discussion of complex dynamic systems theory (CDST) will focus only on the essence of CDST, which is, surprisingly, not as complicated as one would imagine. The real difficulty with CDST begins when it comes to the details of how the general principles operate in practice, with some of the most challenging questions concerning research methodology, which will be addressed in the next chapter (CHALLENGE$_{11}$). As Hiver and Larsen-Freeman (2020) point out, the major contribution of CDST to scholars in the social sciences has been "its way of thinking that represents a radically new foundation for scientific inquiry" (p. 288). A complex dynamic system perspective introduces a holistic approach that takes into account the combined and interactive operation of a number of different factors relevant to a specific situation rather than following the traditional practice of examining cause–effect relations between isolated variables. This ensemble of interactive factors is referred to as the 'system,' and it is considered 'dynamic' if it contains at least two components that are linked together but which also have a certain amount of life of their own in terms of change. The behaviour of such systems is often illustrated by the movement of a 'double pendulum,' which has an upper arm and a lower arm; both arms can move around, but the fact that they are interconnected interferes with their movement and makes the pendulum's overall behaviour seemingly bizarre and unpredictable: when we initiate a regular movement of the upper arm, the linked lower arm also starts moving but in a slightly different rhythm, which will soon upset the regularity of the overall movement (the Internet contains several useful short videos demonstrating this dynamic effect). Given that most systems in the real world have more than two interlinked components, we can expect to find many examples of complex dynamic behavioural patterns (for overviews of the application of CDST in SLA, see e.g. Ortega & Han, 2017; Verspoor, de Bot & Lowie, 2011).

For the sake of illustration, let us imagine Elmira, an international student studying at a Canadian university, and let us consider two important factors in her experience: the amount of contact she has with local people and the development of her English language proficiency. It stands to reason to assume that the two variables are related to each other: on the one hand, the better Elmira's English becomes, the easier it is for her to establish relationships with English speakers; on the other hand, more contact with English speakers means more L2 practice opportunities for her, which in turn leads to further L2 development. Such a relationship would be described as 'linear,' because an increase in one variable causes a proportionate increase in the other.

In reality, however, it is rare to find such a neat linear link, and Elmira's situation is likely to be more 'complex' and 'dynamic,' because both her English proficiency and her contact with L2 speakers will be determined by other factors as well. For example, her L2 proficiency may be affected by her language aptitude, and the amount of contact she has with locals will depend, amongst other things, on her personality features and the availability of contact opportunities. That is, both variables will have their own independent 'movement,' and because the two variables are linked together, the external interferences are likely to cause some nonlinear behaviour, similar to that of the two arms of the double pendulum. For example, due to her, say, lower than average language aptitude, Elmira might find learning English harder than anticipated, which will have a demotivating effect on her and will cause her to reduce the effort to engage in intercultural contact with local people and hang out instead with her peers of the same L1 background (a rather common scenario). The ensuing reduction in the amount of contact with native speakers will, in turn, further slow down the development of her L2 proficiency, placing her thus on a downward spiral. Alternatively, one day Elmira might meet the irresistible local Jimmy, and their budding romantic relationship will lead to a dramatic increase in her participation in host-national networks. This increased contact is likely to have a positive impact on her English, potentially compensating for her limited language aptitude, thereby placing her on an upward spiral.

The hope that underlies the adoption of a complex dynamic systems perspective in applied linguistic research is that it will shed new light on such interacting phenomena, explaining certain observations that simply do not make sense when examined within a linear, cause–effect framework. L2 development is always a function of several interfering factors, and CDST can in principle handle multiple variables as they interact with each other. Unfortunately, however, as we shall see in the next chapter (CHALLENGE$_{11}$), it is not always easy to translate dynamic system principles into specific, workable research designs, as the approach poses considerable research methodological challenges. Yet, as Hiver and Papi (2020) summarise, the new way of systemic thinking has fertilised several strands of L2 motivation research related to issues such as multilingualism, long-term motivation, small group dynamics, demotivation and teacher–learner relationships.

Innovation 2: Placing the agent in the centre of a complex motivational system

Drawing on the work of Evan Thompson, Heidi Byrnes and the Douglas Fir Group, Diane Larsen-Freeman (2019, p. 62) defines agency in SLA as "the capacity to act," particularly with regard to "optimizing conditions for one's own learning and choosing to deploy one's semiotic resources to position oneself as one would wish in a multilingual world." We must realise that this seemingly problem-free definition is actually at odds with some recent claims in the literature about the nonagentive status of L2 learners, which explains why Larsen-Freeman further clarifies her position as follows:

> Let me make clear my position: I do believe we humans are social beings. Communion with others is essential to our survival as individuals. Also, I recognize the need to guard against an ethos of individualism and neoliberalism, and I am aware that SLA's social turn was in part a rejection of the individualism of 'mainstream' SLA theories. I do not wish to be overly agentive, I am not a Cartesian dualist, pitting the social against the individual, and I do not discount collective agency. Nor do I reject the posthumanists' charge that agency is not exclusively human. Finally, I recognize that I am a product of my own noncollectivist culture, and I am aware of my privileged status within it.
>
> p. 63

In other words, Larsen-Freeman foregrounds the role of agency in full awareness of possible objections that such a stance might evoke, and then devotes a whole article to making the case that the agency of language learners should be "respected in SLA theories" (p. 73). In fact, she argues, one of the main functions of educational practices in general is exactly to help students to enact and enhance their agency as proactive learners. In a paper entitled "Human agency: Does the beach ball have free will?" Al-Hoorie (2015) discusses attacks on human agency by scholars investigating unconscious motivation, and his conclusion coincides with Larsen-Freeman's: although there are factors that impose certain limitations on humans exercising their agency, these do not completely diminish this capacity (which is a topic we shall return to in Chapter 4 when exploring unconscious motivation). Hiver and Larsen-Freeman (2020, p. 289) summarise this view in connection with motivation research as follows:

> we believe that the study of human and social systems always implicates agency, whether this is individual or collective. This makes it necessary to include within any human system's boundaries an agent, or agents, capable of exercising intentional action that contributes causally, though not deterministically, to the system's motivational outcomes and processes of change.

The reason for discussing the question of agency at such length is that when we apply the principles of CDST to the understanding of motivation, it is easy to arrive at a position that the individual is but one factor in a larger system in which no single factor has control. For example, regarding the notion of the 'person-in-context' that we discussed earlier (CHALLENGE$_5$/INNOVATION$_5$), Yim, Clément and MacIntyre (2020, p. 227) rightly point out: "But the question then becomes how to distinguish learners from context? Furthermore, how to define the internal, external, and temporal boundaries of context? Any one focal element, such as motivation, potentially makes all other elements part of the context." That this is a pressing issue is reflected by the fact that in a paper specifically devoted to discussing context within a CDST framework, Ushioda (2015, p. 48) poses the same question: "If learners are 'persons-in-context' who are inherently part of, act upon and contribute to shaping the social, cultural and physical environments with which they interact, how do we differentiate meaningfully between learner and context when examining these evolving interactions?" She candidly admits that "There do not appear to be any straightforward solutions to these (and other related) questions" (p. 49) and accordingly, "we are obliged to make certain pragmatic decisions about the contextual elements to be included and excluded, and pragmatic choices about the nested levels of analysis to focus on" (ibid).

This is the point where having an agent (individual or collective) at the centre of the system is, I believe, indispensable, as it offers a firm reference point that can be used to provide cues about how to identify and delimit all the contextual elements that are relevant to the motivational analysis in question. This would be otherwise a real challenge in CDST, because, as Carver and Scheier (2013, p. 131) point out, "you never know all the influences on a system, and the ones you do know are never known with total precision." When Ema Ushioda and I considered practical ways of dealing with this issue (Dörnyei & Ushioda, 2011), we suggested that because the agent has a central position in the complex motivational system, his/her self-report obtained through a qualitative exploratory investigation can offer sufficient clues about the appropriate angle to take and how wide to spread our (research) net to be able to uncover the essence of an intricate motivational set-up. Therefore, we optimistically added, "a carefully executed deep interview study would have the chance to get to the bottom of this. Thus, all we need to do is ask the right questions" (p. 99). This cheerful phenomenological position has been, however, questioned by the recognition in motivational psychology of the salient role played by contextually cued unconscious attitudes and motives, and Chapter 4 will be entirely devoted to exploring this matter further.

References

Ajzen, I., & Fishbein, M. (1980). *Understanding attitudes and predicting social behaviour*. Englewood Cliffs, NJ: Prentice Hall.

Al-Hoorie, A. H. (2015). Human agency: Does the beach ball have free will? In Z. Dörnyei, P. D. MacIntyre & A. Henry (Eds.), *Motivational dynamics in language learning* (pp. 55–72). Bristol: Multilingual Matters.

Ames, C., & Ames, R. (1984). Systems of student and teacher motivation: Toward a qualitative definition. *Journal of Educational Psychology, 76*, 535–556.

Ballard, T., Vancouver, J. B., & Neal, A. (2018). On the pursuit of multiple goals with different deadlines. *Journal of Applied Psychology, 103*(11), 1242–1264.

Bandura, A., & Simon, K. M. (1977). The role of proximal intentions in self-regulation of refractory behavior. *Cognitive Therapy and Research, 1*(3), 177–193.

Boo, Z., Dörnyei, Z., & Ryan, S. (2015). L2 Motivation research 2005–2014: Understanding a publication surge and a changing landscape. *System, 55*, 147–157.

Boudreau, C., MacIntyre, P. D., & Dewaele, J.-M. (2018). Enjoyment and anxiety in second language communication: An idiodynamic approach. *Studies in Second Language Learning and Teaching, 8*(1), 149–170.

Bronfenbrenner, U. (1979). *The ecology of human development: Experiments by nature and design.* Cambridge, MA: Harvard University Press.

Carver, C. C., & Scheier, M. F. (2013). Self-regulatory perspectives on personality. In I. B. Weiner, N. W. Schmitt & S. Highhouse (Eds.), *Handbook of psychology* (2nd ed., Vol. 5, pp. 119–139). Hoboken, NJ: Wiley.

Clément, R. (1980). Ethnicity, contact and communicative competence in a second language. In H. Giles, W. P. Robinson & P. M. Smith (Eds.), *Language: Social psychological perspectives* (pp. 147–154). Oxford: Pergamon.

Clément, R. (1986). Second language proficiency and acculturation: An investigation of the effects of language status and individual characteristics. *Journal of Language and Social Psychology, 5*, 271–290.

Clément, R., & Noels, K. A. (1992). Toward a situated approach to ethnolinguistic identity: The effects of status on individuals and groups. *Journal of Language and Social Psychology, 11*, 203–232.

de Bot, K. (2015). Rates of change: Timescales in second language development. In Z. Dörnyei, P. D. MacIntyre & A. Henry (Eds.), *Motivational dynamics in language learning* (pp. 29–37). Bristol: Multilingual Matters.

Deci, E. L., & Ryan, R. M. (1985). *Intrinsic motivation and self-determination in human behaviour.* New York: Plenum.

Dörnyei, Z. (2000). Motivation in action: Towards a process-oriented conceptualisation of student motivation. *British Journal of Educational Psychology, 70*, 519–538.

Dörnyei, Z. (2005). *The psychology of the language learner: Individual differences in second language acquisition.* Mahwah, NJ: Lawrence Erlbaum.

Dörnyei, Z. (2009). *The psychology of second language acquisition.* Oxford: Oxford University Press.

Dörnyei, Z., & Ottó, I. (1998). Motivation in action: A process model of L2 motivation. *Working Papers in Applied Linguistics (Thames Valley University, London), 4*, 43–69.

Dörnyei, Z., & Ryan, S. (2015). *The psychology of the language learner revisited.* New York: Routledge.

Dörnyei, Z., & Ushioda, E. (2011). *Teaching and researching motivation* (2nd ed.). Harlow: Longman.

Douglas Fir Group. (2016). A transdisciplinary framework for SLA in a multilingual world. *Modern Language Journal, 100*(Supplement 2016), 19–47.

Gardner, R. C. (1985a). *Social psychology and second language learning: The role of attitudes and motivation.* London: Edward Arnold.

Gardner, R. C. (1985b). *The attitude/motivation test battery: Technical report.* London, ON: Univ. of Western Ontario.

Gardner, R. C. (2001). *Psychological statistics using SPSS for Windows.* Upper Saddle River, NJ: Prentice Hall.

Gardner, R. C., & Lambert, W. E. (1959). Motivational variables in second language acquisition. *Canadian Journal of Psychology, 13*, 266-272.

Graham, S. (1996). What's 'emotional' about social motivation: A comment. In Y. Juvonen & K. R. Wentzel (Eds.), *Social motivation: Understanding children's school adjustment* (pp. 346–360). New York: Cambridge University Press.

Gurtner, J.-L., Monnard, I., & Genoud, P. (2001). Towards a multilayer model of context and its impact on motivation. In S. Volet & S. Järvelä (Eds.), *Motivation in learning contexts: Theoretical and methodological implications* (pp. 189–208). Bingley: Emerald.

Heckhausen, H., & Kuhl, J. (1985). From wishes to action: The dead ends and short cuts on the long way to action. In M. Frese & J. Sabini (Eds.), *Goal-directed behaviour: The concept of action in psychology* (pp. 134–160). Hillsdale, NJ: Lawrence Erlbaum.

Hiver, P., & Al-Hoorie, A. H. (2016). A dynamic ensemble for second language research: Putting complexity theory into practice. *Modern Language Journal, 100*(4), 1–16.

Hiver, P., & Larsen-Freeman, D. (2020). Motivation: It *is* a relational system. In A. H. Al-Hoorie & P. D. MacIntyre (Eds.), *Contemporary language motivation theory: 60 years since Gardner and Lambert (1959)* (pp. 285–303). Bristol: Multilingual Matters.

Hiver, P., & Papi, M. (2020). Complexity theory and L2 motivation. In M. Lamb, K. Csizér, A. Henry & S. Ryan (Eds.), *Palgrave Macmillan handbook of motivation for language learning* (pp. 117–137). Basingstoke: Palgrave.

Hofer, M. (2010). Adolescents' development of individual interests: A product of multiple goal regulation? *Educational Psychologist, 45*(3), 149–166.

Juvonen, Y., & Wentzel, K. R. (Eds.). (1996). *Social motivation: Understanding children's school adjustment*. New York: Cambridge University Press.

King, R. B., & McInerney, D. M. (2014). Culture's consequences on student motivation: Capturing cross-cultural universality and variability through personal investment theory. *Educational Psychologist, 49*(3), 175–198.

Lafford, B. A. (2007). Second language acquisition reconceptualized? The impact of Firth and Wagner (1997). (Focus Issue). *Modern Language Journal, 91*, 735–756.

Larsen-Freeman, D. (2007). Reflecting on the cognitive-social debate in second language acquisition. *Modern Language Journal, 91*, 773–787.

Larsen-Freeman, D. (2019). On language learner agency: A complex dynamic systems theory perspective. *Modern Language Journal, 103*(Supplement 2019), 61–79.

MacIntyre, P. D. (2012). The idiodynamic method: A closer look at the dynamics of communication traits. *Communication Research Reports, 29*(4), 361–367.

MacIntyre, P. D., & Serroul, A. (2015). Motivation on a per-second timescale: Examining approach–avoidance motivation during L2 task performance. In Z. Dörnyei, P. D. MacIntyre & A. Henry (Eds.), *Motivational dynamics in language learning* (pp. 109–138). Bristol: Multilingual Matters.

Markus, H. R. (2016). What moves people to action? Culture and motivation. *Current Opinion in Psychology, 8*, 161–166.

Maslow, A. H. (1970). *Motivation and personality* (2nd ed.). New York: Harper and Row.

McClelland, D. C. (1961). *The achieving society*. New York: Van Nostrand.

Milyavskaya, M., & Werner, K. M. (2018). Goal pursuit: Current state of affairs and directions for future research. *Canadian Psychology, 59*(2), 163–175.

Neal, A., Ballard, T., & Vancouver, J. B. (2017). Dynamic self-regulation and multiple-goal pursuit. *Annual Review of Organizational Psychology and Organizational Behavior, 4*, 401–423.

Noels, K. A., Pon, G., & Clément, R. (1996). Language, identity and adjustment: The role of linguistic self-confidence in the acculturation process. *Journal of Language and Social Psychology, 15*, 246–264.

Nolen, S. B., Horn, I. S., & Ward, C. J. (2015). Situating motivation. *Educational Psychologist, 50*(3), 234–247.

Ortega, L., & Han, Z. (Eds.). (2017). *Complexity theory and language development: In celebration of Diane Larsen-Freeman*. Amsterdam: John Benjamins.

Paris, S. G., & Turner, J. C. (1994). Situated motivation. In P. R. Pintrich, D. R. Brown & C. E. Weinstein (Eds.), *Student motivation, cognition, and learning* (pp. 213–237). Hillsdale, NJ: Lawrence Erlbaum.

Pintrich, P. R. (2000). Educational psychology at the millennium: A look back and a look forward. *Educational Psychologist, 35*(4), 221–226.

Pintrich, P. R., & Maehr, M. L. (Eds.). (1995). *Advances in motivation and achievement: Culture, motivation and achievement*. Bingley: Emerald.

Pintrich, P. R., & Schunk, D. H. (2002). *Motivation in education: Theory, research, and applications* (2nd ed.). Upper Saddle River, NJ: Merrill Prentice Hall.

Rauthmann, J. F., Sherman, R. A., & Funder, D. C. (2015). Principles of situation research: Towards a better understanding of psychological situations. *European Journal of Personality, 29*, 363–381.

Rubenfeld, S., & Clément, R. (2020). Identity, adaptation and social harmony: A legacy of the socio-educational model. In A. H. Al-Hoorie & P. D. MacIntyre (Eds.), *Contemporary language motivation theory: 60 years since Gardner and Lambert (1959)* (pp. 109–129). Bristol: Multilingual Matters.

Rueda, R., & Dembo, M. H. (1995). Motivational processes in learning: A comparative analysis of cognitive and sociocultural frameworks. *Advances in Motivation and Achievement, 9*, 255–289.

Ryan, R. M. (2012). Motivation and the organisation of human behavior: Three reasons for the reemergence of a field. In R. M. Ryan (Ed.), *The Oxford handbook of human motivation* (pp. 3–10). New York: Oxford University Press.

Salili, F., Chiu, C.-J., & Hong, Y. (Eds.). (2001). *Student motivation: The culture and context of learning*. New York: Kluwer.

Sampson, R. J. (2016). EFL teacher motivation in-situ: Co-adaptive processes, openness and relational motivation over interacting timescales. *Studies in Second Language Learning and Teaching, 6*(2), 293–318.

Scherer, K. R. (1995). Plato's legacy: Relationships between cognition, emotion, and motivation. *Geneva Studies in Emotion and Communication, 9*(1), 1–7 (https://archive-ouverte.unige.ch/unige:102030).

Scherer, K. R. (2000). Emotions as episodes of subsystem synchronization driven by nonlinear appraisal processes. In M. D. Lewis & I. Granic (Eds.), *Emotion, development, and self-organization: Dynamic systems approaches to emotional development* (pp. 70–99). Cambridge: Cambridge University Press.

Scherer, K. R. (2001). Psychological structure of emotions. In N. J. Smelser & P. B. Baltes (Eds.), *International encyclopedia of the social and behavioral sciences* (pp. 4472–4477). Oxford: Pergamon.

Unsworth, K., Yeo, G., & Beck, J. (2014). Multiple goals: A review and derivation of general principles. *Journal of Organizational Behavior, 35*, 1064–1078.

Urdan, T. C. (2001). Contextual influences on motivation and performance: An examination of achievement goal structures. In F. Salili, C.-J. Chiu & Y.Y. Hong (Eds.), *Student motivation: The culture and context of learning* (pp. 171–201). New York: Kluwer.

Urdan, T. C. (Ed.). (1999). *Advances in motivation and achievement: The role of context*. Bingley: Emerald.

Ushioda, E. (1998). Effective motivational thinking: A cognitive theoretical approach to the study of language learning motivation. In E. A. Soler & V. C. Espurz (Eds.), *Current issues in English language methodology* (pp. 77–89). Castelló de la Plana, Spain: Universitat Jaume.

Ushioda, E. (2009). A person-in-context relational view of emergent motivation and identity. In Z. Dörnyei & E. Ushioda (Eds.), *Motivation, language identity and the L2 self* (pp. 215–228). Bristol: Multilingual Matters.

Ushioda, E. (2015). Context and dynamic systems theory. In Z. Dörnyei, P. D. MacIntyre & A. Henry (Eds.), *Motivational dynamics in language learning* (pp. 47–54). Bristol: Multilingual Matters.

Ushioda, E. (2020a). Researching L2 motivation: Past, present and future. In M. Lamb, K. Csizér, A. Henry & S. Ryan (Eds.), *Palgrave Macmillan handbook of motivation for language learning* (pp. 661–682). Basingstoke: Palgrave.
Ushioda, E. (2020b). Researching L2 motivation: Re-evaluating the role of qualitative inquiry, or the 'wine and conversation' approach. In A. H. Al-Hoorie & P. D. MacIntyre (Eds.), *Contemporary language motivation theory: 60 years since Gardner and Lambert (1959)* (pp. 194–211). Bristol: Multilingual Matters.
Ushioda, E. (in press). *Language learning motivation: An ethical agenda for research*. Oxford: Oxford University Press.
Valsiner, J. (2007). *Culture in minds and societies*. Thousand Oaks, CA: Sage.
Verspoor, M. H., de Bot, K., & Lowie, W. (Eds.). (2011). *A dynamic approach to second language development: Methods and techniques*. Amsterdam: John Benjamins.
Volet, S. (2001). Understanding learning and motivation in context: A multi-dimensional and multi-level cognitive-situative perspective. In S. Volet & S. Järvelä (Eds.), *Motivation in learning contexts: Theoretical and methodological implications* (pp. 57–82). Bingley: Emerald.
Volet, S., & Järvelä, S. (Eds.). (2001). *Motivation in learning contexts: Theoretical and methodological implications*. Bingley: Emerald.
Waninge, F., Dörnyei, Z., & de Bot, K. (2014). Motivational dynamics in language learning: Change, stability and context. *Modern Language Journal, 98*(3), 704–723.
Weiner, B. (1994). Integrating social and personal theories of achievement motivation. *Review of Educational Research, 64*, 557–573.
Wentzel, K. R. (1996). Introduction: New perspectives on motivation at school. In Y. Juvonen & K. R. Wentzel (Eds.), *Social motivation: Understanding children's school adjustment* (pp. 1–8). New York: Cambridge University Press.
Wentzel, K. R. (1999). Social-motivational processes and interpersonal relationships: Implications for understanding motivation at school. *Journal of Educational Psychology, 91*, 76–97.
Williams, M. (1994). Motivation in foreign and second language learning: An interactive perspective. *Educational and Child Psychology, 11*, 77–84.
Wosnitza, M., & Beltman, S. (2012). Learning and motivation in multiple contexts: The development of a heuristic framework. *European Journal of Psychology of Education, 27*, 177–193.
Yashima, T., & Arano, K. (2015). Understanding EFL learners' motivational dynamics: A three-level model from a dynamic systems and sociocultural perspective. In Z. Dörnyei, P. D. MacIntyre, & A. Henry (Eds.), *Motivational dynamics in language learning* (pp. 285–314). Bristol: Multilingual Matters.
Yim, O., Clément, R., & MacIntyre, P. D. (2020). Contexts of SLA motivation: Linking ideologies to situational variations. In M. Lamb, K. Csizér, A. Henry & S. Ryan (Eds.), *Palgrave Macmillan handbook of motivation for language learning* (pp. 225–244). Basingstoke: Palgrave.
Zuengler, J., & Miller, E. R. (2006). Cognitive and sociocultural perspectives: Two parallel SLA worlds? *TESOL Quarterly, 40*(1), 35–58.

3
FUNDAMENTAL CHALLENGES III
Motivation applied

One of the main attractions of researching motivation for me has always been its practical applicability, and since the 1990s, the field has been characterised by ongoing efforts to add an 'applied' dimension to L2 motivation research. Yet, such efforts have not been without difficulties, and this chapter will address three challenging areas: (a) making motivation research relevant to the understanding of specific SLA processes; (b) developing motivational techniques that can produce actual gains in language learning; and (c) measuring the broad and dynamic notion of motivation.

Challenge 9: Motivation and SLA

Looking back at the last two chapters, it is noticeable how generic much of the discussion has been: a great deal of the motivational issues and principles that were drawn on originated in mainstream psychology, without any specific reference to SLA, and, similarly, many of the innovations listed would apply not only to language learning but also to other behaviours. This is no accident: motivation is a higher-order mental function and therefore the motivational principles underlying a behavioural domain are often directly transferrable to another area (e.g. the 'expectancy of success' factor, which is one of the most established sources of motivation in the literature, is equally relevant to performing a language task and, say, a DIY job). Within the study of L2 motivation, we find a situation that is rather similar in nature: the overwhelming bulk of L2 motivation research concerns language learning in general, without specifying any L2 learning subskills or L2 proficiency aspect. As a result, while L2 motivation research has accumulated a great deal of knowledge on how goals, visions and various types of positive incentives can impact on learners' general disposition towards learning an L2, far less is known about how the motivation to develop, say, L2 academic writing skills, is different from the overall L2 motivation construct, and hardly any studies have been conducted on specific procedures such as, say, motivating learners to engage in intensive L2 reading. In a recent position paper, Ushioda (2016) argues that this generic orientation of the field is a limitation that is partly responsible for keeping L2 motivation research outside mainstream SLA:

> a major reason why motivation research has remained somewhat isolated from the core linguistic traditions of the SLA field is because the analysis of motivation and its role in language learning has largely been at the level of global learning behaviours and L2 achievement outcomes, and motivation research has tended not to address more fine-grained processes of language acquisition or linguistic development.
>
> *p. 565*

Having co-authored a systematic literature review of over 400 published papers on L2 motivation between 2005 and 2014 (Boo, Dörnyei & Ryan, 2015), I can attest to the validity of Ushioda's claim; she is right that apart from a few studies on the motivational correlates of L2 pronunciation, little of the existing SLA scholarship has related motivational factors to specific internal processes of L2 development. However, we also need to recognise that the resulting "somewhat limited and tangential" nature of our field (Ushioda, 2016, p. 565) reflects a broader underlying issue concerning the understanding of motivation–cognition relations: in the Introduction of a pioneering edited volume on *Motivation and Cognitive Control* – published in the same year as Ushioda's paper – Braver (2016, p. 15) laments that the "scientific literature that has directly focused on the nature and mechanisms of motivation-cognition interactions, although rapidly growing, is still relatively young and not fully mature." That is, connecting motivational factors with cognitive processes (such as various aspects of learning) has also posed a problem in psychology, not unlike the situation Ushioda describes within SLA.

It is important to emphasise that the absence of relevant scholarship is not an indication of the fact that the motivation–cognition interface is weak or negligible; Braver (2016) argues, for example, that there exist a number of cognitive processes that appear to be considerably enhanced by motivational incentives, including active maintenance in working memory, selective attention and episodic memory encoding. He specifically highlights the potentially special relationship between motivation and 'cognitive control,' which can be defined as "the set of processes that regulate thought and action based on internally maintained task goals" (p. 3); as such, Braver argues, motivational signals can be expected to influence the selection, activation and intensity level of such task goals. In a similar vein, we can make a case for the possibility of identifying fruitful research directions in this area within the field of SLA as well; Innovation 1 will address the question of how to 'sharpen' our research focus in response to the non-L2-specificity challenge, and Innovation 2 will explore the rather undertheorised notion of 'task motivation.'

Innovation 1: Taking a 'small lens' approach

In order to counteract the tendency in the L2 motivation field to investigate language learning and teaching at a rather general level only, Ushioda (2016) proposes an agenda for researching language learning motivation 'through a small lens.' By this she means a 'sharpening' of the empirical research focus by keeping the scope of the study narrow, which can be achieved by zooming in on specific motivational issues and corresponding concrete criterion measures in the research design (e.g. exploring what motives best facilitate the quality and quantity of completed homework). As Ushioda (2020a) argues, such a targeted approach is more likely to develop nuanced insights into locally grounded research issues, and could potentially make a meaningful contribution to our existing knowledge even in relatively small-scale projects (hence the approach would be suitable, she suggests, even for MA dissertations).

Looking at the motivation–cognition connection more closely, parallels between suggestions made by Ushioda (2016) and Braver (2016) are reassuring, as they both begin with highlighting 'attention' as the key aspect to focus on. Braver points out that the relationship between motivation and attention is still insufficiently understood, but the few focused studies conducted on this interaction suggest that motivation *can* enhance attention and the operation of the working memory. Pessoa and Engelmann (2010), for example, provide neuroimaging evidence that motivational signals modulate multiple neural regions involved in attention to guide goal-directed behaviour, and Lewthwaite and Wulf (2017) have also found that when participants were motivated to pay conscious attention to certain aspects of a task, they were more likely to achieve optimal performance. This creates a parallel with a possible connection within the field of SLA, highlighted by Ushioda (2016), namely the interface between motivation and the cognitive process of *noticing*. This link was originally underlined in Crookes and Schmidt's (1991) seminal paper, and given that the 'noticing hypothesis' (Schmidt, 1995, 2001) has been a well-established theoretical principle in mainstream SLA research, establishing the existence of such an interaction would have considerable future potential. Although there has been little follow-up research in this area, Ushioda mentions one valuable exception, Takahashi's (2005) investigation of the motivational effects on L2 learners' attention and awareness when processing *pragmalinguistic features* (i.e. formulaic language associated with certain language functions): in this study, Japanese learners of English with a strong level of intrinsic motivation were found to be particularly attentive to idiomatic expressions, irrespective of their levels of proficiency. This is a good example of the impact of motivation on the acquisition of specific target L2 features, and thus a fitting illustration of the small lens approach.

Innovation 2: Task-based motivation

Another logical approach to linking the study of motivation to concrete elements of the L2 instructional process is focusing on the basic unit of instructed SLA, *the learning task*. There has been a steady flow of studies on task motivation over the past two decades (e.g. Dörnyei, 2002; Dörnyei & Kormos, 2000; Kormos & Dörnyei, 2004; Lambert & Zhang, 2019; Lambert, Philp & Nakamura, 2017; Mozgalina, 2015; Poupore, 2016; Yanguas, 2011; for a review, see Kormos & Wilby, 2020), but the results have remained somewhat episodic; they highlighted a number of important factors and considerations without integrating them into a broader construct. This can be partly explained by the theoretical challenge of conceptualising motivation at such a highly situated, context- and content-dependent manner. In a recent overview, I argued (Dörnyei, 2019a) that this challenge is partly due to the fact that task behaviour is determined by a wide range of variables, involving *learner-specific factors* (e.g. cognitive, motivational and emotional factors; level of L2 competence; personality traits; parental support); *learning situational factors* (e.g. teacher, class size, composition of the learner group, school ethos, norms and regulations); *task-related factors* (e.g. task content, task structure, expected task outcome, task participants, the availability of support structures); and *other miscellaneous factors* (e.g. various time/timing-related issues, different types of distractions and disruptions).

The difficulty of conceptualising motivation at the task level lies in the need to take all (or most of) the above factors into account simultaneously. In order to capture the outcome of the complex network of interacting task influences, Dörnyei (2019a) has drawn on the theory of student engagement (Mercer & Dörnyei, 2020; see CHALLENGE$_{10}$/INNOVATION$_2$) and 'directed motivational currents' (Dörnyei, Henry & Muir, 2016; see Chapter 6), and formulated a set of guidelines for delineating the character of an engaging task under six categories:

- *Task presentation* – introducing a task in a motivating manner.
- *Task goals* – setting personally meaningful goals linked to tangible outcomes.
- *Task content* – designing tasks with content that is not only interesting but also both relevant and real to students.
- *Task ownership and challenges–skills balance* – making sure that students approach the task in an autonomous manner and that their skills match the task demands.
- *Task structure* – making the required outcome transparent and including distinct subphases whose completion provides a clear sense of progress.
- *Positive emotional tenor* – increasing the students 'social wellbeing' through healthy group dynamics.

Challenge 10: How to enhance motivation meaningfully, without carrots and sticks

Using 'carrots' and 'sticks' – that is, incentives and punishments – as motivational tools has been an age-old practice, so what's wrong with them? That is, why would it be not meaningful to offer someone a reward for accomplishing something, and why would we want to do away with the threat of the 'stick' when someone fails to reach a target? These questions feature prominently in modern educational psychology and we should be clear on one point to start the discussion with, namely that 'not meaningful' does not mean 'doesn't work.' Carrots and sticks *can* enhance achievement – and therefore, they *can* motivate – irrespective of the nature of the task. Indeed, monetary rewards (financial enticements, bonuses, tips, bribes, etc.) are known to work as powerful incentives and can get jobs done; likewise, educational rewards (grades, prizes, certificates, etc.) have been used – along with their negative counterparts, such as various forms of penalties – as some of the chief engines of institutionalised learning for several millennia. And yet, there is a serious problem with these practices. If we think about it, offering a reward is an implicit acknowledgement that achieving the outcome of a task would *not* be rewarding enough in itself; therefore, the task needs to be reinforced externally, by tagging an additional prize to its successful accomplishment. However, by offering grades and prizes, we are not making the learning activity itself any more rewarding but are simply offering a compensation for the engagement. In fact, grades can actually *divert* attention *away* from the task, which becomes evident when learners spend more creative energy figuring out how to maximise their rewards without any additional learning effort than how to master the material. Covington (1999) rightly points out that school children can become obsessed with grades: "many students are grade driven, not to say, 'grade grubbing,' and this preoccupation begins surprisingly early in life" (p. 127).

The main point for the current discussion is that while the 'carrot and stick' approach may work in the short run, rarely does it lead to genuine, long-term commitment. This being the case, what would be a 'meaningful' approach to motivating learners? Following the logic of the above discussion, such an approach would need to turn the learning activity itself into being more rewarding. Admittedly, this would be a tall order at any time, but achieving it has become even more of a challenge in our current age when students are continuously bombarded with information and communications through multiple channels, all intended to captivate their attention and offer immediate gratification. All is not lost, however: there have been several successful attempts in education to combat this negative trend, and the four innovations described below offer concrete ways of enhancing motivation meaningfully; they will be complemented by a fifth line of relevant research on strategies enhancing one's vision in Chapter 5.

Innovation 1: Applying motivational strategies

Boo et al.'s (2015) review of the L2 motivation literature between 2005 and 2014 concluded that published papers on the *theory* of motivation outnumbered the articles that discussed issues on how to *increase* the learners' motivation in some practically minded manner at a ratio of 2:1. Yet, if we look back at the history of motivation research in psychology, the (perhaps) surprising fact is that, as Danziger (1997) explains, the initial driving force for introducing and exploring the notion of 'motivation' in the first decades of the 20th century was the desire to understand how people could be *motivated*:

> The specific reference of this term was at that time directed at the growing literature on the improvement of advertising and salesmanship, industrial

efficiency, teaching practice, and personal advancement. It was recognized that these improvements could not be achieved simply by force or by the manipulation of the environment. One had to play upon what individuals wanted, what they were interested in, what they privately wished for. Everyday terms like desire, want, interest, and also motive, were used to represent what it was one had to influence.

p. 113

Thus, as Danziger (1997) continues, the main demand for a theoretical psychological account of motivation came from professionals who were interested in influencing and controlling human behaviour and who wanted to have a scientific basis to build their practical strategies on. With the growing sophistication of the field of psychology, the scientific accounts of motivation became increasingly elaborate, theoretical and diverse, yet the field never lost touch with practical implications. Furthermore, educational psychology has always been at the forefront of motivation research, keeping thus alive the need to generate applicable knowledge for classroom practitioners. This being the case, there has been a steady flow of works in motivational psychology offering strategies to motivate learners.

Within the field of SLA, motivation researchers interested in educational applications traditionally faced two challenges. First, because of the peculiar circumstances of the genesis of L2 motivation research pioneered by primarily Canadian social psychologists (see CHALLENGE$_5$/INNOVATION$_4$), the initial emphasis was not so much on educational factors as on psychological variables implicated in the macro-context of L2 learning such as attitudes towards the L2 and identification with the target ethnolinguistic communities. When I entered the field in the late 1980s, there had been no synthesis of the educational psychological work on motivation that was relevant to SLA. Therefore, practically minded motivation researchers had to draw on the psychological literature for resources in this respect, which in turn led to the second challenge: how to select from the wealth of potentially useful material and how to offer a cohesive account of this for language teachers? The Dörnyei and Ottó (1998) process model (see CHALLENGE$_2$/INNOVATION$_1$) offered a comprehensive framework in this respect, as it allowed me to organise the relevant strategies along the progression from the initial arousal of the motivation to the completion and evaluation of the motivated action. Accordingly, in a book-length overview of motivational strategies (Dörnyei, 2001a), I took the main stages described in the process model and then added a preliminary stage whose aim was to create appropriate classroom conditions for motivation to thrive. The result was the following framework of four broad clusters, which comprised over 35 strategies that were further broken down into over 100 specific motivational techniques:

1. *Creating the basic motivational conditions.* Motivational strategies cannot be employed successfully in a motivational vacuum; certain pre-conditions must be in place before any further attempts to generate motivation can be effective.
2. *Generating initial motivation.* Unless we are singularly fortunate with the composition of our classes, student motivation will not be automatic for everybody;

consequently, we need to actively generate positive student attitudes towards L2 learning.
3. *Maintaining and protecting motivation.* We can initially whet the students' appetites with appropriate motivational techniques, but unless motivation is actively maintained and protected, it is likely to decrease in strength over time and can even disappear altogether.
4. *Encouraging positive retrospective self-evaluation.* The way learners feel about their past accomplishments significantly determines how they approach subsequent learning tasks. However, the students' appraisal of their past does not depend purely on the absolute, objective level of the success they have achieved but also on how they subjectively interpret their achievement. Using appropriate strategies, teachers can help learners to evaluate their past performance in a more positive light, take more satisfaction in their successes and progress, and explain their past failures in a constructive way.

This compilation filled an existing gap in the L2 literature and was well received by classroom practitioners. It also initiated a growing body of research investigating how a motivational teaching practice can have a significant positive impact on student motivation (for recent summaries, see e.g. Cohen & Henry, 2019; Dörnyei & Muir, 2019; Lamb, 2017, 2020).

Innovation 2: Focusing on 'student engagement'

One of the most influential innovations in looking at L2 learner characteristics in the 1990s was the introduction and conceptualisation of the 'willingness to communicate' (WTC) in the L2. As MacIntyre et al. (1998) observed, there are numerous L2 learners who tend to avoid entering L2 communication situations even though they possess a high level of communicative competence in the L2. This warranted, we argued, the introduction of a further layer of mediating factors between having the competence to communicate and putting this competence into practice. In other words, because communicative competence did not in itself guarantee that language learners were ready to engage in L2 communication in the L2, WTC was introduced to bridge the gap between proficiency and actual L2 use. The rationale by Mercer and Dörnyei (2020) for the introduction of *student engagement* in the SLA literature has been similar: in the current era, even if someone has a high level of L2 motivation, this will not necessarily translate into actual language learning behaviour unless the person gets actively *engaged* in the learning process. The reason for the changing perspective has been the exponential growth of academic distractions, as illustrated by Duckworth et al. (2019, p. 378):

> Although the academic duties of students are quite similar across generations, the digital distractions that now compete with them have evolved dramatically in recent years. In one study, undergraduates reported spending more than 7 h per day on their phones. In another study, 92% of undergraduates

admitted to sending or receiving a text message during class. Students aged 13 to 18 now spend more than 5.5 h per day using entertainment media, including television, videogames, laptops, mobile phones, and tablets and excluding reading time; students aged 8 to 12 average more than 3.5 h of entertainment media per day ... Often, when students are on screens, they are also multitasking with academic work. While doing homework, for example, many teenagers simultaneously check their social network accounts (50%), watch television (51%), and send and receive text messages (60%).

Within the classroom, the frequent use of laptops further adds to the problem. Although laptops and tablets can be beneficial for note-taking and online research, Duckworth et al. (2019) report on a study in which more than one-third of the participants' online activity was spent checking email, messaging friends, reading the news, shopping, watching videos and playing games. And this happened despite the fact that students were aware of the fact that their in-class usage was being monitored! As mentioned earlier, in today's globalised, digital age, people are continuously bombarded with information and communications through multiple channels, and the pace of social life has been intensified by social media in an unprecedented manner, resulting in simply too many competing influences on an L2 learner's mind at any time. This has created a new L2 educational landscape, in which even strong motivation can be hijacked by the plethora of other pressing and ever-salient distractions. Therefore, we need to ensure that the students' positive disposition is *realised in action*; as Mercer and Dörnyei (2020, p. 6) state, "motivation is undoubtedly necessary for 'preparing the deal,' but engagement is indispensable for *sealing the deal*."

Engagement can be thus understood as a kind of 'motivation plus,' with the 'plus' element referring to the behavioural outworking of motivation. This is clearly summarised, for example, by Martin, Ginns and Papworth (2017, p. 150): "motivation is defined as the inclination, energy, emotion, and drive relevant to learning, working effectively, and achieving; engagement is defined as the behaviours that reflect this inclination, energy, emotion, and drive." Henry and Thorsen (in press) have put it this way: "since motivation rarely flows completely unhindered into action, it is the behavioural outworkings of various motivational sources that are captured in the engagement construct." This being the case, the main benefit of exploring the notion of 'engagement' over motivation from a practical perspective is that it allows us to address both the motive and its activation *together*, in a *unified* concept: when students are 'engaged,' they are inevitably fuelled by some motivation that has given direction to their action, but the fact that they became engaged also means that this motivational drive has succeeded in cutting through the surrounding multitude of distractions, temptations and alternatives.

A final benefit of focusing on student engagement comes from the fact that, as Mercer and Dörnyei (2020) argue, using the verb 'to engage' offers a valuable benefit in that it is an active verb that can be followed by a *target* within the phrase 'to engage with TARGET'. This allows for a systematic coverage of a target domain by breaking it down into specific facets. For example, I have argued elsewhere (Dörnyei, 2019b) that the L2 Learning Experience component of the L2 Motivational Self System (see Chapter 5) may be defined as the perceived quality of the learners' engagement with various aspects of the language learning process, with the following aspects in particular to engage with:

(a) *school context* (e.g. various aspects of belonging to the school community, adopting school norms and developing general academic confidence);
(b) *syllabus and the teaching materials* (e.g. curiosity about and interest in the content; match between the syllabus and the students' needs; ownership and personalisation of the materials);
(c) *learning tasks* (e.g. utilising the principles of task-based language teaching; application of project/problem-based learning; goal setting and progress checks);
(d) *one's peers* (e.g. relevant areas of group dynamics/classroom management, particularly social acceptance, group cohesiveness, norms of cooperation and tolerance);
(e) *teacher* (e.g. student–teacher rapport; utilising insights from leadership models; conflict resolution).

Innovation 3: Capitalising on role modelling

Ever since Bandura's (1977) seminal work on social learning theory, *role modelling* has been seen in psychology as a powerful teaching tool for passing on knowledge and skills, and role models have also been found to be able to exert considerable influence in shaping others' values, attitudes and beliefs. People continually and actively search for models they perceive as representative of what they wish to achieve, and doing so, Bandura concludes, "guides and motivates self-development" (p. 88). Within the context of SLA, research on role models still needs to reach its full potential, but there have been some promising initial findings. In their pioneering study, Murphey and Arao (2001) have for example argued that role models who are similar to the learner in many ways tend to have the greatest effect, and their research has thus highlighted the significance of 'near peer role models' as "people who might be 'near' to us in several ways: age, ethnicity, sex, interests, past or present experiences, and also in proximity and in frequency of social contact" (p. 1). A recent large-scale survey involving over 8,000 participants by Muir, Dörnyei and Adolphs (in press) has confirmed the relevance of 'near peer role models': although the largest category of role models consisted of famous people such as politicians and celebrities, personally known role models also made up a significant proportion (36%) of the specific cases mentioned by the respondents.

An important aspects of our recent findings was that many of the 'near peer role models' identified by the participants were the learners' teachers, thereby underlining the fact that role modelling can be an important part of a motivational teaching practice. Also, in accordance with Bandura's (1977) suggestion that some people are more likely to be susceptible to modelling influences than others, it was found that certain participant subgroups in our study displayed marked preferences for specific role model types. This points to the conclusion that there is a dynamic interaction between at least some of the characteristics of the role models and the recipients. Intriguingly, survey participants from the two largest countries of the world, China and India, displayed a different response pattern to that observed in the rest of the sample: rather than identifying native speakers of English, these respondents tended to have non-native-speaking role models and they also valued communicative ability over native-like pronunciation. It seems therefore that learners in the two most populous ethnolinguistic communities of the world placed more importance on 'local heroes' than on western celebrities.

Innovation 4: Preventing demotivation and fostering remotivation

One way of enhancing motivation is preventing *demotivation* and fostering the *remotivation* of learners who have become demotivated. The notion of demotivation was first raised in SLA by Dörnyei (2001b), providing a primarily descriptive analysis by mapping, ranking and clustering the various demotivational antecedents. There has been a steady flow of papers on L2 demotivation since then (see e.g. Kim & Kim, 2013), but in their insightful overview, Thorner and Kikuchi (2020) highlight several weaknesses regarding these studies. Most notably, they point out that it is difficult to draw generalisable lessons from the different descriptive studies, because "all factors can be seen by learners as demotivating or motivating to a degree, depending on other variables" (p. 373). This suggests a more complex relationship between 'demotivators' and motivational outcomes than a simple cause–effect link, and indeed, Thorner and Kikuchi also argue that most of the studies tend to be concerned with rather unreliable 'perceptions of causation.' Having said that, let me highlight two lines of inquiry in this sphere that represent sufficiently novel approaches to qualify as innovations proper: the introduction of the notion of 'remotivation' and the association of Dweck's (2006) mindset theory with the notion of demotivation.

Remotivation

Falout (2012, p. 3) defines remotivation simply as a "process of recovering motivation after losing it," and Thorner and Kikuchi (2020) explain that this is different from motivating learners who never had any motivation for the subject matter. This is because remotivation is in essence a purposeful reaction to the demotivating stimuli through 'adaptive coping mechanisms' such as continuing effort, soliciting and volunteering help, controlling negative thoughts, making positive self-statements, building self-efficacy and coping through social modelling (Falout, 2012). In other words, helping learners to become remotivated is a kind of recovery operation that involves demolishing barriers that have been raised by previous negative learning experiences as well as taking remedial action.

Falout (2012) emphasises that teachers can model adaptive processes in a variety of ways. A particularly important aspect of this help is to offer 'attributional retraining' whereby struggling students are guided to blame failure on controllable causes, which can then be remedied with appropriate strategies. Song and Kim (2017) further emphasise the role of generating a 'remotivating learning environment' with a focus on preferred teaching methods and the positive influence of classmates. In their study, however, the greatest remotivational driving force came from participants' "awareness of the necessity of English" (p. 99). This suggests that there is clearly further scope in making remotivation 'tailor-made' to the students' needs, including targeted awareness raising of various attractive aspects of the L2.

Promoting a growth mindset

Dörnyei and Ryan (2015) have argued that one way of revitalising the domain of L2 demotivation would be exploring its dynamics through investigating how certain demotivational factors interact with personal and situational characteristics. Why do some learners bounce back after a demotivating episode, while others completely lose interest? We pointed to the application of Dweck's *mindset theory* as an ideal candidate for supporting adaptive cognitions in demotivated students. The basic idea underlying the theory (also called 'implicit theory'; for a recent, accessible summary, see Dweck, 2017) is that some people constrain their own personal development by the belief that their potentials are limited, for example by birth, early education or manner of upbringing. Most people, for example, would subscribe to the premise that one's IQ is by and large stable and unchangeable, and this therefore limits the things they can strive for. Of course, as an extreme this might be true (e.g. few people are cut out to be nuclear physicists), but Dweck argues convincingly that people *can* grow their brains as they might a muscle, thereby making competence not a question of luck but a controllable factor. This proposal about intelligence has then been extended to apply to any basic human qualities, and the fundamental maxim of mindset theory is that it is people's personal beliefs about how much they can change and learn that will influence what they can actually achieve and become. In other words, as Lou and Noels (2020) explain in their L2-specific review of Dweck's proposal, the 'lay theories' that people have about their own capabilities will determine how people evaluate and take advantage of their learning experiences.

At the heart of mindset theory is the distinction between people having a 'growth mindset,' referring to the belief that one's intellectual abilities and personal qualities can be improved, and a 'fixed mindset,' which concerns a lack of belief in people's changeability, based on the premise that "the way people are now, in terms of their basic qualities, may well be the way they will always be" (Dweck & Yeager, 2018, p. 362). It requires little justification that this latter belief in the static character of one's intelligence, personality and creative ability can be highly demotivational, as it fosters a *what's the point?* mentality and a disposition to make the most of their limited endowment by playing safe. On the other hand, learners with a growth mindset thrive on challenge and are more likely to be motivated as they know that they *can* improve.

The first scholars to highlight the significance of mindset theory in SLA were Mercer and Ryan (2010), and the differences in mindsets have also been specifically linked to variation in L2 motivation (e.g. Lou & Noels, 2017; Waller & Papi, 2017). This makes sense, as we can hear all too often the claim by L2 learners that *I am simply not good at languages*, which is a classic manifestation of a fixed mindset and which usually indicates that the person lacks motivation. Lou and Noels (2020, p. 551) suggest that because the ideal L2 self (see Chapter 5) reflects "growth beliefs about one's future L2 abilities, it is not difficult to see the link between mindsets and the construct of ideal selves," and learners with fixed mindsets "may not be able to envision themselves becoming effective in using the target language." Such an integration of motivation and mindsets offers a promising avenue with regard to combating demotivation. Indeed, Lou and Noels (2017) report on research that demonstrates that even a short mindset-specific intervention (receiving a brief explanation on incremental mindsets) can make learners feel "less anxiety and less helpless in ego-threatening situations" (p. 232). This is consistent with non-L2-related research in educational psychology; as Dweck and Yeager (2018) summarise, mindsets can be primed and induced, and interventions that have taught learners about growth mindsets with their ramifications have indeed produced significant results (e.g. Paunesku et al., 2015).

Innovation 5: Applying technology

Many people, particularly the younger generations, find it inherently motivating to use modern technology, and this has not escaped the attention of applied linguists. Accordingly, there have been proposals in the SLA literature on technology-based and computer-assisted language learning for over half a century (see e.g. Heift & Chapelle, 2012; Otto, 2017), and as Stockwell (2013, pp. 156–157) summarises, "Increased motivation has often been given as the justification for the introduction and use of technology in language learning environments." Despite this ongoing awareness, it does not appear to be the case that technology-based innovations have radically transformed the field of SLA, and it is sobering to note Stockwell's conclusion that problems regarding the implementation of technology for learning purposes seem to be universal, and not present only in countries where resources are scarce but also in industrialised first world contexts (e.g. in Japan). So, the application of technology in SLA is a curious kind of 'innovation': it has been heralded as a 'new' idea for several decades, yet its potential to motivate has largely remained just that: a potential. Nonetheless, in our increasingly digitalised age it simply does not feel right to ignore the promise of technology, particularly because there are some strong points supporting its motivational credentials. Let us briefly summarise these points and then address several factors that caution us against providing an unduly rosy picture about the prospects of technological innovations.

The motivational potentials of technology

Psychologists have long been aware of the strong motivational capacity of certain technologies; for example, Rigby and Ryan's (2011) monograph on the subject has the following expressive title: "Glued to games: How video games draw us in a hold us spellbound." Similarly, in a recent review of the topic within the field of SLA, Henry and Lamb (2020) underline the frequent student experience of becoming immersed in media flows and intensely involved in online interactions such as gaming and using social media, and they also argue that "Navigating within streams of digital information, technologies can provide unparalleled opportunities for creativity and personalized decision-making" (p. 599). Stockwell (2013) adds that through their access to the Internet, networked communication tools can engage users effectively because they allow people to reach real audiences worldwide through a manner of communication that is characterised by reduced anxiety due to the more anonymous nature of the exchanges involved. Indeed, thanks to the Internet, people can become part of virtual communities, take simulated tours in real cultures, satisfy their curiosities in unlimited areas, link to fellow-minded people, express themselves freely, etc. – the list of potential motivating features goes on and on. Lamb and Arisandy (in press) further underline the intrinsically motivating use of the English language through Internet consumption, from information-seeking via search engines and watching YouTube videos to communication via social media and participation in online forums. It is not surprising therefore that in a review of technology types and their effectiveness in SLA, Golonka et al. (2014) point out that the common theme highlighted in articles on computer-assisted language learning (CALL) has not so much been the increased learning outcomes achieved as "the affordances offered by particular types of technology or measuring their effects on students' affective reactions, such as increased motivation or increased enjoyment of learning activities" (p. 92).

Zooming in on specific technological areas, a domain that has been highlighted by scholars as having a particularly promising role in SLA is *online media creation*, whereby high levels of learner motivation can be generated through creating visually appealing and authentic artefacts that promote creative self-expression and which not only document but also elaborate on the learners' personal identities (Henry, 2019). It can indeed be highly appealing to many that by using relatively simple tools they can generate attractive, professional-looking web pages, including authentic blogs illustrated by digital photos and online videos. Stockwell (2013) mentions another unique feature of electronic systems, namely their capacity to track learners' progress and provide personalised feedback about what they have achieved, thereby making improvements salient; as we shall see in Chapter 6 on long-term motivation, this will be an important aspect of generating 'psychological momentum.' Adolphs et al. (2018) highlight the potential of smart phones to produce visual representations of one's ideal L2 self, not unlike an 'L2-speaking selfie,' and Vlaeva (2019) shows that carefully prepared 'success videos' of learners' L2 performance in which they can see themselves using the L2 at an advanced level (created by splicing multiple clips) can give a considerable boost to their motivation and confidence. Finally, Mercer and Dörnyei (2020) report on a highly successful project in Canada by Shelley Hill, in which an online bulletin board ('Padlet') was utilised to engage learners in extra-curricular projects in the community by setting the task of posting short descriptions of their experiences, illustrated by a photo or a video.

Possible issues with the use of technology in SLA

The rosy picture that can so easily be painted about the promise of technology hides a number of persistent issues with regard to the effectiveness of technological applications in SLA. The various concerns can be grouped under five categories: the definition of technology; the novelty element in using technology; superficial engagement and additional distractions; student reluctance; and teacher reluctance.

What exactly do we mean by 'technology'? The various published sources list a very wide range of devices, computer applications and Internet services that may all qualify under the rubric, including: electronic whiteboards; interactive dictionaries; computers, laptops and tablets; smart phones and other hand-held devices; electronic language corpora; e-books; video recorders; online films and videos; PowerPoint and other software supporting writing and art; apps for websearch and web publishing; digital means of communication, including emailing, text messaging, chats, Internet forums, message boards, social networking applications and video conferencing; digital games and multi-user virtual environments, etc. – the options are ever-increasing. Looking at this diverse list, it does not require much justification that the various items have different properties and affordances, and therefore referring to them under the umbrella-term of 'technology' can easily blur the picture and even confuse some issues.

The novelty element. It was mentioned above that many people tend to find the use of modern technological applications inspiring, and that the novelty element of such tasks can definitely be harnessed for the purpose of engaging learners. Yet, one wonders how long this novelty effect will last. Stockwell (2013, p. 158) compares the initial enthusiasm for using a new technology to a child having a new toy, and then raises the same question: "The learners were at first attracted to the so called 'bells and whistles' of learning through a means that was unfamiliar to them, but what about the long-term effects of this attraction?" He also points out that while this effect was more pronounced in the 1990s, in the current age there is no real novelty about computers or smart phones any more, as the vast majority of learners in industrialised nations will view these technologies as part and parcel of everyday life, and will be unlikely to be impressed with technology per se. His overall evaluation is sobering: "if technologies in themselves have an inherent motivating effect, this effect is likely to be relatively short-lived, and certainly not long enough for any kind of meaningful language learning to take place" (p. 159).

In a similar vein, Marek and Wu (2019) argue that many of our students in the current age are 'digital natives' who are surrounded by technology in their daily lives and use it naturally and automatically for a wide range of purposes. They therefore expect a 'technology-rich' learning environment as a default, but surrounding students with technology only for the sake of using technology might be counterproductive:

> A swamp of meaningless technology will just trap students in the quicksand of worthless time and effort and reduce their motivation for learning, because they are already surrounded by technology and are skilled at making judgments about what is beneficial and what is not.
>
> p. 6

This is a reminder that fancy technology cannot replace a motivating teaching practice, because in the end Stockwell (2013) is absolutely right in concluding that "it is not the technology that motivates learners to study, but the manner and the context in which the technology is used" (p. 6).

Superficial engagement and additional distractions. Ushioda (2013) highlights a further potential shortcoming of technology when she points out that the level of engagement with it tends to be broadly superficial or casual rather than deep. This superficiality may have several causes, from the design features and constraints of particular devices to the not always very sophisticated nature of the software available for them; for example, with regard to mobile technologies for language learning, Ushioda observes that "the general preference seems to be for dealing with content that is not too demanding or challenging, for working with tools and features that are quick and easy to use, or for engaging with language input in a casual rather than intensive way" (p. 3). We should also note that the superficial use may simply reflect the casual nature of people's use of technologies in their everyday lives, dipping in and out of them all the time and quickly flicking between various applications. Furthermore, technologies can bring about additional distractions; we saw earlier when discussing the emerging importance of student engagement (INNOVATION$_2$) that students have been facing an exponential growth of digital distractions, partly caused by devices that they use in class, which allow for various non-educational uses, for example, sending or receiving quick text messages and checking various websites. In other words, by allowing technology in the classroom we may inadvertently open up the learning environment for the kind of competition for the students' attention that is becoming a standard feature of their social life. One may therefore rightly wonder whether this additional openness to distractions might in fact defeat the motivating purpose of technological applications.

Student reluctance. It has been implied so far that the main concerns with the use of technology in SLA are linked to the imperfect manner in which they are applied, and that if we manage to address these issues, students will welcome technological innovations wholeheartedly. Is this, however, really the case? It may be unexpected to hear, but several reports confirm that students do not always appreciate language instruction invading their digital worlds. Describing the language learning landscape in Sweden, for example, Henry, Sundqvist and Thorsen (2019) explain that while language teachers may view the extracurricular digital world as a rich bounty to explore, some learners may simply see it as their lives, and may resent a teacher's perceived intrusion into a space that they consider private and personal. Stockwell (2013) has observed the same phenomenon in Japan: "While teachers may be enthusiastic about having their learners use their mobile phones or their devices for learning purposes, some learners have expressed resistance to having their own private space being used for educational purposes" (p. 168). Lamb and Arisandy (in press) make a good point in this respect when they submit that the fact that

> young people's home lives are increasingly oriented around smartphones and other IT devices is not in itself a good reason that their school lives should be – in fact it may be an argument for formal classrooms to offer quite different learning experiences.

Teacher reluctance. Finally, let us also consider the teachers' position. Lamb and Arisandy (in press) cite a headline from *The Times* according to which "Analogue academics are failing to inspire students of the digital age." Some teachers are indeed 'analogue academics' simply because they come from a generation that had not been part of the digital revolution. Can we honestly blame those who feel uncomfortable adopting technologies for their classes when their students have more advanced skills in using them? It requires a great deal of confidence for teachers to freely admit to their students that they are only at a novice level when it comes to technological innovations. This, coupled with the multiple sources of concerns described above might amount to such a deterrent that some teachers may simply decide that it is not worth taking the risk.

Challenge 11: How can we measure a dynamic concept such as motivation?

When Gardner and Lambert (1959) launched modern research into L2 motivation, one of the strengths of their approach was the deployment of the sophisticated research methodology available in social psychology at the time. In the 1960s, there were established procedures for constructing valid and reliable questionnaires for the purpose of measuring attitudes, values, beliefs and other respondent characteristics, and the analysis of the collected data was conducted through elaborate statistical methods. Gardner himself was an expert statistician – see for example his coursebook on statistics using SPSS (Gardner, 2001) – and the high standards he set in this area defined the tenor of subsequent research in the field. As a result, the first few decades of L2 motivation research were firmly rooted in quantitative research methodology, mostly characterised by cross-sectional survey designs. As the field evolved, however, the various challenges discussed earlier became increasingly apparent, and there was a growing recognition that quantitative survey methodology and the mostly linear statistical procedures it was associated with were not suitable to answer all the new questions. For example, we have seen earlier how the situated understanding of L2 motivation foregrounded the need for rich contextual data that went beyond what self-report questionnaires could typically yield (CHALLENGE$_5$/INNOVATION$_3$), and also how the dynamic turn in SLA questioned the theoretical validity of the traditional research practice of attributing causality to distinct variables (CHALLENGE$_9$/INNOVATION$_1$).

The new understanding of L2 motivation in relation to its dynamic interaction with specific environmental and temporal factors required new research approaches, and there was a danger that without sufficient alternative research templates developments in the field would stall. Ryan (2012, p. 7) rightly points out that "many of the recent insights in the field of motivation were made possible less by individual genius and more by new and better tools for exploration. Explorers in a dark cave get further when someone provides a better headlamp." The aftermath of the dynamic turn in SLA has felt in many ways like such a metaphorical dark cave and the challenge over the past decade has been to equip the scholarly community with new research headlamps. For space limitations, the following discussion cannot offer detailed technical descriptions of issues in research methodology – interested readers should refer to recent book-length analyses such as Verspoor, de Bot and Lowie (2011) and Hiver and Al-Hoorie (2020). Instead, the innovations listed below are intended to outline promising directions that can help the field to find its bearings.

Innovation 1: Conducting qualitative, longitudinal and intervention studies

The first set of innovations to be mentioned with regard to researching L2 motivation are not really 'innovations' proper, because qualitative, longitudinal and intervention designs have been part of the research methodological arsenal for several decades. Yet, they could be considered novel against the background of the dominant survey methodology characterising the field of L2 motivation research before the new millennium. We have seen in Chapter 2 (CHALLENGE$_5$/INNOVATION$_3$) that the growing significance attached to exploring the context of L2 motivation started to give rise to *qualitative research*, and qualitative methodology assumed further importance when it became clear that the nonlinear, adaptive and systemic nature of complex dynamic systems was not compatible with the measurement principles of linear modelling, cause–effect relations and statistical probability (i.e. the characteristics of the quantitative research practice rooted in the social psychological era) (Ushioda, 2020a). While qualitative research is by no means the only option for accounting for the dynamic complexity of motivation, it did offer a relatively easily adaptable approach; this is well reflected by the fact that in their overview of research methods suited for the study of dynamic systems, MacIntyre et al. (2017) list as many as five variations on qualitative methodology – longitudinal qualitative interview design, retrodictive qualitative modelling, qualitative comparative analysis (QCA), two-stage qualitative interview design and qualitative interview design gathering data on multiple timescales – and Hiver and Al-Hoorie (2016) introduce further options such as process tracing, concept mapping and agent-based modelling. The description of retrodictive qualitative modelling in Innovation 3 below will offer a concrete illustration of the strengths of qualitative research for such innovative practice.

Longitudinal research has been a frequently called-for research design in SLA (see e.g. Ortega & Iberri-Shea, 2005), which is explained by the fact that acquisition by definition has a prominent time dimension. Unfortunately, in an era characterised by strong pressures on scholars to produce a high number of publications (for a revealing insight into this pressure, see e.g. Weiner, 2019), the time-consuming and labour-intensive nature of longitudinal research meant that few scholars chose to pursue it in actual practice. Moreover, as Ryan and Legate (2012) remind us, the widespread use of experimental laboratory studies in contemporary motivation research in psychology has inevitably foregrounded short timescales and proximal outcomes. However, longitudinal designs have recently received a new emphasis on account of their capability to document the *ongoing change* and *transformation* aspect of complex dynamic systems. Accordingly, in their pioneering paper on "Research methodology on language development from a complex systems perspective," Larsen-Freeman and Cameron (2008, p. 208) advocated a "longitudinal, case-study, time-series approach," and MacIntyre et al. (2017, p. 103) also list "longitudinal qualitative interview design" as a recommended option for investigations in a dynamic vein. It is important to note here that longitudinal research, even with small participant samples, does not have to be qualitative but can also be conducted in a quantitative manner – as highlighted by Ortega and Iberri-Shea (2005) – and for example Hiver and Al-Hoorie (2020) recommend latent growth curve modelling and time series analysis, amongst others, as potentially fruitful methods in this vein. The quest for new longitudinal design options is ongoing, and for example in their fascinating recent twin study of two participants, Lowie et al. (2017) have experimented with 'permutation tests' by performing Monte Carlo permutation analyses.

According to Ryan and Legate (2012), *intervention studies* (i.e. experimental designs) have been one of the most often mentioned future directions by the contributors to the *Oxford Handbook of Human Motivation*. They justify this popularity by the fact that controlled and randomised clinical trials allow scholars to measure potential mediators and moderators of obtained effects, while also helping to establish the generalisability and relevance of theory to representative populations and everyday contexts. Similar to longitudinal research, experimental designs involving interventions have been a known option in research methodology for several decades, but they have been underutilised in motivation research because of the demanding nature of organising treatment and control groups.

However, in the new research climate where the notion of causality has been under increased scrutiny, the rigour of intervention studies in this respect would be most welcome, although we need to bear in mind that experimental designs are still anchored in traditional research methodology in that they are variable-based. Yet, it also appears to be a characteristic of the new era that no single approach is likely to be able to address every issue raised by complex dynamic systems, which makes Kikuchi's (2017) conclusion particularly timely: after employing a variety of methods (questionnaires, interviews and journal entries) to explore the complexity of the motivational/demotivational disposition of five language learners in Japan, he highlighted the necessity of approaching an issue via several different avenues simultaneously:

> I would like to emphasize the importance of using several methods. For example, Mio was usually quiet in the interview session, especially in the fall semester. Her response pattern to the questionnaire was not easy to interpret. However, she wrote openly in the reflective journal to explain about her depression at the beginning of the fall semester and how she dealt with it. Neither focus group interviews nor the questionnaire were easy methods for her to express herself through.
>
> *p. 143*

Innovation 2: Conducting mixed methods research

As described in Dörnyei (2007) in more detail, the origins of mixing methodologies go back to the concept of *triangulation* introduced in the 1970s, referring to the process of combining several data sources for the study of the same social phenomenon. Not only was this practice meant to offer a richer and more rounded understanding of the research topic than single-method investigations, but it was also assumed that method integration had the potential to maximise both the internal and the external validity of the research through offsetting the inherent weaknesses of individual methods by the strength of another. *Mixed methods research* has taken this assumption as its starting point and has gained considerable popularity in SLA over the past decade, because it was seen as an 'ecumenical' and inclusive solution to the qualitative–quantitative debate. After Dörnyei's initial treatment of the principles of the approach, several detailed guides have been published offering practical advice (e.g. Brown, 2014; Riazi, 2017). The methodology has been endorsed by both qualitative and quantitative scholars as an approach that allows one to investigate reality from two different, yet complementary, perspectives: words can be used to add meaning to numbers and numbers can be used to add precision to words. Mixed methods research has also been considered a potential response to the challenge of researching complex dynamic systems, as it allows for a multi-level analysis of complex phenomena by converging numeric trends from large-scale quantitative data and specific details from in-depth qualitative data. Finally, the method has also been found as a suitable basis for other innovative research approaches – for example, both the 'idiodynamic method' (MacIntyre, 2012; see CHALLENGE₆/INNOVATION₁) and 'q methodology' (e.g. Irie & Ryan, 2015) combine quantitative and qualitative data.

Thus, the zeitgeist has been positive for applying mixed methods research to the study of L2 motivation, and as Ushioda (2020a) summarises, the 'questionnaire + interviews' structure has become almost a standard research design in the field. Indeed, Boo et al. (2015) report a nearly 600% growth rate of mixed methods studies from 2005 to 2014, and an edited volume specifically devoted to motivational dynamics (Dörnyei et al., 2015) contains no fewer than five studies displaying integrated methodologies (Gregersen & MacIntyre, 2015; Irie & Ryan, 2015; Nitta & Baba, 2015; Piniel & Csizér, 2015; You & Chan, 2015). However, we should note MacIntyre et al.'s (2015) caution that "a mixed methods study is *not* inherently dynamic in nature" (p. 425) and should also bear in mind that the popular belief that the sum is greater than its parts is not always true. Indeed, as pointed out more than once (e.g. by Boo et al., 2015; Hiver & Al-Hoorie, 2020), much of the current practice of method integration involves rather superficial mixing of relatively independent qualitative and quantitative components within a study, without maximising the full potential of the approach.

Innovation 3: Retrodictive qualitative modelling

Retrodictive qualitative modelling (Dörnyei, 2014) has been proposed as a practical approach to researching complex dynamic systems. It capitalises on these systems' *self-organisation capacity*, which increases the orderly nature of the initially transient, fluid and nonlinear system behaviour. As a result of this process, in most complex situations we will find a relatively small number of well-recognisable outcome patterns or 'attractor states' rather than the unlimited variation that one could, in theory, anticipate in a completely erratic system. The researcher's task is then to identify these archetypes along with the specific mechanisms that drove the system behaviour to them. As Ushioda (2020b) succinctly explains, the method therefore takes the complex system's observable end state as the starting point for analysis and involves a backward search (hence the 'retrospective' part in the label) for the underlying 'signature dynamics,' which is the name given to the powerful patterns or trends within the system that make the different components end up in one of the outcome archetypes.

How can signature dynamics be identified? This is where qualitative research comes into the picture. The main tools for researchers to uncover relevant mechanisms are in-depth qualitative interviews with representatives of each archetype (hence the 'qualitative' part in the label), and the principal aim of the subsequent analysis of the obtained qualitative data is to distinguish holistic patterns and interactions that are specific to each case. The benefit of detecting such signature dynamics is that these can then be viewed as the central part of a model of the researched domain (hence the 'modelling' part in the label). In sum, the essence of the method is that tracing back the reasons why the system has ended up with a small number of particular outcome options allows the researcher to produce a retrospective qualitative model of the system's evolution, which may serve as a lesson for other, similar situations (for illustrations of the application of the method, see Chan, Dörnyei & Henry, 2015; Hiver, 2017).

Innovation 4: Identifying motivational conglomerates

From a research perspective, the ultimate challenge regarding complex dynamic systems is the limited predictability of system behaviour. If the behaviour of a system is unpredictable or random, there is no point researching it, because there are no systematic elements to uncover in the situation. If, however, the system's behaviour is predictable, then it may be possible to find systematic trends that can be analysed meaningfully (for a more detailed explanation, see Dörnyei, 2014). When is a system's behaviour predictable enough to make researching it meaningful? System development often involves stable and predictable phases when the system is governed by strong attractors and is settled in a non-dynamic attractor state; for example, the complex movement patterns of children in a playground are likely to come to a halt if a low-flying helicopter passes over and everybody stops to watch it. Such settled states often occur when the various factors in operation within a system form powerful *conglomerates* to function in concert, and as we saw in Chapter 1 (CHALLENGE₃), such composites are highly relevant to the construct of motivation because motivation typically involves a blended operation of cognitive, affective and motivational components. A case in point is the notion of 'interest': it has been included in several mainstream motivation theories (e.g. in self-determination theory), but it also contains a salient cognitive aspect (e.g. curiosity, knowledge and attention with regard to a specific domain) as well as a prominent affective dimension (e.g. the joy of engaging with a topic of interest). Therefore, when people say in everyday communication that someone is "interested" in doing something, they use a verbal shortcut to refer to this complex, integrated meaning. Identifying conglomerates is thus an inherently *systemic* approach, because it aims to examine the joint operation of constellations of different factors. If we recognise a powerful conglomerate in action, this is likely to be associated with predictable – and therefore researchable – system behaviour.

References

Adolphs, S., Clark, L., Dörnyei, Z., Glover, T., Henry, A., Muir, C., Sánchez-Lozano, E., & Valstar, M. (2018). Digital innovations in L2 motivation: Harnessing the power of the Ideal L2 Self. *System*, 78, 173–185.

Bandura, A. (1977). *Social learning theory*. Englewood Cliffs, NJ: Prentice Hall.

Boo, Z., Dörnyei, Z., & Ryan, S. (2015). L2 Motivation research 2005–2014: Understanding a publication surge and a changing landscape. *System*, 55, 147–157.

Braver, T. S. (2016). Motivation and cognitive control: Introduction. In T. S. Braver (Ed.), *Motivation and cognitive control* (pp. 1–19). New York: Routledge.

Brown, J. D. (2014). *Mixed methods research for TESOL*. Edinburgh: Edinburgh University Press.

Chan, L., Dörnyei, Z., & Henry, A. (2015). Learner archetypes and signature dynamics in the language classroom: A Retrodictive Qualitative Modelling approach to studying L2 motivation. In Z. Dörnyei, P. D. MacIntyre & A. Henry (Eds.), *Motivational dynamics in language learning* (pp. 238–259). Bristol: Multilingual Matters.

Cohen, A. D., & Henry, A. (2019). Focus on the language learner: Styles, strategies and motivation. In N. Schmitt & M. P. H. Rodgers (Eds.), *An introduction to applied linguistics* (3rd ed., pp. 165–189). Abingdon: Routledge.

Covington, M. (1999). Caring about learning: The nature and nurturing of subject-matter appreciation. *Educational Psychologist, 34,* 127–136.

Crookes, G., & Schmidt, R. (1991). Motivation: Reopening the research agenda. *Language Learning, 41,* 469–512.

Danziger, K. (1997). *Naming the mind: How psychology found its language.* London: Sage.

Dörnyei, Z. (2001a). *Motivational strategies in the language classroom.* Cambridge: Cambridge University Press.

Dörnyei, Z. (2001b). *Teaching and researching motivation.* Harlow: Longman.

Dörnyei, Z. (2002). The motivational basis of language learning tasks. In P. Robinson (Ed.), *Individual differences in second language acquisition* (pp. 137–158). Amsterdam: John Benjamins.

Dörnyei, Z. (2007). *Research methods in applied linguistics: Quantitative, qualitative and mixed methodologies.* Oxford: Oxford University Press.

Dörnyei, Z. (2014). Researching complex dynamic systems: 'Retrodictive qualitative modelling' in the language classroom. *Language Teaching, 47*(1), 80–91.

Dörnyei, Z. (2019a). Task motivation: What makes an L2 task engaging? In Z. Wen & M. J. Ahmadian (Eds.), *Researching L2 task performance and pedagogy: In honour of Peter Skehan* (pp. 53–66). Amsterdam: John Benjamins.

Dörnyei, Z. (2019b). Towards a better understanding of the L2 learning experience, the Cinderella of the L2 Motivational Self System. *Studies in Second Language Learning and Teaching, 9*(1), 19–30.

Dörnyei, Z., & Kormos, J. (2000). The role of individual and social variables in oral task performance. *Language Teaching Research, 4,* 275–300.

Dörnyei, Z., & Muir, C. (2019). Creating a motivating classroom environment. In X. A. Gao (Ed.), *Second handbook of English language teaching.* New York: Springer.

Dörnyei, Z., & Ottó, I. (1998). Motivation in action: A process model of L2 motivation. *Working Papers in Applied Linguistics (Thames Valley University, London), 4,* 43–69.

Dörnyei, Z., & Ryan, S. (2015). *The psychology of the language learner revisited.* New York: Routledge.

Dörnyei, Z., Henry, A., & Muir, C. (2016). *Motivational currents in language learning: Frameworks for focused interventions.* New York: Routledge.

Dörnyei, Z., MacIntyre, P. D., & Henry, A. (Eds.). (2015). *Motivational dynamics in language learning.* Bristol: Multilingual Matters.

Duckworth, A. L., Taxer, J. L., Eskreis-Winkler, L., Galla, B. M., & Gross, J. J. (2019). Self-control and academic achievement. *Annual Review of Psychology, 70,* 373–399.

Dweck, C. S. (2006). *Mindset: The new psychology of success.* New York: Random House.

Dweck, C. S. (2017). *Mindset: Changing the way to fulfil your potential* (Rev. ed.). London: Robinson.

Dweck, C. S., & Yeager, D. S. (2018). Mindsets change the imagined and actual future. In G. Oettingen, A. T. Sevincer & P. M. Gollwitzer (Eds.), *The psychology of thinking about the future* (pp. 362–376). New York: Guilford Press.

Falout, J. (2012). Coping with demotivation: EFL learners' remotivation processes. *TESL-EJ, 16*(3), 1–29.

Gardner, R. C. (2001). *Psychological statistics using SPSS for Windows*. Upper Saddle River, NJ: Prentice Hall.

Gardner, R. C., & Lambert, W. E. (1959). Motivational variables in second language acquisition. *Canadian Journal of Psychology, 13*, 266–272.

Golonka, E. M., Bowles, A. R., Frank, V. M., Richardson, D. L., & Freynik, S. (2014). Technologies for foreign language learning: A review of technology types and their effectiveness. *Computer Assisted Language Learning, 27*(1), 70–105.

Gregersen, T., & MacIntyre, P. D. (2015). 'I can see a little bit of you on myself': A dynamic systems approach to the inner dialogue between teacher and learner selves. In Z. Dörnyei, P. D. MacIntyre & A. Henry (Eds.), *Motivational dynamics in language learning* (pp. 260–284). Bristol: Multilingual Matters.

Heift, T., & Chapelle, C. A. (2012). Language learning through technology. In S. Gass & A. Mackey (Eds.), *The Routledge handbook of second language acquisition* (pp. 555–569). New York: Routledge.

Henry, A. (2019). Online media creation and L2 motivation: A socially situated perspective. *TESOL Quarterly, 53*(2), 372–404.

Henry, A., & Lamb, M. (2020). L2 motivation and digital technologies. In M. Lamb, K. Csizér, A. Henry & S. Ryan (Eds.), *Palgrave Macmillan handbook of motivation for language learning* (pp. 599–619). Basingstoke: Palgrave.

Henry, A., & Thorsen, C. (in press). Disaffection and agentic engagement: 'Redesigning' activities to enable authentic self-expression. *Language Teaching Research*.

Henry, A., Sundqvist, P., & Thorsen, C. (2019). *Motivational practice: Insights from the classroom*. Lund, Sweden: Studentliteratur.

Hiver, P. (2017). Tracing the signature dynamics of language teacher immunity: A retrodictive qualitative modeling study. *Modern Language Journal, 101*(4), 669–690.

Hiver, P., & Al-Hoorie, A. H. (2016). A dynamic ensemble for second language research: Putting complexity theory into practice. *Modern Language Journal, 100*(4), 1–16.

Hiver, P., & Al-Hoorie, A. H. (2020). *Research methods for complexity theory in applied linguistics*. Bristol: Multilingual Matters.

Irie, K., & Ryan, J. (2015). Study abroad and the dynamics of change in learner L2 self-concept. In Z. Dörnyei, P. D. MacIntyre & A. Henry (Eds.), *Motivational dynamics in language learning* (pp. 343–366). Bristol: Multilingual Matters.

Kikuchi, K. (2017). Reexamining demotivators and motivators: A longitudinal study of Japanese freshmen's dynamic system in an EFL context. *Innovation in Language Learning and Teaching, 11*(2), 128–145.

Kim, Y.-K., & Kim, T.-Y. (2013). English learning demotivation studies in the EFL contexts: State of the art. *Modern English Education, 14*(1), 77–102.

Kormos, J., & Dörnyei, Z. (2004). The interaction of linguistic and motivational variables in second language task performance. *Zeitschrift für Interkulturellen Fremdsprachenunterricht [Online], 9*(2), pp. 19.

Kormos, J., & Wilby, J. (2020). Task motivation. In M. Lamb, K. Csizér, A. Henry & S. Ryan (Eds.), *Palgrave Macmillan handbook of motivation for language learning* (pp. 267–286). Basingstoke: Palgrave.

Lamb, M. (2017). The motivational dimension of language teaching. *Language Teaching, 50*(3), 301–346.

Lamb, M. (2020). Motivational teaching strategies. In M. Lamb, K. Csizér, A. Henry & S. Ryan (Eds.), *Palgrave Macmillan handbook of motivation for language learning* (pp. 287–305). Basingstoke: Palgrave.

Lamb, M., & Arisandy, F. E. (in press). The impact of online use of English on motivation to learn. *Computer Assisted Language Learning*.

Lambert, C., & Zhang, G. (2019). Engagement in the use of English and Chinese as foreign languages: The role of learner-generated content in instructional task design. *Modern Language Journal*, *103*(2), 391–411.

Lambert, C., Philp, J., & Nakamura, S. (2017). Learner-generated content and engagement in second language task performance. *Language Teaching Research*, *21*(6), 665–680.

Larsen-Freeman, D., & Cameron, L. (2008). Research methodology on language development from a complex systems perspective. *Modern Language Journal*, *92*(2), 200–213.

Lewthwaite, R., & Wulf, G. (2017). Optimizing motivation and attention for motor performance and learning. *Current Opinion in Psychology*, *16*, 38–42.

Lou, N. M., & Noels, K. (2017). Measuring language mindsets and modeling their relations with goal orientations and emotional and behavioral responses in failure situations. *Modern Language Journal*, *101*(1), 214–243.

Lou, N. M., & Noels, K. (2020). Language mindsets, meaning-making, and motivation. In M. Lamb, K. Csizér, A. Henry & S. Ryan (Eds.), *Palgrave Macmillan handbook of motivation for language learning* (pp. 537–559). Basingstoke: Palgrave.

Lowie, W., van Dijk, M., Chan, H., & Verspoor, M. (2017). Finding the key to successful L2 learning in groups and individuals. *Studies in Second Language Learning and Teaching*, *7*(1), 127–148.

MacIntyre, P. D. (2012). The idiodynamic method: A closer look at the dynamics of communication traits. *Communication Research Reports*, *29*(4), 361–367.

MacIntyre, P. D., Clément, R., Dörnyei, Z., & Noels, K. A. (1998). Conceptualizing willingness to communicate in a L2: A situated model of confidence and affiliation. *Modern Language Journal*, *82*, 545–562.

MacIntyre, P. D., Dörnyei, Z., & Henry, A. (2015). Conclusion: Hot enough to be cool: The promise of dynamic systems research. In Z. Dörnyei, P. D. MacIntyre & A. Henry (Eds.), *Motivational dynamics in language learning* (pp. 419–429). Bristol: Multilingual Matters.

MacIntyre, P. D., MacKay, E., Ross, J., & Abel, E. (2017). The emerging need for methods appropriate to study dynamic systems: Individual differences in motivational dynamics. In L. Ortega & Z. Han (Eds.), *Complexity theory and language development: In celebration of Diane Larsen-Freeman* (pp. 97–122). Amsterdam: John Benjamins.

Marek, M. W., & Wu, W.-C. V. (2019). Creating a technology-rich English language learning environment. In X. A. Gao (Ed.), *Second handbook of English language teaching*. New York: Springer.

Martin, A. J., Ginns, P., & Papworth, B. (2017). Motivation and engagement: Same or different? Does it matter? *Learning and Individual Differences*, *55*, 150–162.

Mercer, S., & Dörnyei, Z. (2020). *Engaging language learners in contemporary classrooms*. Cambridge: Cambridge University Press.

Mercer, S., & Ryan, S. (2010). A mindset for EFL: Learners' beliefs about the role of natural talent. *ELT Journal*, *64*, 436–444.

Mozgalina, A. (2015). More or less choice? The influence of choice on task motivation and task engagement. *System*, *49*, 120–132.

Muir, C., Dörnyei, Z., & Adolphs, S. (in press). Role models in language learning: Results of a large-scale international survey. *Applied Linguistics*.

Murphey, T., & Arao, H. (2001). Changing reported beliefs through near peer role modeling. *TESL-EJ*, *5*(3), 1–15.

Nitta, R., & Baba, K. (2015). Self-regulation in the evolution of the ideal L2 self: A complex dynamic systems approach to the L2 Motivational Self System. In Z. Dörnyei, P. D. MacIntyre & A. Henry (Eds.), *Motivational dynamics in language learning* (pp. 367–396). Bristol: Multilingual Matters.

Ortega, L., & Iberri-Shea, G. (2005). Longitudinal research in second language acquisition: Recent trends and future directions. *Annual Review of Applied Linguistics, 25*, 26–45.

Otto, S. E. K. (2017). From past to present: A hundred years of technology for language learning. In C. A. Chapelle & S. Sauro (Eds.), *The handbook of technology and second language teaching and learning* (pp. 10–25). Hoboken, NJ: Wiley Blackwell.

Paunesku, D., Walton, G. M., Romero, C., Smith, E. N., Yeager, D. S., & Dweck, C. S. (2015). Mind-set interventions are a scalable treatment for academic underachievement. *Psychological Science, 26*(6), 784–793.

Pessoa, L., & Engelmann, J. B. (2010). Embedding reward signals into perception and cognition. *Frontiers in Neuroscience, 4*(17), 1–8.

Piniel, K., & Csizér, K. (2015). Changes in motivation, anxiety, and self-efficacy during the course of an academic writing seminar. In Z. Dörnyei, P. D. MacIntyre & A. Henry (Eds.), *Motivational dynamics in language learning* (pp. 164–194). Bristol: Multilingual Matters.

Poupore, G. (2016). Measuring group work dynamics and its relation with L2 learners' task motivation and language production. *Language Teaching Research, 20*(6), 719–740.

Riazi, A. M. (2017). *Mixed methods research in language teaching and learning*. Sheffield: Equinox.

Rigby, C. S., & Ryan, R. M. (2011). *Glued to games: How video games draw us in and hold us spellbound*. Santa Barbara, CA: Praeger.

Ryan, R. M. (2012). Motivation and the organisation of human behavior: Three reasons for the reemergence of a field. In R. M. Ryan (Ed.), *The Oxford handbook of human motivation* (pp. 3–10). New York: Oxford University Press.

Ryan, R. M., & Legate, N. (2012). Through a fly's eye: Multiple yet overlapping perspectives on future directions for human motivation research. In R. M. Ryan (Ed.), *The Oxford handbook of human motivation* (pp. 554–564). New York: Oxford University Press.

Schmidt, R. (1995). Consciousness and foreign language learning: A tutorial on the role of attention and awareness in learning. In R. Schmidt (Ed.), *Attention and awareness in foreign language learning* (pp. 1–63). Honolulu, HI: University of Hawaii Press.

Schmidt, R. (2001). Attention. In P. Robinson (Ed.), *Cognition and second language acquisition* (pp. 3–32). New York: Cambridge University Press.

Song, B., & Kim, T.-Y. (2017). The dynamics of demotivation and remotivation among Korean high school EFL students. *System, 65*, 90–103.

Stockwell, G. (2013). Technology and motivation in English-language teaching and learning. In E. Ushioda (Ed.), *International perspectives on motivation: Language learning and professional challenges* (pp. 156–175). Basingstoke: Palgrave Macmillan.

Takahashi, S. (2005). Pragmalinguistic awareness: Is it related to motivation and proficiency? *Applied Linguistics, 26*(1), 90–120.

Thorner, N., & Kikuchi, K. (2020). The process of demotivation in language learning: An integrative account. In M. Lamb, K. Csizér, A. Henry & S. Ryan (Eds.), *Palgrave Macmillan handbook of motivation for language learning* (pp. 367–388). Basingstoke: Palgrave.

Ushioda, E. (2013). Motivation matters in mobile language learning: A brief commentary. *Language Learning & Technology, 17*(3), 1–5.

Ushioda, E. (2016). Language learning motivation through a small lens: A research agenda. *Language Teaching, 49*(4), 564–577.

Ushioda, E. (2020a). Researching L2 motivation: Past, present and future. In M. Lamb, K. Csizér, A. Henry & S. Ryan (Eds.), *Palgrave Macmillan handbook of motivation for language learning* (pp. 661–682). Basingstoke: Palgrave.

Ushioda, E. (2020b). Researching L2 motivation: Re-evaluating the role of qualitative inquiry, or the 'wine and conversation' approach. In A. H. Al-Hoorie & P. D. MacIntyre

(Eds.), *Contemporary language motivation theory: 60 years since Gardner and Lambert (1959)* (pp. 194–211). Bristol: Multilingual Matters.

Verspoor, M. H., de Bot, K., & Lowie, W. (Eds.). (2011). *A dynamic approach to second language development: Methods and techniques.* Amsterdam: John Benjamins.

Vlaeva, D. (2019). *Enhancing L2 motivation through 'video self-modeling': Insights from an exploratory study.* MA thesis, University of Nottingham, Nottingham.

Waller, L., & Papi, M. (2017). Motivation and feedback: How implicit theories of intelligence predict L2 writers' motivation and feedback orientation. *Journal of Second Language Writing, 35*, 54–65.

Weiner, B. (2019). My journey to the attribution fields. In A. J. Elliot (Ed.), *Advances in motivation science* (Vol. 6, pp. 185–211). Cambridge, MA: Academic Press.

Yanguas, Í. (2011). The dynamic nature of motivation during the task: Can it be captured? *Innovation in Language Learning and Teaching, 5*(1), 35–61.

You, C. J., & Chan, L. (2015). The dynamics of L2 imagery in future motivational self-guides. In Z. Dörnyei, P. D. MacIntyre & A. Henry (Eds.), *Motivational dynamics in language learning* (pp. 397–418). Bristol: Multilingual Matters.

4
RESEARCH FRONTIERS I
Unconscious motivation

We saw in Chapter 1 (CHALLENGE₄) that although a great deal of human behaviour is not consciously driven, the lion's share of research in psychology to explain why people act as they do has been centred on conscious and reportable experiences of intention and motivation (Ferguson, Hassin & Bargh, 2008). Over the past 15 years, however, the research climate has undergone considerable transformation in this respect, and the current environment is highly favourable for researching unconscious motivation, as reflected in Ryan and Legate's (2012) summary in the *Oxford Handbook of Human Motivation*, which characterises the unconscious strand as "the most saliently expressed future direction in the field" (p. 563). It has thus been widely accepted that the human mind contains two distinct processing channels that can have different effects on motivation, but this does not mean that the area is without any challenges. Questions abound about how the joint operation of the conscious and the unconscious mind takes place in actual practice, and there are heated arguments in the scholarly community about which is ultimately in charge of shaping human behaviour: the conscious or the unconscious. Views also differ on how unconscious attitudes, goals and motives can be identified and investigated, given that the particular person who beholds them is actually unaware of them.

This chapter is intended to offer an overview of these matters in order to create the foundation for further research on the role of unconscious motivation within the field of SLA. As a preliminary, let us set the scene by recognising that there is a massive imbalance between unconscious and conscious processes in the brain: within the immense interconnected network of simultaneously active neurons – that is, the 'neural system' – the vast majority of all the neural processes happening at any given moment are unconscious. Baars (1997) illustrates the enormous size of the unconscious mind by the working of our visual memory. Humans tend to be rather good at recognising scenes from films they have seen in the past, which requires by definition matching a scene they see with a scene they store in their visual memory. In order to do so, they must hold unconscious records of literally millions and millions of images, and the recognition of a specific scene involves ultra-quick scanning of this unconscious store to find a match, so that it can be brought into the spotlight of consciousness. Anybody who has downloaded or copied films digitally will know how data-rich and memory-intensive this process is and how quickly the films fill up any available storage space with huge files. Therefore, the human act of being able to say with almost certainty within a split second whether we have seen a certain filmstrip or not is comparable to the achievement of a supercomputer – and most of this processing power is unconscious!

In contrast, the conscious part of our mind is surprisingly limited in its capacity, as there are severe bottlenecks in our immediate memory and attentional focus: we can, for example, keep only a rather restricted amount of material active in our working memory, we can listen to only one dense flow of information at a time and we cannot do two demanding voluntary actions simultaneously – in other words, we can be conscious of only one unified experience at a time. This being the case, the human brain is characterised by a stark contrast between a huge and powerful neural system that works in the background without any consciousness and a narrow, sharply focused conscious 'window' into this system – that is, our conscious attention – which functions as a metaphorical spotlight that can direct the enormous unconscious processing power to focus on some narrowly defined aspect. Although this conscious 'navigational system' is of limited capacity, it is still an amazing aspect of being human; as Baumeister and Bargh (2014, p. 35) expressively put it, "Human consciousness is one of the wonders of the world. It integrates sensation, perception, emotion, and interpretation, often understanding events in sequences that include causal analyses and extended narrative structures."

In sum, there is clearly close cooperation between conscious and unconscious processes in driving human behaviour, but the crucial (metaphorical) question in this respect is which of them drives the car. As the answer to this question is central to defining the nature of human motivation, we shall begin the exploration with examining the notion of *human agency*, that is, the capacity of people to act independently, to exercise their free will and to make their own individual choices. In sociology the limitations of human agency are usually seen in terms of variables such as social class, socioeconomic status, ethnicity and gender, whereas our current focus will be on the limits set by unconscious motives.

Human agency and its unconscious limits

The research community is deeply divided about how much control conscious intentions have on human behaviour, and in the fast-moving pace of the evolution of the field, even leading scholars keep modifying their positions; Baumeister and Bargh (2014), for example, openly admit that "Our views about the role of consciousness in the genesis of action have changed several times and no doubt may evolve further" (p. 45). As these scholars summarise, the various stances in the ongoing debate cover the full spectrum, from consciousness having complete control to being completely irrelevant. The intuitive view that most people would subscribe to is that consciousness is in full (or almost full) control of what one does. This is to be expected, because the whole point about *un*conscious motives is that people are *not* aware of them. Yet, as was pointed out in Chapter 1 (CHALLENGE₄), even nonspecialists will realise that some of our behaviours are not completely governed by conscious decisions; for example, sometimes there is simply not enough time to deliberate and behaviour is activated automatically (see e.g. Hornstra et al., 2018) or is guided by impulses that originate in the unconscious (e.g. Baumeister, Masicampo & Vohs, 2011). Indeed, the phrases 'acting on instinct' and 'acting on intuition' are common in everyday language, reflecting the recognition that a particular action was performed without the support of explicit knowledge or fully conscious reasoning. Because this unconscious aspect is the less-known side of the mind, let us begin the exploration of human agency with a description of unconscious motivation, to be followed by considerations related to the other, conscious, side of the coin.

The case for unconscious motivation

It was mentioned earlier that despite the fact that unconscious motivation has been acknowledged in academic psychology only relatively recently, the notion itself has a long history. It is therefore useful to present a brief overview of its main historical precursors, from Freud's notion of the subconscious to McClelland's proposal for implicit motivation, before surveying some influential modern research findings starting with Benjamin Libet's seminal work on the subject.

Historical precursors

The study of the unconscious mind has a long tradition in clinical psychology, going back to the work of Sigmund Freud (1856–1939). Although Freud was not the only psychologist working in this area at the time, he was the most influential champion for achieving scientific recognition of the unconscious by highlighting the importance of repressed ideas and motives that are removed from consciousness and yet remain operative in shaping the individual's thinking, feelings and behaviour. The Freudian view was that the unconscious mind is the primary source of human behaviour, and in the popular culture it was his notion of dreams opening up a window into the subconscious parts of the mind that had a particularly lasting impact (Freud, 1955). The well-known phrase 'Freudian slip' – referring to an unintentional verbal error that is thought to reveal some unconscious feeling that a person might have – demonstrates perfectly just how wide-ranging Freud's influence has been.

Freudian psychology was sidelined in academic psychology by the prominent movement of behaviourism, but the curious fact is that although behaviourist psychologists considered psychoanalytic theory unscientific as it was not based on observable behaviours and several of its tenets could not be verified experimentally, behaviourism itself did not favour consciousness as the cause of behaviour; as Custers and Aarts (2005) explain, behaviourist psychology focused on the role of various environmental stimuli and conditioning/reinforcement influences on the occurrence of different behaviours, without making any assumptions about the mental processes involved. In the 1960s, behaviourism was eclipsed by cognitive psychology, which, as its name implies, foregrounded conscious cognition as the foundation of human action. However, as we shall see later, the behaviourist emphasis on the action-shaping potential of environmental cues has been reaffirmed by recent research on unconscious goal setting and pursuit.

Interestingly, at the genesis of modern motivation research in mainstream psychology in the 1960–70s, the construct of classic achievement motivation did include a component – 'need for achievement' – that had strong unconscious overtones and which was accordingly referred to by its main champion, David McClelland, as 'implicit motivation' (se e.g. McClelland, Koestner & Weinberger, 1989). Need for achievement was conceived as an underlying urge to achieve that amplified conscious motives; as Neumann and Schultheiss (2015) explain, such an implicit disposition was seen to imbue stimuli and situations with additional affective value, and it was thought to operate in facilitating behaviour and learning not unlike hunger facilitates a rat learning a maze. Need for achievement was typically measured using the 'Thematic Apperception Test' (TAT), which involved first asking participants to write narratives about ambiguous pictures and then coding every sentence for its achievement content. However, as we shall discuss later in detail, despite considerable efforts to fine-tune the TAT measure, it never achieved sufficient reliability and, more generally, implicit motivation measures did not provide sufficient correlations with self-reported conscious motivation measures. As a result, explicit approaches gradually sidelined the implicit measures in research, and subsequent theories of motivation typically ignored the implicit strand.

Modern research findings

Despite the various early indications that unconscious motives might matter more than what they had been credited for, something more dramatic was needed to propel the notion of unconscious motivation into the psychological limelight. This 'something dramatic' was provided by the ground-breaking study of Libet and his colleagues in the early 1980s (Libet, Wright & Gleason, 1982; Libet et al., 1983). In this thought-provoking investigation, participants, whose electrical brain activity was measured throughout the process, were asked to do an abrupt, voluntary movement of the fingers and/or the wrist at a time of their choice while looking at a screen where a spot of revolving light simulated a clock. Once they performed the movement of their choice, they were asked to report what the clock's position was when the self-initiated act happened. The astounding result of the experiment was that the participants' conscious decision to act was preceded by about 300 milliseconds by an electric signal in the 'supplementary motor area' of the brain, leading Libet to argue that the brain had already unconsciously made a decision to move even before the participants became aware of it. On the basis of this finding, Libet proposed that human action begins outside of consciousness. The key findings of the experiment were replicated consistently in various laboratories (see e.g. Dominik et al., 2018; for responses to criticisms, see Libet, 2002, 2004), and some 25 years later, Soon et al. (2008) went even further when they reported that the outcome of a decision-making task (pressing one of two buttons) could be detected in brain activity up to 10 seconds before it entered awareness (that is, far exceeding Libet's finding of one-third of a second).

These and other carefully executed laboratory studies created a fair amount of stir in the research community even though it was generally acknowledged by all sides that the exact manner by which self-initiated behaviour is encoded by neuronal circuits in the human brain leaves many questions open. Scholars also agreed that because the brain is such a complex and interconnected system, it might be impossible to offer an incontestable interpretation of measured changes in neural activity. However, an experiment by Fried, Mukamel and Kreiman (2011) did get very close to offering conclusive results in this respect, as it involved a 'single neuron study.' Such investigations are rather rare and difficult to conduct because they require an invasive procedure of planting electrodes in the brain (for a review, see Fried et al., 2014); for this reason, single neuron studies can only be done linked to some medical surgery (e.g. when treating brain tumours or epilepsy). In Fried et al.'s (2011) case, the researchers examined 12 epilepsy patients implanted with depth electrodes to localise the focus of seizure onset, and recorded the activity of over 1,000 single neurons while the participants performed self-initiated finger movements following a research design similar to that of Libet and his colleagues (1982, 1983). The findings confirmed the earlier results that conscious volition was preceded by changes in neural activity: Fried and his colleagues were able to predict an impending decision to move with an accuracy greater than 80% already 700 milliseconds before the subjects' awareness of it. Accordingly, they concluded:

> Taken together, these findings lend support to the view that the experience of will emerges as the culmination of premotor activity (probably in combination with networks in parietal cortex) starting several hundreds of ms before awareness.
>
> p. 557

Priming

The neuroscientific investigations outlined above have successfully tipped the balance of scholarly belief in favour of accepting that the unconscious mind matters, but in order to act upon this belief researchers needed a workable methodology to examine the various characteristics of unconscious processes. The technique of *priming* has provided this capability. We shall talk about the methodological aspects of priming at the end of this chapter when discussing research issues related to unconscious motivation, but the essence of the method is relevant here. The process of priming is based on the idea that participants can be presented with a stimulus which is registered in their brain but which remains outside their awareness. Such cues can be, for example, visual (e.g. a small picture in the corner of a computer scene when the person's attention is captured by information presented in the centre of the screen) or auditory (e.g. a special word that has been used in an unrelated task), and they can even be presented subliminally (e.g. a stimulus flashed for less than 500 ms embedded in some other visual flow).

Significantly for the current discussion, priming can be used to generate subconscious motivation in people; that is, a prime can trigger a motive that the person will act upon without realising what the cause of the behaviour was. In fact, as described by Dörnyei and Al-Hoorie (2017), when people are asked in such experiments why they behaved as they did, they would often misattribute their action to some cause such as a preference or disposition (even though the researchers know that this was not the case); that is, people would fabricate a conscious explanation in retrospect that had nothing to do with the real antecedent of their action. Thus, priming studies can produce compelling evidence that human behaviour is subject to manipulation at the unconscious level, and that people can be motivated to do things without them being aware of the underlying motives. The technique has lent itself to a wide range of laboratory studies, as a result of which the past decade has seen a surge of experiments examining various aspects of unconscious motivation.

Does free will exist?

The converging evidence produced by neuroscientific and priming studies regarding the significance of unconscious motives raised the stakes high, because it questioned the role – and sometimes even the existence – of conscious agency, that is, of free will. Assigning a decisive role to the unconscious mind in governing behaviour is easily perceived to undermine some of the basic assumptions about being human, because it implies that the subjective experience of having free will is no more than an illusion; as Soon et al. (2008) rightly point out, "The impression that we are able to freely choose between different possible courses of action is fundamental to our mental life" (p. 543), and Fried et al.'s (2011) caution echoes this point: "Volitional control is at the root of our notion of self. Impairments in the ability to express or detect volitional output can be devastating" (p. 548). We must realise, however, that even if conscious action emerges gradually from unconscious precursors in the brain, consciousness may not be merely a false impression. The processes involved are still poorly understood, and the results may well be attributed to some variation of a scenario whereby the unconscious mind only prepares the ground for the conscious executive system, not unlike administrators in a corporation would assemble the necessary background material prior to a meeting where important decisions will be taken by the senior managers. In any case, the foregrounding of the role of the unconscious mind has forced the research community to take a fresh look at the role of consciousness in human behaviour, something that had been taken for granted before. Let us look at some of the conclusions that scholars have arrived at in this respect.

The case for conscious motivation

One of the most systematic responses to the challenge caused by research findings concerning the unconscious mind was offered by Baumeister, Masicampo and Vohs (2011), who conducted a comprehensive literature review of studies addressing the conscious causation of behaviour. Reflecting on this paper, Baumeister and Bargh (2014) conclude that in the light of the evidence presented, it is hard to dispute the capability of conscious agency to control behaviour. Reviewing the business management literature, Latham, Stajkovic and Locke (2010) came to a similar conclusion: not only did they find that consciously set goals lead to significant increases in job performance, but these goals also appeared to *exceed* their subconscious counterparts in terms of their impact. Baumeister et al. (2011) highlight several mental functions in which the role of consciousness is particularly salient, and the following list describes the most important processes:

- *Planning, mentally rehearsing and imagining future actions.* The available evidence is fairly conclusive that conscious deliberation of future behaviour has a definite impact on whether and how a particular act will be performed. Such conscious thought can involve making plans, envisaging future scenarios (a topic that will be elaborated on in Chapter 5, discussing the notion of vision) and mentally rehearsing certain action sequences.
- *Saying no.* Another area where conscious agency can exercise control is saying 'no' to one's inclinations and stopping certain actions before they happen. In his insightful overview of agency in complex dynamic systems theory, Al-Hoorie (2015) has highlighted this 'vetoing' aspect of agency as the most salient consciously performed human function, and Libet himself (e.g. 2004) also subscribed to this view. Reflecting on this matter, Sheldon (2014) explains that even if conscious experience may emerge relatively late in a mental preparatory sequence, "it appears to have the capacity to at least approve or disapprove of the behavioural possibilities that emerge within its view" (p. 360). This monitoring function is of particular significance when it comes to self-regulation as it allows consciousness to mediate between conflicting motives, a theme that will be further elaborated on in Chapter 6 when we consider the role of self-control in long-term motivation. Kihlstrom (2019) further adds that such conscious resistance to distractions or temptations may become particularly effective if it is itself automatised with practice and is thus unconsciously deployed, an argument which feels a bit like coming full circle.
- *Confronting obstacles and trouble shooting.* While many of our actions are undoubtedly driven by unconscious mechanisms, conscious awareness will

be directed at them if there is a problem. As Ellis (2007, p. 26) expressively summarises, "when automatic capabilities fail, there follows a call for recruiting additional collaborative conscious support: We only think about walking when we stumble, about driving when a child runs into the road, and about language when communication breaks down." Thus, his conclusion is that "In unpredictable conditions, the capacity of consciousness to organize existing knowledge in new ways is indispensable" (ibid). In other words, when encountering obstacles, automatic/unconscious operation can shift into a conscious mode to take care of the problematic or unresolved issue (see also Kihlstrom, 2019).

- *Communicating and discussing things with others.* Baumeister and Bargh (2014) make an important point when they underline the crucial function of consciousness in communication. As they point out, "Although many things can be done while conscious thought is directed elsewhere, talking does not appear to be one of them (nor does writing!)" (p. 45) Indeed, interpersonal brainstorming coupled with logical reasoning and persuasion is an effective conscious source of directing action towards optimal outcomes.
- *Deliberating on multiple motives.* Consciousness also appears to be relied on intensively when one needs to decide between alternative courses of action, fuelled by competing motivations (Baumeister et al., 2011). In fact, Sheldon (2014) emphasises that consciousness provides a particularly useful platform to compare different options, and indeed, one can intentionally juxtapose various elements at a level of abstraction to make an informed choice. As Sheldon concludes, consciousness is required for a person to be able to throw one's weight behind a particular option, particularly when a highly consequential act is being considered.
- *Goal setting.* The study of the role played by goals in guiding human behaviour has a long history in motivational psychology and, indeed, goal setting theory (e.g. Locke & Latham, 1994, 2006) is an established cognitive theory of motivation. In many ways, assuming a goal-directed characterisation of behaviour is one of the main pillars of the conscious understanding of human motivation; as Custers and Aarts (2005, p. 257) summarise, "Modern views on human behaviour assume that people's goal pursuits are governed by consciousness ... that goal setting is characterised by a conscious reflection process, and that goal adoption and enactment are associated with conscious intent." Yet, they go on, one wonders where our goals actually come from: "Although we might be conscious of setting goals, adopting them, or acting on them, it is often unclear what leads us to do so. We are, so to speak, often unconscious of the sources of our conscious thoughts and pursuits" (p. 258). Thus, while goals have traditionally been part of the discourse of scholars arguing in favour of consciousness in motivation research, the situation has changed dramatically in the new millennium, and the nature of goals and goal setting has become a (if not *the*) primary research frontier with regard to unconscious motivation. This special status warrants a more detailed discussion of the topic.

Unconscious goal setting and goal pursuit

Consciously set *goals* (or as they are often called nowadays, 'targets') have been seen as a lynchpin of enhancing human performance because of (at least) four main reasons (see e.g. Dörnyei, 2001): (a) they direct attention and effort towards goal-relevant activities at the expense of irrelevant or distracting actions; (b) they regulate the amount of effort people expend as people adjust their effort to the difficulty level and the demands of the task; (c) they encourage persistence until the goal is accomplished; and (d) they promote the search for relevant action plans or task strategies. Thus, goals have been seen both in educational and organisational (i.e. work) psychology as a highly useful concept for the purpose of initiating action and then keeping people's attention and commitment focused during goal pursuit. As such, setting and pursuing goals appear to be a thoroughly conscious human affair. However, this widely held and intuitively convincing position has been increasingly qualified over the past two decades by the growing body of research on goal priming and unconscious goal pursuit, which suggest that unconsciously activated goals play a far greater role in everyday life than previously suspected (Custers & Aarts, 2014).

The focal issue in studies on unconscious goals has been the identification of the factors that can trigger such goals as well as understanding the processes that guide their unconscious pursuit. The principal finding in this respect has been the discovery that goal pursuit can be directly triggered and then guided by *environmental cues* such as certain events, people, situational factors and other external stimuli whose impact the actor is unaware of. This human dependence on environmental regulation is reminiscent of the conditioning principles of behaviourism, but Custers and Aarts (2005) argue that modern views differ from the behaviourist position in one crucial aspect: instead of treating the mind as a 'black box' and focusing primarily on the outcome of environmental effects, cutting-edge research is exploring the mental processes and representations that make up the unconscious motivational mechanisms.

Perhaps the best illustration of the magnitude of the change in scholarly views on unconscious goals has been the dramatic transformation of the position of one of the founders of conscious goal setting theory, Gary Latham. In a recent paper he recounts his initial scepticism about priming goals and his subsequent "transition from sceptic to believer" (Latham, 2018, p. 392). Having spent his academic career studying consciously set goals, Latham was initially highly doubtful about the applicability of the findings of priming experiments to real-life, work settings. He attributed the published results to experimental bias and demand effects, and because most priming studies have a rather short time-frame between the manipulation and the outcome measure, he reckoned that even if there was a small effect, it was so fragile and short-lived that it would be negligible for goal setting in the workplace. In other words, he was convinced that the findings of priming research were not generalisable beyond tightly controlled laboratory experiments. Therefore, in order to test whether his doubts were valid, he conducted a field experiment with his doctoral student, Amanda Shantz, in a call centre where employees were given standardised instructions to solicit money from potential donors. The priming condition involved printing the instructions across the photograph of a racer winning a race, and to the researchers' self-confessed surprise, it worked: there was a main effect for the primed goal even though employees reported that they had not even noticed the photograph as they were too busy to pay any attention to the picture of the racer (Shantz & Latham, 2009). To be on the safe side, Latham's lab conducted three further field replications and two laboratory studies to reinforce the results and eliminate rival hypotheses (for a review, see Latham, 2018), and as a result, Latham concludes that the success of these experiments

> have made it impossible for me to remain a sceptic of the primed goal-job-task-performance relationship. These six experiments include both exact and conceptual replications. The participants were unaware of the prime-performance hypothesis. This was not only evident in the funnel-debrief, but it was also particularly evident in the employees' great surprise when they were made aware of the hypothesis at the end of the debrief.
>
> *Latham, 2018, p. 399*

Thus, Latham became a believer in goal priming because research has demonstrated a causal relationship between primed goals and job performance in real field settings. The generalisability of goal priming to work environments was further substantiated in a recent study by Stajkovic et al. (2019) in a for-profit customer service organisation, which answered phone calls to offer solutions to customer inquiries and complaints. In his weekly, Monday-morning email to all the employees, the CEO used goal priming to motivate job performance by including 12 achievement-related words (out of a total of 100) in a message sent to the experimental group; the control group also received a 100-word message, which did not contain achievement-related words. The results showed that the primed goal significantly increased the two key measures with which job performance was assessed in the company, 'Average Call Handling Time' and 'Average Call Resolution Time,' indicating a 35% performance improvement in goal pursuit.

Automatised and chronic goals

At the outset of research into unconscious motives, Bargh (1990) suggested that in the case of habitual action, an originally conscious goal can be automatised and can thus get stored in the unconscious. Subsequently, this subconscious goal can be activated by certain environmental cues (i.e. 'primes') without an individual's intention or awareness, and the primed unconscious goal will, in turn, trigger its associated behaviours; as a result, action unfolds automatically, without conscious guidance (see Stajkovic & Sergent, 2019). The process of automatisation has also been discussed in a different context, skill learning theory (e.g. Anderson, 2000), which holds that the essence of the progression of learning any skill is a gradual move from the laboured, conscious and overtly controlled declarative processes of the novice to the smooth, unconscious and covertly controlled procedural processes of the expert. A good illustration of this process is the rapid development of most learner drivers as they automatise their initial declaratively learnt knowledge and turn it into unconsciously applied procedures whose execution requires relatively little attentional control.

Automatised goals are thus believed to acquire a 'chronic state' – that is, an ongoing state of permanent accessibility across a variety of contexts – through consistent and habitual pursuit (Moskowitz, 2014), but what is important for the current discussion is that the frequency of pursuit is not the only avenue for a goal to become chronically accessible. As Markus and Kunda (1986) submit, if powerful goals and visions exceed a critical threshold of personal importance, they can become chronically accessible in the self-concept and subsequently automatic regulators of behaviour (see also Dörnyei et al., 2016). Custers and Aarts (2007) offer supporting evidence that deep-seated goals/visions can function like an unconscious goal-orientation which can "spontaneously trigger the preparation of goal-directed actions" (p. 624); they illustrate this chronic accessibility in analogy with a thermostat maintaining the temperature in a room: "the chief advantage offered by a thermostat is not that it achieves the desired temperature once we have set it but that it maintains it by automatically reacting to discrepancies with the goal state" (p. 632). Bargh (2017) sums up chronically accessible goals in an expressive way:

> Your important goals never sleep. They operate unconsciously in the background, without your needing to guide them or even being aware of them, vigilantly monitoring your environment for things that might help meet that need. Answers to problems can then pop into your mind out of seemingly nowhere. Sleep is a big chunk of downtime when conscious activities are at a minimum, and your mind uses that time unconsciously to continue to work on problems. The good news is that sometimes it is successful, providing a breakthrough answer or solution to a problem or puzzle you've worked on consciously for quite a while.
>
> *p. 258*

We should note, however, that Bargh goes on to mention the 'bad news' as well: some other times the subconscious can reach an impasse, which will cause worries and anxiety. Such an impasse can only be broken by "conscious work in the form of making a concrete plan for how to solve that problem in the near future" (p. 258). Melnikoff and Bargh (2018) further caution that even if unconscious goal pursuit works, it can sometimes be rather inefficient. For example, when the solving of a puzzle requires discovering a certain rule, people may be able to achieve the solution without having conscious awareness of it, but it is often a more effective way to work out the rule and then apply it consciously. The growing consensus is, thus, that conscious and unconscious processes *interact* with each other, passing the baton from one to the other. This brings us to the significance of the *blended cooperation* of the conscious and the unconscious mind, to be discussed below.

Dual-process theories and the interaction of the conscious and the unconscious mind

Dual-process theories first appeared in psychology in the 1970s, and Sherman, Gawronski and Trope (2014) begin their high-profile anthology on the subject by submitting that the emergence of these theories "has been one of the most significant developments in the history of scientific psychology" (p. xi). The assumption underlying these theories is highly ambitious and not a little controversial: it is postulated that psychological processes can be divided into two distinct categories: efficient, unintentional, uncontrollable and unconscious (Type 1) and inefficient, intentional, controllable and conscious (Type 2) (see e.g. Melnikoff & Bargh, 2018). The Type 1/Type 2 distinction has been identified in a number of different cognitive areas, suggesting that "experience, thought, and action can be influenced by processes that operate either automatically and unconsciously or under deliberate, conscious control" (Kihlstrom, 2019). Although framing psychological processes in such a dichotomous manner may not be accurate in the strict sense – as argued, for example, by Melnikoff and Bargh, amongst others – the division has been highly effective in directing attention to the subconscious mind and to the potential interaction between conscious and unconscious processes.

It is this cooperation of the two dimensions of mental functioning that has increasingly emerged over the past decade as the crucial aspect of human motivation. According to this view, while behaviour may well originate in the unconscious sphere, its execution is usually determined by "a blend of conscious and unconscious processes working together to meet the person's critical needs and facilitate important goal pursuits" (Baumeister & Bargh, 2014, p. 46). Some theoreticians would, in fact, go as far as to say that performing *any* task requires a certain amount of contribution from both automatic and conscious processes, with the balance between them depending on the nature of the task and other situational considerations (see Kihlstrom, 2019). This, however, is a contentious area, as other scholars believe that there is relatively little cross-talk between the two largely independent processes (see e.g. Sheldon, 2014). Moreover, even the views that support a complementary interaction between conscious and unconscious processes show some variation between assigning the dominant role to consciousness and viewing unconscious/automatised processes as a modifying factor on the one hand, and regarding unconscious processes as the default source of action on the other, while "consciousness can occasionally intervene to override, regulate, redirect, and otherwise alter the stream of behaviour – often at a distance, with unconscious processes filling in" (Baumeister & Bargh, 2014, p. 37).

In sum, the jury is still out about the extent to which unconscious and conscious processes work together to direct and energise action. However, it is unlikely that any clear-cut and uniform answer will emerge for every task, because Bargh (2017) is right that the two types of functioning do different things well and support each other dynamically:

> For example, conscious experiences in one situation linger into the next situation without our realising it and become the unconscious influences

in that subsequent setting. Unconscious processes work on our important problems and goals, and pop answers and solutions into our conscious minds. Unconscious goals direct our conscious attention to things relevant to our goals, and cause us to notice and then make use of those things. *Both* forms of thought are part of you, not only the conscious part.

pp. 280–281

Researching unconscious motivation

The scientific study of the unconscious sources of human behaviour is a relatively new line of inquiry that has acquired fully recognised status only during the past decade or so. It is therefore still full of as yet unrealised potential, and this is increasingly true of conducting empirical research in this area. Researching unconscious motivation is difficult for the very reason that it *un*conscious: most people simply cannot recognise, let alone report, the causes of their behaviour accurately, and when they try to understand why they do (or do not do) something, they are susceptible to personal bias, social desire effect and misattribution (see e.g. Hoffman, 2015). What is currently needed is further testing and data-driven elaboration on the various theoretical hypotheses. Because traditional techniques used for assessing explicit motives are only of limited use for this purpose, the main challenge in the field has been to create new research templates that enable the investigation of the unconscious mind. The good news is that the past two decades have seen a great deal of progress in two areas of relevant research methodology: (a) developing research designs that allow for the *priming* – that is, consciously generating – unconscious motives, and (b) developing *research instruments* to identify and assess unconscious attitudes and motives. We shall survey these two areas before narrowing down our focus to the study of unconscious L2 motivation.

Priming

It was the technique of *priming* which has provided researchers with the necessary methodology to examine the characteristics of unconscious mental processes. Priming can be divided into two broad types, *subliminal* and *supraliminal*. The former involves presenting a cue below the threshold of perceptibility (e.g. flashing a picture so swiftly that the viewer is not aware of it); the latter, supraliminal priming, is the more common type applied in contemporary psychological research, and it involves presenting a perceptible cue either in a manner that the participants do not notice it consciously (e.g. because their attention is otherwise engaged or because the cue is unobtrusively hidden) or in a way that its relationship to the primary task is not readily obvious (e.g. doing a language task that contains certain key words that will only be relevant for the next task).

Priming is a versatile technique, as it can involve both visual cues and language ones (e.g. after hearing the word 'black,' people are quicker to perceive the word 'white' than without hearing 'black' first). Holland, Hendriks and Aarts (2005) report on three intriguing studies that even applied olfactory (i.e. odour) primes: when participants were unobtrusively exposed to the smell of a citrus-scented all-purpose cleaner, not only was the mental accessibility of the concept of cleaning enhanced (as evidenced by faster identification of cleaning-related words in a subsequent lexical decision task) but the unconscious prime also caused the participants to keep their direct environment tidier during an eating task. Priming can also be *cross-modal*, that is, when two sensory modes are activated at the same time (e.g. watching something and listening to something else through earphones) and the subject's attention is intentionally kept on one of the tasks (e.g. because they need to answer comprehension questions) while providing the prime through the other sensory mode.

The target of priming can be varied, ranging from attitudes, internal norms and traits to desired outcomes and specific behaviours, and the recipients of the primes typically display some relevant reaction, for example by displaying a prime-related attitude or preference, or doing something consistent with the attainment of the primed goal. To give but one illustration, in an online Microsoft training course Sitzmann and Bell (2017) primed (a) subconscious achievement goals by supraliminally presenting pictures portraying people exerting effort and attaining success (e.g. cyclists racing up a hill and runners leaping across a finish line) as well as (b) subconscious underachievement goals through pictures conveying laziness, lethargy, sluggishness and sleepiness (e.g. people yawning or napping). The results showed that the subconscious achievement goals facilitated task performance, whereas the subconscious underachievement goals triggered increased goal abandonment. We should also note that even classical behaviourist conditioning can be connected to priming, because an unconscious link is developed through repeated exposure between an environmental cue and a specific reaction to it (e.g. the sound of a metronome and the salivation of a dog in anticipation of food in Pavlov's famous experiment); this reaction is then automatically activated when encountering the stimulus again.

Thus, priming is a powerful and versatile technique, but we need to also be aware of some scholars' caution that currently the use of priming is often a rather unprincipled 'fishing' adventure along the lines of "Let's prime people with achievement, cooperation, food, or computers and see what happens" (Custers & Aarts, 2005, p. 258) The absence of sufficient understanding of how exactly primes operate becomes salient when a prime does *not* work. For example, Custers and Aarts report that priming does not always affect every goal-related measure: in a study they found that although priming did facilitate the perception of goal-related opportunities, it did not seem to increase people's explicit desire to achieve the goal. Priming only creates more accessibility to a certain content, and the hope is that this "more accessible content *can* influence a subsequent response" (Janiszewski & Wyer, 2014, p. 97; emphasis added); however, further research is needed to determine the conditions under which "*can* influence" becomes "*does* influence."

Traditional assessment of implicit motivation through projective tests

Although psychological testing has traditionally been dominated by objective tests involving self-report measures, some scholars were aware of the fact that consciously formulated responses to items in motivation tests may not reflect the whole breadth of a respondents' underlying disposition. As the label suggests, 'self-report' responses represent what the respondents *report* to feel or believe, rather than what they *actually* feel or believe, and the two might not coincide for a number of reasons. One salient cause for a potential discrepancy is the *social desirability* or *prestige bias*, which refers to the general human tendency of trying to present ourselves in a better, socially more acceptable light. A second issue that is directly relevant to the subject of this chapter is that respondents are not always aware of their deep-seated motives and therefore they are not in a position to provide explicitly formulated insights about them. People can easily misattribute their actions that have been caused by unconscious motives, which means that in some cases respondents unintentionally provide inaccurate or false information. In response to such concerns, researchers in personality psychology have experimented with alternative assessment methods for over a century. The best-known early technique to focus on the unconscious realm of the mind was the *projective test*, involving tasks whereby respondents are asked to react to ambiguous stimuli (such as the famous Rorschach test, in which respondents describe ten irregular but symmetrical inkblots) and their unique responses are then analysed to discern manifestations of hidden, internal psychological content.

The most famous projective test in motivation research has been the Thematic Apperception Test (TAT), which involves a picture-story task that invites participants to make up short stories about ambiguous pictures. As Morgan (2002) describes, such picture-story tasks were first applied at the beginning of the twentieth century and were then turned into scientific research instruments by Henry Murray and his colleagues in the late 1930s and early 1940s. The technique was adapted for the assessment of implicit motives by David McClelland in the 1950s, and the resulting Picture-Story Exercise, along with the motivation-specific scoring system, became the principal methodology in the study of unconscious motivation. It involves a series of picture cues (about four to eight) showing people engaged in motive-relevant behaviours in various social situations. Participants are asked to write an imaginative story inspired by these cues, and the content of the stories is coded using specially designed coding schemes to assess motive-relevant imagery. While the technique has produced a wealth of insights over the decades, its main shortcoming has been that the scoring could not be made sufficiently reliable even after providing raters with training, and therefore the instrument fell short of modern psychometric standards (see e.g. Latham et al., 2010).

In the field of the social psychology of language, a specialised procedure – the Matched-Guise Technique (MGT) – was introduced by Lambert et al. (1960) to measure unconscious language-related and ethnolinguistic attitudes. The technique is simple and ingenious: participants listen to recordings of a text read out in different languages or accents, and are then asked to evaluate the character of the different speakers based on what they hear. The trick is that the 'different speakers' are actually all the same person and therefore different evaluations of this person are seen to be caused by the attitudes and prejudices attached to the specific accent/language used. Nejjari et al. (2019) offer an overview both of past research using the MGT and various technical aspects of the procedure, also including suggestions for making the selection of the matched guises more principled.

Modern assessment procedures

The new wave of interest in unconscious attitudes, goals and motives in the 1990s generated an impetus for the development of research tools that were based on altogether different principles and which produced scores that were compatible with the requirements of quantitative data analysis. Three widely recognised and used instruments have emerged from these efforts: the Implicit Association Test (IAT; Greenwald, McGhee & Schwartz, 1998), the Affect Misattribution Procedure (AMP; Payne et al., 2005) and the Evaluative Priming Task (EPT; Fazio et al., 1995). A key method of tapping into the unconscious domain has been to measure *reaction times* to various stimuli presented on a computer screen in milliseconds, with the subtle differences in speed in reacting to various cues believed to reflect differences in unconscious dispositions (for a review, see e.g. De Houwer et al., 2009). This has been a logical development, because measuring reaction times has traditionally been one of the most common methods of psycholinguistic experimentation; the new tests could therefore draw upon an established measurement tradition while circumventing the introspective limits and distortions of self-report measures. Although Teige-Mocigemba et al. (2017) are right to conclude that none of the new tools possess all the features typically ascribed to them, their utility in research has received sufficient confirmation over the past two decades. Let us have a quick look at the three specific instruments:

The Implicit Association Test (IAT; Greenwald et al., 1998) is arguably the best-known of the new tools of unconscious motivation assessment, and it has also been utilised in studies on L2 motivation (e.g. Al-Hoorie, 2016a; Waninge, 2017). Similar to many psycholinguistic measures, it involves special software that assesses the respondent's response time in making quick decisions regarding cues appearing on a computer screen; by pressing one of two buttons, the respondent has to assign each appearing cue to one of two categories. A clever combination of cues and response categories ensures that the respondent's underlying implicit disposition will influence the speed of the responses, and because the software measures response time in milliseconds, even tiny differences show up and are recorded by the program. After the participant has responded to all the items, the IAT software computes a score on the basis of some complex algorithm (for a detailed description of the procedure, see e.g. https://en.wikipedia.org/wiki/Implicit-association_test; for downloadable material, including a pilot version of the test, see http://faculty.washington.edu/agg/iat_materials.htm).

A unique feature of IAT is that it compares unconscious attitudes towards two pre-set categories (e.g. English and Hungarian) and the outcome measure generated by the instrument reflects the respondents' *preferences* between the two. This is because the assessment is based on comparisons of various contrasts, but a shortcoming of such a 'relative' measure is that it cannot offer a straightforward index of a person's attitude towards a single-target concept. For example, with English and Hungarian as the two categories to compare, the IAT score can only tell us that a person is more keen on, say, English than Hungarian, rather than *how* keen he/she is on English; accordingly, a positive score for English can mean three different things:

- the person likes English and dislikes Hungarian;
- the person likes both languages but likes English more;
- the person dislikes both languages but dislikes English less.

Despite this evaluation of relative strength, the IAT still yields a useful measure of unconscious dispositions and has therefore been applied in a wide range of studies in the social sciences (see e.g. De Houwer et al., 2009). There have been several attempts to produce a version of the test that can yield an independent evaluation of a single target: Karpinski and Steinman (2006) developed the Single Category Implicit Association Test, Penke, Eichstaedt and Asendorpf (2006) the Single-Attribute Implicit Association Test and several studies (e.g. Al-Hoorie, 2016b; Huijding & de Jong, 2006; Lüke & Grosche, 2018) report on the use of an unpublished version of the IAT, the Single-Target Implicit Association Test (by Wigboldus, Holland & van Knippenberg). These versions, however, have not been widely verified yet.

The Affect Misattribution Procedure (AMP; Payne et al., 2005; for downloadable material, see http://bkpayne.web.unc.edu/research-materials/) is also a computer-based test, but it follows a different principle from the IAT. The procedure is simple: participants first see a prime stimulus (picture) on the screen briefly but not subliminally, followed by an ambiguous target item (usually a Chinese pictograph); they are then asked to make a simple judgement about the target item (usually on a binary response scale such as pleasant/unpleasant). Because the target item is neutral, the response will follow the lead of the unconscious original prime (i.e. the picture preceding the target item), but the respondents are unaware of this and believe that they are evaluating the target pictograph. In order to make sure that any unwanted influence of the pictograph is eliminated, prime and target items are paired randomly and thus the averaged responses reflect only the systematic influence of the primes. The term 'misattribution' in the name of the procedure refers to the fact that the unintentional evaluation of the prime is misattributed to the target stimuli (i.e. the respondents are mistaking the effect of the prime for the effect of the target pictograph). Payne et al. (2005) point out that the procedure is reminiscent of classic projective tests in the sense that the appraisal of the pictographs is shaped by unrelated, subjective content similar to how respondents to a Rorschach test imbue the ambiguous inkblots with their unrelated subjective evaluation. However, unlike projective tests, the scoring of the AMP is objective and reliable, and studies conducted over the past decade utilising this tool have shown that the AMP is indeed a valid instrument (Payne & Lundberg, 2014; Teige-Mocigemba et al., 2017).

The Evaluative Priming Task (EPT; Fazio et al., 1995) is similar to the AMP in that the results are derived from the combination of a prime and a target stimulus. However, while in the AMP the target stimulus (e.g. the Chinese pictograph) had a neutral evaluative content and therefore when participants were asked to evaluate it, they in effect appraised the previous prime, the EPT involves a distinctly evaluative target stimulus (e.g. a cockroach). Accordingly, the evaluation of this target will be straightforward, but researchers are interested in the speed of this evaluation: if the unconscious evaluation of the prime preceding the target is similarly negative, the appraisal will be faster than when there is a dissonance in the evaluation of the prime and the target. In other words, when participants classify a target as emotionally positive or negative, responses are faster if a preceding prime stimulus had the same affective loading. An overall measure of someone's attitudes towards the prime is reflected by the relative difference in the speed of evaluating a negative target paired with the prime versus a positive target paired with the same prime. Kiefer et al. (2017) offer a good overview of the procedure as well as a neuroimaging comparison of priming with pictures and words.

The relationship between explicit and implicit motivational measures: Research implications

One of the most important lessons emerging from the study of unconscious attitudes and motivation over the past decades has been the finding that they are only weakly, if at all, related to conscious measures concerning the same targets; that is, the correlation between an explicit, self-report variable assessed by means of a questionnaire and an unconscious, indirect measure of the same variable obtained by means of one of the tools described in the previous section will usually be rather low and quite often nonsignificant (see e.g. Kihlstrom, 2019; McClelland et al., 1989; Teige-Mocigemba et al., 2017). This result, consistently obtained across different targets and assessment instruments, has (at least) two fundamental implications for research design in motivation studies. First, it indicates that measuring only one type of motivation – whether conscious or unconscious – will result in a one-sided overall picture, because it does not take into account the *incremental value* of the two motivational dimensions. Second, the weak correlation implies a *mixed* association between conscious and unconscious motives: in certain learning and achievement situations there is undoubtedly a great deal of *congruence* between conscious and unconscious motives, but this positive correlation is offset by the existence of considerable *dissonance* in other situations and conditions. In other words, while the conscious and unconscious motives of an individual sometimes operate in harmony, at other times they pull the person in different directions. Let us examine the research implications of these points:

- *Incremental value.* In their overview of the relationship between explicit and implicit motives, McClelland et al. (1989) explain that implicit motives such as need for achievement constitute broad underlying orientations, whereas self-attributed (i.e. self-report) desires reflect more specific areas in which these orientations can be realised. For example, someone's general achievement orientation may find an outlet in the person's wish to do well in a concrete social domain such as work or school. Accordingly, the authors argue that accounting for the strength of both the explicit and the implicit motives will improve the accuracy of the prediction of performance. This makes sense, because regardless of how one conceptualises implicit/unconscious motives, it is clear that they predict different aspects of behaviour from explicit/conscious motives. If this is, however, the case, then past research on motivation, whether in mainstream psychology or in SLA, has been incomplete and offered an insufficient description of the interplay of forces shaping human behaviour. Yet, we should note that the relationship between unconscious and conscious motives is likely to be more complex than merely being additive (i.e. having to be simply summed up), and focusing on the *dissonance* and *congruence* between them offers a useful inroad into understanding the associations between the two motivational dimensions.
- *Dissonance versus congruence.* Certain conditions may create harmony between the conscious and unconscious motives underlying some behaviour, whereas others might bring them into conflict, and this contrast might explain aspects of a person's action that did not make sense before. McClelland et al. (1989) for example offer the illustration of people who express a desire to act in a certain way but seem unable to do so consistently, arguing that their lack of consistency originates from a discordance between their explicit and implicit motives. The advantage of considering how conscious and unconscious motives are aligned with each other is that this can potentially reveal whether a low motivation score is simply the reflection of an overall lack of commitment or whether there *are* some powerful motives in operation in the situation in question but they are dampened by some negative unconscious counterparts. The research implication of the dissociation of explicit and implicit goals/motives is that people with incompatible dispositions are likely to do worse than those with nonconflicting goals (Latham et al., 2010). For example, Shah and Kruglanski (2002) showed that priming participants to pursue goals that were alternative to their conscious commitment impacted their goal-directed behaviour, resulting in the waxing and waning of goal focus, whereas if the primed goal had a facilitative relation to the focal pursuit, this had an amplifying effect.

Unconscious motivation in SLA

We have seen earlier in this chapter that the 'matched-guise technique' was an effective way of identifying unconscious language attitudes, but this line of inquiry has not been integrated in modern research on L2 motivation. This was, as Al-Hoorie (2020) summarises, partly because of concerns with research methodological aspects of the technique and partly because the emerging findings were inconclusive. Given, however, the changing research climate regarding the unconscious mind in mainstream psychology, it was only a question of time before the issue of unconscious L2 attitudes and motivation was revisited. The initiative was taken by Al-Hoorie (2015) in his conceptual overview of conscious and unconscious agency in complex dynamic systems, and he then conducted two empirical investigations to demonstrate that unconscious language attitudes matter. The first study (Al-Hoorie, 2016a) pioneered the employment of the Implicit Association Test (described earlier) in SLA, to compare the impact of explicit and implicit attitudes towards L2 speakers. Adopting the congruence/dissonance paradigm discussed above, the results provided evidence that accounting for the learners' level of implicit attitudes had substantial effects on the explanatory power of the results: students with *harmonious* positive explicit and implicit attitudes were more favourably disposed towards the L2 group than those who reported a positive explicit disposition but held negative implicit attitudes. This result was further corroborated in a follow-up study (Al-Hoorie, 2016b), which also included academic achievement as a criterion measure. Using a single-target version of the IAT in an instructed SLA environment (i.e. where English was taught as a school subject), Al-Hoorie confirmed not only that learners with favourable implicit attitudes towards L2 speakers expressed more openness to the L2 community but that they also achieved higher grades in their English class.

In analysing the motivation to learn languages other than English (LOTEs), Dörnyei and Al-Hoorie (2017) argued that in some linguistic environments the spread of Global English is likely to generate widespread unconscious resistance. As we pointed out, some countries such as Japan display a deep-seated discrepancy between the dominant explicit discourse of internationalisation through the promotion of English and subtle and often unconscious social resistance to language globalisation, resulting in a marked incongruity between the efforts and resources invested in the instruction of English and the rate of success observed in the area. The impact of Global English also affects the study of other languages in general, as learners are bound to make conscious and unconscious comparisons with English. This has been evidenced in a study that compared L2 attitudes towards learning English and Mandarin in Hong Kong (Boo, 2018), which demonstrated the existence of significant discrepancies of the learners' explicit and implicit disposition in this context, and which confirmed that learners with congruent attitudes reported more intended effort to study an L2 than learners whose conscious and unconscious motives clashed with each other. Unconscious L2 motivation has also surfaced in the study of directed motivational currents (DMCs), which will be discussed in Chapter 6 with respect to long-term motivation. As we shall see there, these motivational currents derive their energy partly from behavioural routines that become an automatic part of the action sequence, and Dörnyei et al. (2016) further highlight the fact that the powerful visions and goals guiding DMC acquire 'chronic goal' status and thus operate as unconscious goal-orientations that automatically regulate goal pursuit.

Summary

The topic of unconscious attitudes, goals and motivations is a new and potentially exciting (or scary) development not only in L2 motivation research but also in mainstream motivational psychology. Although it admittedly requires a substantial change of research perspective, I hope that the previous discussion has offered convincing arguments that such a change is warranted in the light of the role that the unconscious mind can play in shaping human behaviour. Having said that, we need to also recognise that several of the fundamental questions about the relationship between conscious and unconscious motives are still open. For example, Latham et al. (2010) rightly point out that there has virtually been no research to date to *compare* the effects of conscious and unconscious goals on specific performance. The good news, however, is that psychologists have been developing useful methodologies and instruments for the purpose of studying the unconscious regulators of behaviour, thereby offering usable research templates for SLA applications.

References

Al-Hoorie, A. H. (2015). Human agency: Does the beach ball have free will? In Z. Dörnyei, P. D. MacIntyre & A. Henry (Eds.), *Motivational dynamics in language learning* (pp. 55–72). Bristol: Multilingual Matters.

Al-Hoorie, A. H. (2016a). Unconscious motivation. Part I: Implicit attitudes toward L2 speakers. *Studies in Second Language Learning and Teaching, 6*(3), 423–454.

Al-Hoorie, A. H. (2016b). Unconscious motivation. Part II: Implicit attitudes and L2 achievement. *Studies in Second Language Learning and Teaching, 6*(4), 619–649.

Al-Hoorie, A. H. (2020). Motivation and the unconscious. In M. Lamb, K. Csizér, A. Henry & S. Ryan (Eds.), *Palgrave Macmillan handbook of motivation for language learning* (pp. 561–578). Basingstoke: Palgrave.

Anderson, J. R. (2000). *Learning and memory: An integrated approach* (2nd ed.). Hoboken, NJ: John Wiley & Sons.

Baars, B. J. (1997). *In the theater of consciousness.* New York: Oxford University Press.

Bargh, J. A. (1990). Auto-motives: Preconscious determinants of social interaction. In E. T. Higgins & R. M. Sorrentino (Eds.), *Handbook of motivation and cognition: Foundations of social behaviour* (Vol. 2, pp. 93–130). New York: Guilford Press.

Bargh, J. A. (2017). *Before you know it: The unconscious reasons we do what we do.* New York: Atria.

Baumeister, R. F., & Bargh, J. A. (2014). Conscious and unconscious: Toward an integrative understanding of human mental life and action. In J. W. Sherman, B. Gawronski & Y. Trope (Eds.), *Dual-process theories of the social mind* (pp. 35–49). New York: Guilford Press.

Baumeister, R. F., Masicampo, E. J., & Vohs, K. D. (2011). Do conscious thoughts cause behavior? *Annual Review of Psychology, 62*, 331–361.

Boo, Z. (2018). *Implicit-explicit attitudes: Understanding Hong Kong language learners' motivation*. Paper presented at the Third International Conference on Psychology and Language Learning (PLL3), Tokyo.

Custers, R., & Aarts, H. (2005). Beyond priming effects: The role of positive affect and discrepancies in implicit processes of motivation and goal pursuit. *European Review of Social Psychology, 16*(1), 257–300.

Custers, R., & Aarts, H. (2007). Goal-discrepant situations prime goal-directed actions if goals are temporarily or chronically accessible. *Personality and Social Psychology Bulletin, 33*, 623–633.

Custers, R., & Aarts, H. (2014). Conscious and unconscious goal pursuit: Similar functions, different processes? In J. W. Sherman, B. Gawronski & Y. Trope (Eds.), *Dual-process theories of the social mind* (pp. 386–399). New York: Guilford Press.

De Houwer, J., Teige-Mocigemba, S., Spruyt, A., & Moors, A. (2009). Implicit measures: A normative analysis and review. *Psychological Bulletin, 135*(3), 347–368.

Dominik, T., Dostál, D., Zielina, M., Mahaj, J., Sedláčková, Z., & Procházka, R. (2018). Libet's experiment: A complex replication. *Consciousness and Cognition, 65*, 1–26.

Dörnyei, Z. (2001). *Motivational strategies in the language classroom*. Cambridge: Cambridge University Press.

Dörnyei, Z., & Al-Hoorie, A. H. (2017). The motivational foundation of learning languages other than global English: Theoretical issues and research directions. *Modern Language Journal, 101*(3), 455–468.

Dörnyei, Z., Henry, A., & Muir, C. (2016). *Motivational currents in language learning: Frameworks for focused interventions*. New York: Routledge.

Ellis, N. C. (2007). The weak interface, consciousness, and form-focused instruction: mind the doors. In S. S. Fotos & H. Nassaji (Eds.), *Form-focused instruction and teacher education* (pp. 17–34). Oxford: Oxford University Press.

Fazio, R. H., Jackson, J. R., Dunton, B. C., & Williams, C. J. (1995). Variability in automatic activation as an unobtrusive measure of racial attitudes: A bona fide pipeline? *Journal of Personality and Social Psychology, 69*(6), 1013–1027.

Ferguson, M. J., Hassin, R., & Bargh, J. A. (2008). Implicit motivation: Past, present, and future. In J. Shah & W. Gardner (Eds.), *Handbook of motivation science* (pp. 150–166). New York: Guilford Press.

Freud, S. (1955). *The interpretation of dreams* (J. Strachey, Trans.). New York: Basic Books.

Fried, I., Mukamel, R., & Kreiman, G. (2011). Internally generated preactivation of single neurons in human medial frontal cortex predicts volition. *Neuron, 69*, 548–562.

Fried, I., Rutishauser, U., Cerf, M., & Kreiman, G. (2014). *Single neuron studies of the human brain: Probing cognition*. Cambridge, MA: MIT Press.

Greenwald, A. G., McGhee, D. E., & Schwartz, J. L. K. (1998). Measuring individual differences in implicit cognition: The implicit association test. *Journal of Personality and Social Psychology, 74*(6), 1464–1480.

Hoffman, B. (2015). *Motivation for learning and performance*. San Diego, CA: Academic Press.

Holland, R. W., Hendriks, M., & Aarts, H. (2005). Smells like clean spirit: Nonconscious effects of scent on cognition and behavior. *Psychological Science, 16*(9), 689–693.

Hornstra, L., Kamsteega, A., Pota, S., & Verheija, L. (2018). A dual pathway of student motivation: Combining an implicit and explicit measure of student motivation. *Frontline Learning Research*, *6*(1), 1–18.

Huijding, J., & de Jong, P. J. (2006). Automatic associations with the sensory aspects of smoking: Positive in habitual smokers but negative in non-smokers. *Addictive Behaviors*, *31*, 182–186.

Janiszewski, C., & Wyer, R. S. J. (2014). Content and process priming: A review. *Journal of Consumer Psychology*, *24*(1), 96–118.

Karpinski, A., & Steinman, R. B. (2006). The single category implicit association test as a measure of implicit social cognition. *Journal of Personality and Social Psychology*, *91*(1), 16–32.

Kiefer, M., Liegel, N., Zovko, M., & Wentura, D. (2017). Mechanisms of masked evaluative priming: Task sets modulate behavioral and electrophysiological priming for picture and words differentially. *Social Cognitive and Affective Neuroscience*, *12*(4), 596–608.

Kihlstrom, J. F. (2019). The motivational unconscious. *Social and Personality Psychology Compass*, *13*, e12466.

Lambert, W. E., Hodgson, R. C., Gardner, R. C., & Fillenbaum, S. (1960). Evaluational reactions to spoken languages. *Journal of Abnormal and Social Psychology*, *60*(1), 44–51.

Latham, G. P. (2018). The effect of priming goals on Organizational-related behavior: My transition from skeptic to believer In G. Oettingen, A. T. Sevincer & P. M. Gollwitzer (Eds.), *The psychology of thinking about the future* (pp. 392–404). New York: Guilford Press.

Latham, G. P., Stajkovic, A. D., & Locke, E. A. (2010). The relevance and viability of subconscious goals in the workplace. *Journal of Management*, *36*(1), 234–255.

Libet, B. (2002). The timing of mental events: Libet's experimental findings and their implications. *Consciousness and Cognition*, *11*, 291–299.

Libet, B. (2004). *Mind time: The temporal factor in consciousness*. Cambridge, MA: Harvard University Press.

Libet, B., Gleason, C. A., Wright, E. W., & Pearl, D. K. (1983). Time of conscious intention to act in relation to onset of cerebral activities (readiness-potential): The unconscious initiation of a freely voluntary act. *Brain*, *106*, 623–642.

Libet, B., Wright, E. W., & Gleason, C. A. (1982). Readiness-potentials preceding unrestricted 'spontaneous' vs. pre-planned voluntary acts. *Electroencephalography and Clinical Neurophysiology*, *54*, 322–335.

Locke, E. A., & Latham, G. P. (1994). Goal setting theory. In H. F. O'Neil Jr & M. Drillings (Eds.), *Motivation: Theory and research* (pp. 13–29). Hillsdale, NJ: Lawrence Erlbaum.

Locke, E. A., & Latham, G. P. (2006). New directions in goal-setting theory. *Current Directions in Psychological Science*, *15*(5), 265–268.

Lüke, T., & Grosche, M. (2018). Implicitly measuring attitudes towards inclusive education: A new attitude test based on single-target implicit associations. *European Journal of Special Needs Education*, *33*(3), 427–436.

Markus, H., & Kunda, Z. (1986). Stability and malleability of the self-concept. *Journal of Personality and Social Psychology*, *51*(4), 858–866.

McClelland, D. C., Koestner, R., & Weinberger, J. (1989). How do self-attributed and implicit motives differ? *Psychological Review*, *96*(4), 690–702.

Melnikoff, D. E., & Bargh, J. A. (2018). The mythical number two. *Trends in Cognitive Sciences*, *22*(4), 280–293.

Morgan, W. G. (2002). Origin and history of the earliest thematic apperception test pictures. *Journal of Personality Assessment*, *79*(3), 422–445.

Moskowitz, G. B. (2014). The implicit volition model: The unconscious nature of goal pursuit. In J. W. Sherman, B. Gawronski & Y. Trope (Eds.), *Dual-process theories of the social mind* (pp. 400–422). New York: Guilford Press.

Nejjari, W., Gerritsen, M., van Hout, R., & Planken, B. (2019). Refinement of the matched-guise technique for the study of the effect of non-native accents compared to native accents. *Lingua, 219,* 90–105.

Neumann, M.-L., & Schultheiss, O. C. (2015). Implicit motives, explicit motives, and motive-related life events in clinical depression. *Cognitive Therapy and Research, 39,* 89–99.

Payne, B. K., & Lundberg, K. (2014). The affect misattribution procedure: Ten years of evidence on reliability, validity, and mechanisms. *Social and Personality Psychology Compass, 8*(12), 672–686.

Payne, B. K., Cheng, C. M., Govorun, O., & Stewart, B. D. (2005). An inkblot for attitudes: Affect misattribution as implicit measurement. *Journal of Personality and Social Psychology, 89*(3), 277–293.

Penke, L., Eichstaedt, J., & Asendorpf, J. B. (2006). Single-attribute implicit association tests (SA-IAT) for the assessment of unipolar constructs: The case of sociosexuality. *Experimental Psychology, 53*(4), 283–291.

Ryan, R. M., & Legate, N. (2012). Through a fly's eye: Multiple yet overlapping perspectives on future directions for human motivation research. In R. M. Ryan (Ed.), *The Oxford handbook of human motivation* (pp. 554–564). New York: Oxford University Press.

Shah, J. Y., & Kruglanski, A. W. (2002). Priming against your will: How accessible alternatives affect goal pursuit. *Journal of Experimental Social Psychology, 38,* 368–383.

Shantz, A., & Latham, G. P. (2009). An exploratory field experiment of the effect of subconscious and conscious goals on employee performance. *Organizational Behavior and Human Decision Processes, 109,* 9–17.

Sheldon, K. M. (2014). Becoming oneself: The central role of self-concordant goal selection. *Personality and Social Psychology Review, 18*(4), 349–365.

Sherman, J. W., Gawronski, B., & Trope, Y. (2014). Preface. In J. W. Sherman, B. Gawronski & Y. Trope (Eds.), *Dual-process theories of the social mind* (pp. xi–xii). New York: Guilford Press.

Sitzmann, T., & Bell, B. S. (2017). The dynamic effects of subconscious goal pursuit on resource allocation, task performance, and goal abandonment. *Organizational Behavior and Human Decision Processes, 138,* 1–14.

Soon, C. S., Brass, M., Heinze, H.-J., & Haynes, J.-D. (2008). Unconscious determinants of free decisions in the human brain. *Nature Neuroscience, 11*(5), 543–545.

Stajkovic, A. D., & Sergent, K. (2019). *Cognitive automation and organizational psychology: Priming goals as a new source of competitive advantage.* New York: Routledge.

Stajkovic, A. D., Latham, G. P., Sergent, K., & Peterson, S. J. (2019). Prime and performance: Can a CEO motivate employees without their awareness? *Journal of Business and Psychology, 34,* 791–802.

Teige-Mocigemba, S., Becker, M., Sherman, J. W., Reichardt, R., & Klauer, K. C. (2017). The affect misattribution procedure: In search of prejudice effects. *Experimental Psychology, 64*(3), 215–230.

Waninge, F. (2017). *Emotion and motivation in language learning.* PhD thesis, University of Nottingham, Nottingham.

5

RESEARCH FRONTIERS II

Vision

In the English language, the word 'vision' is commonly used both in everyday parlance and in a variety of professional contexts, and it is a term that most people can readily relate to, even beyond its core meaning of 'eyesight.' Indeed, the notion of vision has been employed widely in a number of different domains, from politics to business management. In an insightful review article, van der Helm (2009, p. 96) rightly concludes that "visions show up in diverse contexts, taking many different shapes" so much so that we can talk about "the vision phenomenon" to cover "the ensemble of claims and products which are called 'visions' or could be called as such." The widespread familiarity with the notion is partly due to the fact that mental visualisation is closely connected to one of the most common human behaviours, *daydreaming*. Eric Klinger's seminal research in psychology reveals that various forms of daydreaming are a surprisingly common part of our mental activities, with as much as half of human thought qualifying for it (for an overview, see Klinger, 2009). Our daydreams are often visual, and interestingly, although daydreams appear to emerge in our vision seemingly spontaneously – for example, when we are doing a monotonous task – we do have some control over the daydreaming flow as we can influence not only when to stop it but also what to daydream about.

Vision is not restricted to daydreaming only, and as will be shown below, visualisation processes are involved in many mental functions, with some visionary experiences producing remarkable outcomes. To cite a famous example, Albert Einstein developed his theory of relativity from a vision he had when he was 16 as he repeatedly imagined himself chasing after a beam of light in space and visualised how the scene would look from this perspective. He recalled later that this thought experiment had played a decisive role in his development of the theory of special relativity (Norton, 2013), and in a letter written to French mathematician Jacques Hadamard, Einstein explicitly stated:

> The words or the language, as they are written or spoken, do not seem to play any role in my mechanism of thought. The psychical entities which seem to serve as elements in thought are certain signs and more or less clear images which can be "voluntarily" reproduced and combined.
>
> Hadamard, 1945, p. 142

In politics, one of the most memorable examples of the role of vision occurred in a speech given by the Rev. Dr Martin Luther King, Jr. about civil rights and racial equality in Washington in 1963. At around the halfway point of the speech, the gospel singer Mahalia Jackson unexpectedly called out, "*Tell 'em about the dream, Martin!*" and it was as if an electric switch had been turned on: Rev. King put aside his prepared text, changed gear in his pace, pitch and emotion, and finished by describing an extended vision of a brighter future, punctuated eight times by the now legendary phrase, *"I have a dream…"* His vision of an alternative future touched his hearers in a way that rational arguments, however convincing, could not have.

So, what exactly is vision and how is it related to human motivation? In answering these questions, the following discussion will begin with an initial stocktaking of the multiple meanings covered by the term, before making the case that vision is more than merely a powerful metaphor for imaginative thinking; it will be argued that vision – or as it is usually referred to in cognitive science, *mental imagery* – concerns one of the most intriguing human faculties that has solid neuroscientific validity. As we shall see, this unique capability is involved in a variety of mental functions and it has been specifically associated with motivational enhancement in several fields in the social sciences, for example in sport psychology and business management. It has also been applied in educational contexts, and within SLA the vision-based construct of the L2 Motivational Self System (Dörnyei, 2005, 2009) has been a frequently employed motivational paradigm over the past decade (see e.g. Boo et al., 2015). The curious fact is, however, that in spite of the widely held assumption that visualising future scenarios promotes the motivation to reach an envisaged destination, there is relatively little understanding about the specific mechanisms whereby vision achieves this purpose. Therefore, the second half of this chapter will survey the main theoretical views in this respect, before concluding with a summary of the existing research on vision in SLA, with an emphasis on issues concerning future L2 self-images.

What is vision?

Even the most cursory exploration of the term 'vision' reveals that it has several different meanings; in contemporary English, the word occurs in at least three distinct senses:

- *Physical perception*, which is commonly used to refer to someone's eyesight, for example in sentences such as *"My vision has deteriorated since last time"* or *"Pilots need perfect vision."*

- *Mental picture*, which concerns various forms of internal images and visualisations such as memory images, daydreams, fantasies, creative imagination and spiritual revelations. This 'internal sight' has been captured expressively in the phrase 'mind's eye,' as coined by Shakespeare in a dialogue at the beginning of his play *Hamlet*, where the title character explains: "*My father – methinks I see my father. / Where, my lord? / In my mind's eye, Horatio.*"
- *Future aspiration*, which is a meaning frequently ascribed to the ambitions of politicians or business leaders in contexts such as "*Walt Disney's vision was to establish a theme park in California.*"

Thus, 'vision' can refer to seeing something either through one's *physical eyes* or in the *mind's eye*, and in the latter case it can also denote *foreseeing* a picture of a desired future in one's imagination. In the *British National Corpus* we find more than 4,000 occurrences of the word, mostly corresponding to these three semantic domains, and the meaning that most people would probably judge to be the basic reference of the term, physical perception, is in fact only the second most common usage. The most popular sense in which vision is used concerns the third option listed above, a hoped-for, desirable future state or plan.

When people report visionary experiences, they will usually use visual terms (Hall et al., 2006), but such experiences also include other sensory modalities, not just visual. Auditory images (or 'auditions') are common, because people frequently imagine conversations (Pearson et al., 2013). The case of Beethoven offers a particularly remarkable illustration of this modality: as is well known, Beethoven began to lose his hearing at the age of 26 and composed some of his best-known music, such as his Ninth Symphony, while being totally deaf, thereby providing evidence that hearing in the head 'through the mind's ear' can reach unprecedented elaborateness. Interestingly, however, Robertson (2002) reports that when people rate the vividness of imagery in the various senses, it is not visual images or auditions that come first, but the sense of smell, followed by taste. In sport psychology, 'motor imagery' (or kinesthetic imagery) has particular relevance, as it concerns the bodily sensations of movement, allowing athletes to rehearse certain action sequences mentally (Cumming & Ste-Marie, 2001).

The ability to simulate mentally any of their senses allows people to generate rich mental scenarios of various types. These may include replaying what has happened in the past and thus reliving memories; visualising written narratives (e.g. novels); counterfactual thinking (i.e. imagining a counterfactual scenario such as Hungary winning the football World Cup); conjuring up fantasy scenes and mixtures of real and hypothetical events such as mentally rerunning an argument and imagining what one should have said (see e.g. Taylor et al., 1998). Thus, 'vision' appears in a wide range of meanings and functions that are seemingly only loosely related to each other; however, we shall see in this chapter that the various facets of the notion are ultimately interlinked as they are all connected to one of humanity's most remarkable capabilities, the 'faculty of mental imagery.' Let us examine this faculty and its unique properties in more detail.

The neuropsychology of vision

Mental imagery is an experience of subjective perception when the source of the actual stimulus is not present. Moulton and Kosslyn (2009) explain that, quite remarkably, such mental representations preserve the perceptible properties of the stimulus by producing a realistic image, similar to what people experience through their physical senses. The resemblance between actual sensation and the formation of mental images was already noticed by the famous American psychologist, William James (1842–1910), who speculated as to whether the two processes share the same regions in the brain (see Modell, 2003), a question formulated by Gazzaniga, Ivry and Mangun (2002, p. 237) as follows: "When we imagine our beachside sunset, are we activating the same neural pathways and performing the same internal operations as when we gaze upon such a scene with our eyes?" It took almost a century to develop the necessary technology – most importantly, various methods of neuroimaging – to be able to assess this matter scientifically, but contemporary research has confirmed that optical vision and visual imagery do indeed utilise similar neural circuitry, activating about two-thirds of the same brain areas (see e.g. Cattaneo & Silvanto, 2015; Kosslyn, Thompson & Ganis, 2006).

The overlap between visual perception and internal vision has been studied extensively in neuropsychology and cognitive neuroscience, using a variety of research designs. For example, in one study using functional MRI, Meister et al. (2004) compared music performance and music imagery; they found considerable overlap in the brain activation when the participants played music on a silent keyboard and when they imagined playing the same music. Similar results have been obtained about motor execution and motor imagery in a variety of areas, pointing to the general conclusion that the actual production of action and imagining the same action share a number of mental operations and rely upon common neural structures (see e.g. Decety & Grèzes, 2006). In their review of the psychology of mental imagery in the *International Encyclopedia of the Social and Behavioral Sciences*, Cattaneo and Silvanto (2015) argue that perhaps the strongest single piece of evidence for the overlap between the neuronal basis of visual perception and imagery was offered by Kreiman, Koch and Fried (2000) in the journal *Nature*. These scholars examined single imagery neurons, which is (as mentioned already in Chapter 4) a rare and difficult technique because it requires an 'invasive' procedure of planting electrodes in the brain; for this reason, single neuron studies can only be done during the treatment of clinical conditions such as brain tumour or epilepsy (see Fried et al. 2014). Kreiman and his colleagues found many neurons in four brain regions that were activated *both* by visual and imaginary stimuli, which suggests "a common substrate for the processing of incoming visual information and visual recall" (p. 358). In other words, mental imagery was found to be sensory in nature.

The fact that the brain uses largely the same processing regions to generate an 'imaginary' experience as for processing the concrete experience of the world equips the faculty of vision with a unique ability: it can create a representation of an envisaged reality that may be as vivid and life-like as the material reality that people perceive through their physical senses. Thus, this alternative reality can have the same intensity of impact on humans as the material environment. This intensity is experienced most commonly in dreams, and neuroimaging research by Horikawa et al. (2013) reported in *Science Magazine* confirms that the vivid visual content experienced by the sleeping dreamer is represented by the same neural substrate as observed during waking perception of mental imagery. However, despite the unquestionable commonalities between mental imagery and physical perception, the two mental representations are not indistinguishable. The overlap between the perceptual and the imaginative domains is not complete, and studies of patients with brain damage also produced cases when the lesion resulted in a loss of mental imagery without a corresponding loss of perception and vice versa (Brogaard & Gatzia, 2017). Thus, in most cases the brain *can* distinguish between a physical perception and a mental image, and when this fails to happen, for example in some types of schizophrenia, it is regarded as a symptom of a mental condition (Robertson, 2002). Indeed, in normal cases, an imagined action does not activate our muscles like real behavioural intentions do, although sometimes a particularly strong imagined impulse might lead to involuntary muscle movement.

In conclusion, human beings are hard-wired to generate, behold and manipulate vision, and research shows that this faculty is not a special skillset of a selected few but a generic feature of the whole human species. Furthermore, this faculty is not something that we learn during our lifetime but rather a capability that we are born with, as evidenced for example by the fact that even the congenitally blind, who have never experienced sight, are able to visualise to some extent. In an article on "Visual imagery without visual perception?" Bértolo (2005) reports evidence that blind people can create powerful mental images that have a lot in common with visual images. For example, he was told by several blind subjects that when they sign their names they do not use a memorised set of movements but rather 'visualise' their signature and reproduce it. Moreover, one of his participants revealed that during dreaming he had experienced visual images but he added that he was generally reluctant to share these experiences with others because his revelation typically met with disbelief.

Vision and human mental functioning: Dual coding theory and working memory

The human faculty of vision is not merely a virtual 'picture projector' but also forms an integral part of higher-order mental functioning in general. Already Aristotle claimed that "The soul never thinks without a mental image [*phantasma*]" (*De Anima*, III, 7), and contemporary psychology confirms the claim that aspects of imagery have an essential role to play in all forms of thinking. To illustrate this, let us briefly look at two influential theories in cognitive psychology: Allan Paivio's *dual coding theory* and Alan Baddeley's concept of the *working memory*, both of which have a salient imagery component.

Dual coding theory

Paivio (1986) was initially interested in the 'mnemonic' benefits of imagery – that is, the use of imagery as a potent memory aid (employed to great effect by magicians, for example) – but his research expanded into a more comprehensive theory of memory and cognition. He suggested that cognition is made up of two interacting mental subsystems, *verbal* and *nonverbal/perceptual*, with mental imagery playing a central role in the nonverbal/perceptual system. According to this division, therefore, people process environmental information in two different modes, with the verbal and the nonverbal/perceptual information stored separately within the long-term memory. People can experience the importance of perceptual memory through the ease with which they can recall pictures, sounds, smells and even tastes from memory, as this can only happen if tracers of those perceptions are linked to the memories in storage.

From our current perspective, the main lesson of Paivio's (1986) dual coding theory is the acknowledgement that the nonverbal/perceptual system is one of the basic dimensions of human mental operations, with its critical functions including "the analysis of scenes and the generation of mental images (both functions encompassing other sensory modalities in addition to visual)" (pp. 53–54). Reviewing the significance of this proposal, Pearson and Kosslyn (2015, p. 10089) underline the theory's importance in recognising that humans do not rely only on "language-like 'propositional' representations" (i.e. meaning that can be expressed in verbal statements), but also on information "stored in a depictive, pictorial format." They further emphasise that Paivio's extensive experimental research has provided strong empirical evidence that memory is enhanced when both types of codes – verbal and pictorial – are used at the same time (see also Kosslyn & Moulton, 2009). Interestingly, this complementary dichotomy is reminiscent of the first modern investigation on mental imagery in psychology by Francis Galton (1822–1911), who observed a contrast between the faculties of seeing pictures and abstract thoughts that only "the highest minds" can sufficiently integrate:

> My own conclusion is, that an over-ready perception of sharp mental pictures is antagonistic to the acquirement of habits of highly-generalised and abstract thought, especially when the steps of reasoning are carried on by words as symbols, and that if the faculty of seeing the pictures was ever possessed by men who think hard, it is very apt to be lost by disuse. The highest minds are probably those in which it is not lost, but subordinated, and is ready for use on suitable occasions.
>
> Galton, 1892/1907, pp. 60–61

Working memory

Working memory refers to the "temporary storage and manipulation of information that is assumed to be necessary for a wide range of complex cognitive activities" (Baddeley, 2003, p. 189), and it is thus seen to underpin our overall capacity for thinking. In Baddeley's original model, the construct of working memory included three main components, an attentional control system called the 'central executive' and two subsidiary slave systems: the 'phonological loop,' which is the specialised verbal component of working memory, concerned with the temporary storage of verbal and acoustic information, and the 'visuospatial sketchpad,' which is responsible for integrating spatial, visual and kinesthetic information into a unified representation. Since the 1970s when the model was first proposed, the description of the construct has become more elaborate, but the visuospatial sketchpad retained its central position (see e.g. Baddeley & Andrade, 2000).

The parallels between Paivio's and Baddeley's theories on long-term memory and working memory, respectively, are obvious in that both contain a prominent dimension where visual information is represented and manipulated. However, because of the unfortunate practice of compartmentalisation in psychological research, the two lines of inquiry have not been sufficiently integrated either with each other or with the neuropsychological study of mental imagery. Pearson et al.'s (2015) recent work indicates, though, that while the different conceptual systems and research designs make it difficult to establish the commonalities in the three separate literatures (i.e. on dual coding theory, working memory and mental imagery), a process of establishing a more integrated perspective has begun (see also Cattaneo et al., 2006; Richardson, 1999).

The absence of vision: Aphantasia

Ever since mental imagery became an established part of the cognitive scientific landscape, deficiencies in the faculty of vision have also been documented, and over the past decade it has emerged that there are a number of people who lack the faculty of vision (see e.g. Palombo et al., 2015; Zeman et al., 2010). As Zeman, Dewar and Della Sala (2015) report, these people "typically became aware of their condition in their teens or twenties when, through conversation or reading, they realised that most people who 'saw things in the mind's eye'... enjoyed a quasi-visual experience" (p. 378). Their condition has been termed 'aphantasia' and we receive an insightful personal account of it from Nicholas Watkins (2018), who confirms that although aphantasia is "limited in its scope, and hasn't stopped me living an essentially normal life" (p. 49), it is a definite deficit of the mind. Watkins was in fact one of three high-functioning aphantasic adults investigated by Palombo et al. (2015), and as these scholars report:

> Their self-reported selective inability to vividly recollect personally experienced events from a first-person perspective was corroborated by absence of functional magnetic resonance imaging (fMRI) and event-related potential (ERP) biomarkers associated with naturalistic and laboratory episodic recollection, as well as by behavioural evidence of impaired episodic retrieval, particularly for visual information.

p. 105

Interestingly, although formal memory testing of people with aphantasia indicates a modality-specific deficit on visual memory tasks, this does not appear to cause any impairment for verbal memory, pointing to the separate nature of the two processing systems (Palombo, Sheldon & Levine, 2018). And given that people like Watkins were successful human beings in most real-life memory tasks, the verbal and the non-verbal/visual systems seem to perform effective compensatory roles. Similarly, Jacobs, Schwarzkopf and Silvanto (2018) have found that while aphantasic people performed significantly worse than controls on the most difficult visual working memory trials, their performance on a task designed to activate mental imagery was average. This again indicates that aphantasia can be compensated for under some conditions; indeed, as the authors conclude, for many tasks involving mental imagery there are alternative cognitive strategies that can lead to equally successful performance.

Envisioning the future: Mental time travel and possible selves

Arguably, the most remarkable role that vision plays in the lives of most ordinary people is *envisioning the future*. Research indicates that people spend a great deal of time conjuring up images of possible future scenarios (see e.g. Oettingen, Sevincer & Gollwitzer, 2018; Schacter, Benoit & Szpunar, 2017); for example, D'Argembeau, Renaud and Van der Linden (2011) found that people think about the future approximately once every 16 minutes on average during a day, and they also report that thoughts about the future occur about two to three times more often than thoughts about the past. This foresight appears to be a hallmark of being human: in a pioneering article on 'prospection' in *Science Magazine*, Gilbert and Wilson (2007, p. 1351) point out that while all animals can predict "the hedonic consequences of events they've experienced before," humans can predict "the hedonic consequences of events they've never experienced by simulating those events in their minds." As they submit, similar to how 'retrospection' refers to our ability to re-experience the past, "prospection refers to our ability to 'pre-experience' the future by simulating it in our minds" (p. 1352). Their description of the different mental representations is closely related to the discussion on mental time travel below:

> The brain combines incoming information with stored information to build 'mental representations,' or internal models, of the external world. The mental representation of a past event is a memory, the mental representation of a present event is a perception, and the mental representation of a future event is a simulation ... Simulations allow people to 'preview' events and to 'prefeel' the pleasures and pains those events will produce.
>
> *p. 1352*

Mental time travel

'Mental time travel' is a new line of inquiry that has exploded in psychology over the past 15 years, with over a hundred articles published on various aspects of the topic in high-ranking research journals. It is related to the role that mental imagery plays both in episodic memory (i.e. memory of experienced events and the associated emotions that people can recall and relive) and hypothetical future scenarios. As Michaelian, Klein and Szpunar (2016) summarise in the introduction of an edited volume devoted to the subject (*Seeing the Future: Theoretical Perspectives on Future-Oriented Mental Time Travel*), re-experiencing past events shares "striking similarities" (p. 2) with imagining future episodes; scholars therefore argue that episodic memory shapes the simulation of possible future events in the sense that people draw on "elements of past experiences in order to envisage and mentally 'try out' one or more versions of what might happen" (Schacter, Addis & Buckner, 2008, p. 40). Schacter and his colleagues further submit that the brain is a fundamentally 'prospective' organ (in the sense explained above by Gilbert & Wilson, 2007) that uses memory as a key component for the formation of plans and predictions. The strongest link between episodic memory and episodic foresight, as Miloyan, McFarlane and Suddendorf (2019) explain, is that both processes depend on a common neural mechanism involving the hippocampus, which plays a role in the combination of information acquired through past experience. It was this commonality of a neural system supporting the retrieval of episodic memories and the simulation of possible futures that has inspired the catchy phrase of 'mental time travel,' with one process projecting back into the past, the other forwards into the future (Suddendorf & Corballis, 2007).

The significance of mental time travel for the current discussion lies in its connection to mental imagery. We have seen earlier in Paivio's work that visual imagery plays a key role in memory for past events, and the highly situated nature of episodic memory makes this type of memory particularly dependent on imagery elements; in a similar vein, as episodic future thinking is closely related to representing future episodes of achievement, it also relies on mental imagery (Rasmussen & Berntsen, 2014). Indeed, D'Argembeau and Van der Linden (2006) have demonstrated that the effects of individual differences in visual imagery on the two kinds of representations were remarkably similar; as they conclude, "For both past and future events, individual differences in the vividness of visual imagery were positively related to the amount of visual and other sensory details experienced while representing the events" (p. 348). In other words, individuals with a higher capacity for mental imagery experienced more sensory details both when remembering past events and when imagining future events, which is consistent with the basic tenet of the mental time travel paradigm that projecting oneself in the past and the future relies on similar neural mechanisms.

Possible future selves

While the central link between vision and mental time travel is the reliance on mental imagery to generate episodic details of specific situations one remembers or foresees, another influential psychological paradigm linked to vision, *possible selves theory*, represents a different connecting point with vision, namely one's *self-image*. Of course, the self is not absent from mental time travel either, as the projected hypothetical episodic scenarios are typically self-related – and accordingly, D'Argembeau and Van der Linden (2006) maintain that "mental time travel, whether it be into the past or the future, crucially involves the notion of experiencing the self in time" (p. 343) – but the emphasis of most research on episodic future thinking to date has been on identifying parallel mechanisms with remembering past events. In contrast, possible selves theory, as the term suggests, concerns people's views of what they might possibly become in the future, with a special emphasis on what they *would like to* become and what they are *afraid of* becoming (Markus & Nurius, 1986). Oyserman and James (2009, p. 373) offer a clear definition:

> Possible selves are the future-oriented aspects of self-concept, the positive and negative selves that one expects to become or hopes to avoid becoming. They are the desired and feared images of the self already in a future state – the 'clever' self who passed the algebra test, the 'unhealthy' self who failed to lose weight or quit smoking, and the 'off-track' self who became pregnant. Individuals possess multiple positive and negative possible selves.

Possible selves have become a familiar notion in SLA ever since they were used as theoretical building blocks for the L2 Motivational Self System (Dörnyei, 2005, 2009), and they will be further discussed at the end of this chapter; in this section the main point to be made about them is that they have not been conceptualised merely as abstract, goal-related notions but rather as constructs that involve *mental imagery* as a crucial component. Markus and Nurius (1986) have specifically underlined that possible selves are represented in the mind in the same imaginary and semantic way as the here-and-now self, and this being the case, they are a *reality* for the individual: people can see and hear their possible future selves. This conceptualisation of possible selves shares key aspects with one's visions about oneself, and indeed, Markus and Nurius (1987, p. 159) confirm that "Possible selves encompass within their scope visions of desired and undesired end states"; thus, they can be seen as the "vision of what might be."

Applications of vision in the social sciences

A mental faculty that is as potent and versatile as vision will have multiple applications in a number of different areas of human operation, and in order to round up our overview of the notion, let us consider its involvement in three domains in particular: psychology, sports and business studies. Regarding psychology, given that many of the theories presented so far and to be presented later concerning the motivational role of vision are ultimately psychological in nature, the current overview will focus on offering a historical summary to set the scene. The special relevance of sport science and business management for the current chapter lies in the explicit motivational content that these fields have assigned to the notion of vision.

Vision in psychology

The study of mental imagery is currently an active and highly respected area in psychology and, more generally, in cognitive neuroscience. This is reflected by the fact that arguably the most influential clinical psychologist specialised in mental imagery and daydreaming, Jerome Singer, has been Professor of Psychology at the Yale School of Medicine and a former President of Division 10 of the American Psychological Association, while one of the leading researchers on the neuropsychology of vision, Stephen Kosslyn, has been Head of Psychology and then Dean of Social Sciences at Harvard University. However, this high status did not always characterise the subject in the past; as Baddeley and Andrade (2000) summarise, the study of imagery has seen "more extreme fluctuation in its scientific respectability than almost any other aspect of cognitive psychology" (p. 126).

As mentioned earlier, the first research project on vision in the modern sense was conducted by Francis Galton, who wrote an article on "Statistics of mental imagery" in 1880, and in his subsequent book on *Inquiries into Human Faculty and Its Development* (1892/1907) he further discussed the subject. Galton investigated vision from an individual differences perspective:

> The particular branch of the inquiry to which this memoir refers, is Mental Imagery; that is to say, I desire to define the different degrees of vividness with which different persons have the faculty of recalling familiar scenes under the form of mental pictures, and the peculiarities of the mental visions of different persons.
>
> *Galton, 1880, p. 21*

His main finding on imagery was that humans differ considerably in terms of their visualisation skills, with some image reports having great vividness and clarity while others being hardly more than sketches if that. For this reason, he is seen by many (e.g. Zeman, MacKisack & Onians, 2018) as the forerunner of research on aphantasia (discussed earlier).

The initial interest in imagery was taken up by clinical psychologists as they recognised the capacity of mental imagery to open up a window into the subconscious parts of the mind and that an appropriate interpretation of the arising images and fantasies has definite healing potential. This line of psychotherapy was made popular by Freud and Jung's relevant work (see e.g. Hall et al., 2006; Thomas, 2016), and since these beginnings, visualisation techniques have been integrated into almost all schools of psychotherapy, with currently cognitive behavioural therapy in particular being known for the systematic use of mental simulation. In academic psychology, however, the study of mental imagery became sidelined, if not banished, during the behaviourist period (roughly between the 1910s and 1960s), which placed an emphasis on the experimental study of human behaviour (for good overviews, see Curtis, 2016; Thomas, 2016). During this period the notion of mental imagery was typically amalgamated with hallucination, which was seen as a pathological manifestation and was thus relegated to psychotherapy.

The turning point in psychological research was signalled by a paper written by Robert Holt (1964) on "Imagery: The return of the ostracized," based on his Presidential Address to Division 12 of the American Psychological Association. Holt explained the turn of the tide partly by a renewed interest from brain researchers and partly by the widespread appearance of psychedelic drugs and the parallel growth of psychopharmacology, which attracted a great deal of attention to imaginal phenomena in the popular press, leading to bestselling publications such as *Seeing with the Mind's Eye* by Mike and Nancy Samuels (1975). There was also growing evidence that mental practice (i.e. imagery rehearsal) could be used to improve certain motor skills, which had considerable implications for sports performance (Feltz & Landers, 1983), and this was also the period when humanistic psychology emerged as a major branch of the field of psychology, challenging the hegemony of behaviourism (e.g. Maslow, 1968; Rogers, 1965). The humanistic movement introduced therapies that drew upon a wide repertoire of imagery techniques and was therefore indirectly instrumental in unleashing a flood of literature facilitating self-actualisation and self-fulfilment containing visualisation techniques (often sold in airport bookshops). Thus, these converging trends led to a surge of work on images and imagination in a variety of fields and, consequently, mental imagery was reclaimed by psychology; as Thomas (2016) summarises:

> Faced with this evidence, behaviourists started to revise their hard-line position and began to study how imagery was implicated in behavioural change. In a very short space of time there was an explosion of interest in mental imagery. After a dearth of interest and publications, almost overnight, mental imagery was reclaimed with enthusiasm across several disciplines including psychology.
>
> *pp. 20–21*

A good illustration of the ensuing popularity of vision in psychology was offered by a landmark paper by four UCLA psychologists, Taylor, Pham, Rivkin and Armor, in 1998 on "Harnessing the imagination." The authors began by asserting that:

> Of the many skills that humans possess, one of the most intriguing is the process by which we envision the future and then regulate our behaviour and emotions so as to bring it about.
>
> *p. 429*

As they explained, the human faculty to imagine future events has been explored in virtually every area of psychology, from *developmental psychology* (e.g. examining how children fantasise and make plans) and *cognitive psychology* (e.g. studying how people deploy mental resources to manage vision-related tasks) to *personality* and *social psychology* (e.g. exploring how visioning oneself in the future can shape one's self-concept and actions), and last but not least, *clinical psychology* (e.g. helping clients to rehearse coping skills in order to manage potentially problematic future situations). If we add to this impressive spectrum the interest in the neural processes underlying mental imagery displayed in *cognitive neuroscience*, we may agree with Taylor and her colleagues that the capacity to generate, behold and manipulate vision about the future is indeed a most intriguing and quite frankly astounding human skill, linked to a wide range of psychological research perspectives.

Vision and sport performance

The stakes in professional sports are high and therefore a great deal of research has been conducted in this field on how mental imagery can be used to facilitate achievement. On balance, studies have found that imagery is an effective procedure to promote sport performance (Gregg & Hall, 2006), and as a result, virtually every elite athlete in the world applies some sort of imagery enhancement technique during training. For example, Weinberg and Gould (2015) report that in a study conducted at the United States Olympic Training Centre, 90% of Olympic athletes used some form of imagery and 91% of them considered this practice useful. The proportion of coaches using imagery training was even higher, 94%, with one-fifth applying imagery at every training session. In fact, it has been found that imagery training is the most widely applied psychological skills training technique amongst both athletes and coaches/sport psychologists (Morris, 2010).

To illustrate the reason for this keen interest, let us consider a fascinating classic investigation by Woolfolk, Parrish and Murphy (1985) into the effect of imagery instruction on a simple motor skill accuracy task: putting a golf ball. The researchers asked some college students to imagine the backswing and putting stroke, with half of them visualising the ball going into the cup (i.e. positive imagery), while the other half imagined the ball narrowly missing the cup (i.e. negative imagery). There was also a control group which received no imagery instruction. The golfers then participated in a ten-putt trial on each of six consecutive days. The results were dramatic: over the six days the scores of the participants in the control group (i.e. no imagery) showed a level of improvement of around 10% that one would expect as a result of practice; in contrast, the golfers who exercised positive imagery improved by around 30%, while members of the negative imagery group actually got worse over the six-day period by as much as 20%!

Interestingly, as Munroe-Chandler and Guerrero's (2017) review highlights, most of the recent research on sport performance has been based on an analytic model developed by Allan Paivio, the author of dual coding theory described earlier. The strength of Paivio's (1985) model is that it brings together a number of different imagery functions employed in sports along two central dimensions: *cognitive* and *motivational*. The former involves imagery used by athletes for mental rehearsal to plan, refine and practise various strategies, routines and motor skills (e.g. specific movements such as putting in golf, as mentioned earlier), while motivational functions concern keeping up the athletes' general commitment or psyching them up for specific events in order to achieve specific goals (e.g. winning a gold medal at the Olympics). Paivio further divided the two main dimensions of imagery functions (i.e. cognitive and motivational) into two subcategories, *general* and *specific*, and Hall, Mack, Paivio and Hausenblas (1998) extended the 'motivational general function' to include two subtypes, thus resulting in the following five-component framework:

1. *Cognitive General* function: using mental imagery to familiarise oneself with the competition site or to rehearse team strategies and entire game plans (e.g. set pieces in football such as a corner kick).
2. *Cognitive Specific* function: imagining oneself correctly executing a specific sport skill (e.g. a basketball free throw).
3. *Motivational General–Arousal* function: imagery associated with managing stress or arousal associated with performing (e.g. relaxing or psyching up).
4. *Motivational General–Mastery* function: imagining oneself in a situation exhibiting the ability to remain mentally tough, focused and confident (e.g. coping in an important competition or remaining positive in the face of a tough challenge or a previous disappointment).
5. *Motivational Specific* function: imagining oneself in a highly motivating situation, accomplishing an individual goal (e.g. scoring the winning point in the national championship, achieving a personal best time or stepping onto the podium to receive a gold medal).

Let us conclude this section by considering what is arguably the most astonishing impact of imagery in sport, namely that it can contribute to actual muscle gain – that is, people can increase their physical strength through mental imagery without going to the gym! The neuroscientific basis of this remarkable fact is that by going through a training routine mentally, many of the same brain circuits will be activated as in real participation, and the brain signals drive the muscles to a higher activation level and thus increase their strength (see e.g. Ranganathan et al., 2004; Robertson, 2002). According to a recent review by Slimani et al. (2016), laboratory studies have evidenced strength gain within the range of 2.6 to 136.3% as a result of mental imagery (for specific experiments, see e.g. Clark et al., 2014; Lebon, Collet & Guillot, 2010; Yao et al., 2013).

Vision and business management

Over the past four decades, the notion of vision has become a central theme in the business world, because envisaging an attractive future has been found highly effective for promoting motivation and performance in the workplace. Indeed, the success of legendary business leaders such as Steve Jobs or Walt Disney has typically been ascribed to their visionary capacity. However, a closer look at the meaning of the term 'vision' in business management contexts shows that it tends to be used rather broadly, in close association with terms like 'goal' (e.g. *'the company's goal/vision is to become the market leader'*) or 'mission' (e.g. *'the organisation's vision/mission statement'*). We saw at the beginning of this chapter that this extended use of picturing a desired future is in fact the most frequent occurrence of the word 'vision' in the *British National Corpus*, but this usage raises the question of how to distinguish between a goal and a vision.

Visions and goals are similar in that they both represent desired future states, but a fundamental difference between the two concepts is that unlike an abstract, cognitive goal, a vision includes a strong *sensory element*: it involves tangible images related to achieving the goal. Thus, as Dörnyei and Kubanyiova (2014) illustrate, the vision of becoming a doctor would involve actually seeing oneself receiving the medical degree or practising as a qualified doctor. Thus, even when we talk about future aspirations, a vision has a strong picture-like quality, and despite its somewhat inconsistent use in the world of business (or in politics), the various meanings tend to contain elements of an envisaged ideal future state. Indeed, Kouzes and Posner (2017) define vision in their highly influential seminal book on leadership – which is already on its sixth edition and has sold over two million copies in over 20 languages since its original publication in 1987 – as "an ideal and unique image of the future" (p. 97), and variations on this definition are included in most relevant works in the business management literature (see e.g. Berg 2015; Strange & Mumford, 2002). While this conception is compatible with previous discussions of mental imagery, Kouzes and Posner go one step further when they describe vision as follows:

> Visions are images of the mind; they are impressions and representations. They become real as leaders express those images in concrete terms to their constituents. Just as architects make drawings and engineers build models, leaders find ways of giving expression to collective hopes for the future.
>
> *p. 132*

This understanding extends the meaning of vision in an important way: vision in the business sense involves some form of *sharing* with an audience for a *purpose*; as Kouzes and Posner (2017) put it in the above quotation, business visions only "become real" when leaders convey them to the workforce. Levin (2000) also argues that vision is not simply a destination to seek but "a field that permeates the entire organization, affecting all who bump up against it" (p. 103). In other words, while mental imagery in psychology is a private experience of an individual, a business leader's personal vision is only the initial seed that will need to grow into a *corporate vision*, that is, into the collective perspective of the people involved in the business enterprise in question. Thus, while vision in the business sense is similar to mental imagery in psychology in terms of its sensory nature, it also has an explicit motivational dimension, a point made by Kurland, Peretz and Hertz-Lazarowitz (2010) very clearly:

> vision is more than an image of the future. It has the power to inspire, motivate, and engage people. Vision rallies people for a joint effort, motivates them to become involved and committed, promoting quality performance, causing them to exert additional efforts and devote time…
>
> *p. 13*

How does vision motivate?

The previous overview of vision in business management has highlighted its capacity to exert motivational power and, as we have seen earlier, the notion has also been used in sports to motivate athletes and to enhance their performance. Curiously, however, while there is a general agreement amongst scholars about the motivational potency of envisaged future pictures and plans, there is less certainty about the specific mechanisms that mediate the impact of this mental imagery to action. The quote by Kurland et al. (2010) cited above is typical in this respect in that the motivational force of vision is taken for granted and is simply declared rather than explained. Indeed, in a recent paper entitled "The motivating power of visionary images," Rawolle et al. (2017) conclude:

> Relatively little is known about what makes visionary images effective … The idea that imagining a desired future promotes motivation has guided decades of research but has produced inconsistent findings.
>
> *pp. 769–770*

Thus, a key question to be addressed is *why* a mental image of a future scenario would be instrumental in realising a desired outcome; or, in van der Helm's (2009) words, "How can a bunch of ideas depicting an idealised future provoke and sustain behaviour, which tends to strive for this particular future?" (p. 101). The following overview will summarise several proposals in the literature that have aimed at explaining why and how vision can energise and guide behaviour. As we shall see, rather than having a single powerful answer, the strength of vision's motivational capacity seems to be provided by the fact that it can trigger a number of different mechanisms. This in turn ensures that most people will be positively affected by at least some of these processes – to put it broadly, vision can stir up something in virtually everybody. I believe that it is in this sense that Jerome Singer (2006, p. 128) was right when he declared in his seminal book on the subject that "Our capacity for imagery and fantasy can indeed give us a kind of control over possible futures!"

Possible future selves and self-discrepancy theory

Arguably the most popular psychological approach to explaining the motivational capacity of vision has been offered by linking it to the notion of *possible selves* (discussed earlier) and *self-discrepancy theory* (Higgins, 1987). This latter theory suggests that if there is a perceived discrepancy between one's actual self and the image of one's desired self – which is usually referred to as the 'ideal self' and which represents an envisaged 'best-case' scenario (i.e. the best that one can conceivably be) – this difference creates unease and an ensuing urge in the person to reduce the gap by trying to approach the desired self (for an insightful recent analysis, see Thorsen, Henry & Cliffordson, in press). According to this paradigm, therefore, motivation is perceived "as a reflection of what individuals hope to accomplish with their life and the kind of people they would like to become" (Leondari, Syngollitou & Kiosseoglou, 1998, p. 154), which in turn energises action to promote the sought-after self-image (see e.g. Manian et al. 2006). Put in another way, by providing a glimpse of a desired outcome, a visionary image can function as a foretaste of the realised future, thereby metaphorically whetting the actor's appetite (see Rawolle et al., 2017).

This intuitively convincing – though perhaps a bit simplistic – theory of self-discrepancy is corroborated by an important finding in research on mental time travel, namely that episodic future thoughts tend to be *positively biased* in the sense that imagined future episodes are consistently rated as more positive than past memories of personal events (e.g. Schacter et al., 2017; Szpunar, 2010). This rosy tint of envisaged future scenes works in favour of supporting forward-pointing motivation, and so does another intriguing feature of future simulations, namely that they are, as Gilbert and Wilson (2007) explain, "essentialised":

> When we imagine 'going to the theatre next week,' we don't imagine every detail of the event, but rather, we imagine the essential features that define it. We imagine seeing a stage filled with actors but we do not imagine parking the car, checking our coat, or finding our seat … Because simulations omit inessential features, people tend to predict that good events will be better … than they actually turn out to be … mental simulations tend to overrepresent the moments that evoke the most intense pleasure…
>
> *p. 1353*

Thus, as Gilbert and Wilson (2007) summarise, envisaging the future is "ingenious but imperfect. The cortex attempts to trick the rest of the brain by impersonating a sensory system" (p. 1354). Yet, this deception works, because, as the authors conclude, the simulated future events "are convincing enough to elicit brief hedonic reactions from subcortical systems" (ibid). We should note, however, that the essentialisation of envisaged future scenes can be a double-edged sword, because Gilbert and Wilson (2007) also warn us that it can also lead to the amplification of negative essential features and can thus potentially overrepresent not only the moments that evoke the most intense pleasure but also those of pain.

Interestingly, possible selves researchers have been aware of the potential 'dark side' of vision, and Markus and Nurius (1986) highlighted the powerful role of 'feared selves' right at the genesis of the theory. In fact, they considered the possible motivational impact of such negative projections so substantial that Oyserman and Markus (1990) devised a way of utilising it to good effect: they proposed that for maximum effectiveness, a desired future self should be offset by a corresponding feared self. That is, future self-guides are most potent if they utilise the cumulative impact of both approach and avoid tendencies: we do something because we want to do it but also because not doing it would lead to undesired results. Dörnyei and Kubanyiova (2014) devote a whole chapter to discussing this principle, underlining the fact that it is deeply engraved in general motivational thinking, as demonstrated by the age-old 'carrot and stick' contrast. Oyserman and Markus (1990) emphasise that the balance between a goal to be achieved and a corresponding goal to be avoided is particularly important in situations when learners are faced with a number of alternative potential visions. The danger here is that they can wander from the pursuit of one desired self to another, without committing themselves sufficiently to any single goal to work towards. Accordingly, the pressure coming from the negative counterbalance is needed to nail down a particular positive vision and to initiate a course of action towards it.

While the above argument makes sense, we need to realise that it undermines to some extent the essence of self-discrepancy theory: it is easy to see how the gap between a desired future and a mundane present can imbue the discrepancy with a motivating pulling power, but what sort of a discrepancy are we talking about when the future seems *bleaker* than the present? A negative one? And while it may be possible to tweak the theory by stipulating that this negative discrepancy evokes some sort of a 'pushing' (rather than pulling) power, in the light of the number of other issues we shall see below that fall outside the original terms of reference of the theory, it might be more sensible simply to accept the limitations of a self-discrepancy based explanation: while it offers an appropriate explanation in some situations, it is not the only possible avenue for vision to exert its motivational power. In order to expand the spectrum of motivational mechanisms, let us first look at mental simulation more closely, examining what difference the fine-tuning of the vision content can make through 'mental contrasting' and 'process imagery.'

Mental contrasting and process imagery

As seen above, there has been a strong sense in the research community that vision possesses motivational power, a belief amplified by the numerous self-help books one can find in airport bookshops that suggest unequivocally that *'You can do it, just dream it!'* It was therefore rather unexpected when highly respected German psychologist Gabriele Oettingen and her colleagues published evidence that 'positive fantasies' may not only be motivationally *ineffective* but might even be *counterproductive* (e.g. Kappes & Oettingen, 2011; Oettingen, Pak & Schnetter, 2001; Oettingen & Sevincer, 2018). Terminological nuances are important here, because these scholars have not been talking about future self-images but about 'positive fantasies,' yet a claim that "positive fantasies sap the energy needed to fulfil them" (Oettingen & Sevincer, 2018, p. 135) is sufficiently surprising to warrant a closer look.

What exactly do Oettingen and her colleagues claim? Oettingen et al. (2001, p. 737) argue that "solely fantasizing about a positive future" is counterproductive, because it "seduces a person to mentally enjoy the desired future in the here and now." Locke (2018) concurs when he points out that engaging in pure fantasy may lead to a subconscious belief that the desired future has been achieved and that therefore no action is necessary. What is missing, according to Oettingen et al. (2001, p. 737), is "reflections on present reality that would point to the fact that the positive future is not yet realised." Thus, they conclude, in order to evoke the motivational power of a positive fantasy, one needs to pursue the strategy of 'mental contrasting,' which involves a deliberate juxtaposing of a positive future outcome with an identified obstacle standing in the way or realising that outcome (e.g. Oettingen & Sevincer, 2018). Oettingen emphasises that it should not suffice to merely notice that there is a dissonance – the obstacle needs to be explicitly attended to and mentally elaborated on. Interestingly, the principle behind beholding such deliberate contrasts is not in itself incompatible with self-discrepancy theory, as the latter also focuses on an existing gap between present and future. However, the thrust of the elicited motivational force in the two approaches is different: in self-discrepancy theory the energy stems from trying to reach the desired goal, whereas when positive fantasies are mentally contrasted with current obstacles, "they trigger the energy needed to overcome the identified obstacles standing in the way of the desired future … When an obstacle can potentially be overcome, people become energized and put in the effort needed to fulfil their wishes" (p. 135).

Thus, the crux of the problem with indulging in positive fantasies is that they tend to idealise a desired future outcome *along with the process to get there* (Kappes & Oettingen, 2011), which is consistent with Gilbert and Wilson's (2007) argument about the essentialised and tinted nature of envisaged futures (discussed earlier); in Kappes and Oettingen's (2011) words, "fantasies are mute to the realism of their content" (p. 719) and "positive fantasies allow people to embellish idealized paths to idealized future outcomes" (p. 720). This is indeed a serious problem that can potentially derail even the most noble plans, and the gravity of the issue is shown by the fact that another line of research concerning making possible self-images more effective – 'process imagery' – focuses on the very same topic.

Process imagery emerged from the recognition that sometimes even when people have good intentions, they fail to achieve their goals. One lesson drawn from such cases has been that successful goal completion is promoted more when people are encouraged to focus on the *journey* to the goal rather than merely on the final outcome itself. Gollwitzer (1999) termed the action plan that focuses on a journey an "implementation intention," and the concept of process imagery builds on this strategy by adding sensory details to the action plan; that is, by envisaging an implementation intention, process imagery involves mentally mimicking the experience of progressing towards the final vision state (Knäuper et al., 2009). Taylor et al.'s (1998) seminal research supported this proposal, as it showed that students who envisioned the *steps* leading to successful goal achievement performed considerably better than those who focused exclusively on the targets they wanted to reach. The connection between the two strategies (mental contrasting and process imagery) was acknowledged by Kappes, Singmann and Oettingen (2012) when they submitted that "mental contrasting may prepare people to form particularly effective implementation intentions" (p. 817).

Vision and hope

Another line of relevant research has attributed the motivational power of vision to the *hope* raised by the reality-like nature of envisaged future scenes: the realistic depiction implies that the outcome is *plausible* and can therefore be reached. Hope has been defined as "the perceived capability to derive pathways to desired goals, and motivate oneself via agency thinking to use those pathways" (Snyder, 2002, p. 249), and it is therefore conceptually related to expectancy-based motivation that is at the heart of expectancy-value theories (Wigfield & Eccles, 2000). However, hope is typically mentioned in situations when outcome expectancies are low (see Nelissen, 2017) – indeed, hope does not usually concern things that are bound to happen – and this being the case, hope can be seen to exert its motivational properties almost as a 'substitute expectation.' This scenario applies well to vision-based plans, as they usually concern highly ambitious goals whose attainment expectancy can do with some boosting by hope. An additional motivational effect of hope is that because it is by definition relatively independent of realistic expectations, it is, as Nelissen argues, "both more resistant and more resilient to negative feedback. So, people who experience hope should be less affected by negative feedback on goal-progress and be more persistent in their efforts at goal-striving" (p. 227).

Nelissen's hypothesis has been borne out in a large-scale empirical study assessing the link between resilience and various personality factors by Goodman et al. (2017), who have found hope to exert the largest moderating effect on resilience; it was in fact the only statistically significant personality strength variable in their study. The researchers explain this somewhat unexpected outcome by the fact that hope captures the belief that if there is sufficient vitality, there will be several flexible options to proceed with and to manage obstacles, which is reminiscent of the motivational saying, "where there's a will, there's a way."

Vision and emotions

When engaging with vision, individuals mentally mimic not only perceptual images and motor movements but also *emotional experiences*; in Taylor et al.'s (1998) words, "Imagining a scenario does not produce a dry cognitive representation but rather evokes emotions, often strong ones"(p. 431). In a paper dedicated to "Mental imagery in emotion and emotional disorders," Holmes and Matthews (2010) confirmed that "imagery has more powerful emotional consequences than does the verbal representation of equivalent events" (p. 353), and for example the core characteristics of post-traumatic stress disorder are the powerful disruptive emotions that are produced by imagery in the form of 'flashbacks' to the original traumatic event. Thus, vision and emotions go hand in hand, and it is a widely held view that the motivational power of vision is a function of the emotions it evokes. There is no question that emotions can shape human behaviour – we only need to think of times when we are angry and are bursting to do something about it – and indeed, MacIntyre, Ross and Clément's (2020) recent summary of the subject in the *Palgrave Macmillan Handbook of Motivation for Language Learning* is entitled simply "Emotions are motivating."

Curiously, however, psychology has typically treated the notions of emotion and motivation separately, without focusing sufficiently on the linkage between the two concepts; to give but one telling example, Reeve's (2015) classic volume on *Understanding Motivation and Emotion*, which is now on its sixth edition, discusses the two concepts largely unconnectedly, without any explicit focus on the emotional basis of motivation. This impression is confirmed by Weiner's (2019) recent conclusion that "missing in many theories of motivation is emotion" (p. 191). So, what lies behind the reluctance in psychology to discuss the motivational capacity of emotions? One reason for this situation, I would suggest, is related to an important point made by Taylor et al. (1998): although they acknowledged that the emotional response associated with an envisaged future state can help people to muster the motivation to achieve their goals, these scholars also highlighted the fact that such an emotional arousal in itself – without a suitable action plan – does *not* guarantee productive goal-appropriate behaviour. In other words, emotional arousal is not automatically translated into goal-directed motivated behaviour. Such a view is consistent with Tomkins's (2008) classic observation on emotions, namely that their main impact involves *amplifying* human reactions and responses without necessarily giving them direction:

> Affect amplifies, in an abstract way, any stimulus which evokes it or any response which it may recruit and prompt, be the response cognitive or motoric. Thus, an angry response usually has the abstract quality of the high-level neural firing of anger, no matter what its more specific qualities in speech or action. An excited response is accelerating in speed whether in walking or talking. An enjoyable response is decelerating in speed and relaxed as a motor or perceptual savouring response.
>
> *p. 659*

Indeed, when we are bursting to do something in our anger, it is often unclear what this 'something' should be beyond simply lashing out. Thus, emotions do give people the urge to act but do not set a course for the specific action, and in this sense emotional arousal is distinct from a motivational state, which is, by definition, purposeful and goal-directed. Recent neuroscientific research by Berridge (2018) on the neural mechanisms of emotion and motivation appears to lend some support to the separation of emotional arousal and motivational states: his lab at the University of Michigan has established that 'liking' (in a sensory way) and 'wanting' (as a type of desire) are governed by distinct brain circuits. Although neither construct coincides exactly with emotions and motivation as they have been discussed in this book, their association with reward cues (in the sense that they are related to the attractiveness of these cues) gives them motivational properties. This makes Berridge's proposal that the hedonic (i.e. 'liking') and motivational (i.e. related to incentive salience) facets of reward are neurobiologically dissociable highly relevant to the current discussion. Chiew and Braver's (2011) have arrived at the same conclusion concerning Berridge's findings in their overview of emotional and motivational influences on cognitive control: "This work suggests that the constructs of emotion and motivation might involve separable neural mechanisms, and as such may have distinct influences on cognitive processing" (p. 2).

The other side of the coin is, however, that MacIntyre et al. (2020) are also right in stating that some emotions *do* possess a certain amount of goal-directed quality; for example, as they argue, "fear often motivates protective actions, anger motivates destruction of an obstacle blocking pursuit of a goal, and sadness motivates seeking connections with another person" (p. 186). Weiner (2019) similarly explains that "It was intuitively evident and documented in rich research histories that emotions guide future behaviour, e.g. anger results in 'going against' actions, sympathy in pro-social and 'going toward' behaviour, guilt and regret in reparation performance, and so on" (p. 201). In the light of these considerations, one wonders whether it would perhaps produce a clearer picture if we separated different extents of goal-directedness, and spoke about more general "action tendencies" (Epstein, 2014, p. 63) rather than 'goal-specific action' in connection to emotional influences on behaviour. Indeed, Frijda (2007) for example specifically links emotions to action tendencies, arguing that those "lead to unpremeditated, impulsive behaviours" (p. 26), and this characterisation is in line with Chiew and Braver's (2011, p. 2) general argument:

> Motivations are similar to emotions in that they also serve to define the relation between the individual and the environment, but differ from emotions in being more tightly linked to action and explicit goal associations ... Thus, whereas an emotion may emerge from one's status relative to motivational goals, it may not necessarily be directly relevant to a particular goal.

This 'halfway' position of emotions with regard to motivating behaviour might explain why emotion researchers often use cautious language when talking about the emotion-motivation link; for example, note Izard's (2007) use of the verb 'to influence' instead of something more specific such as 'to guide/direct/motivate' in the following sentence: "Many psychological scientists affirm that discrete emotion like joy, sadness, anger, and fear *influence* thought, decision making, and actions" (p. 260; emphasis added). Similarly, a major review article on the topic by Baumeister et al. (2007) has the telling title: "How emotion *shapes* behaviour: Feedback, anticipation, and reflection, *rather than direct causation*" (emphasis added).

In sum, the common belief – both in lay circles and in the research community – that 'emotions are motivating' is perhaps more accurately stated as 'emotions have motivational qualities': they can sustain and amplify existing motivation (this sustaining function will be further discussed in Chapter 6 with regard to long-term motivation) and they can also instigate the generation of new, goal-directed behavioural scripts (i.e. motives proper) by stirring up people and producing cues for social functioning (Izard, 2007); in MacIntyre et al.'s (2020, p. 185) words, "Intense emotional arousal energizes the body, focusses the mind, and *often* can *provoke action*" (emphasis added). We can also think of three specific mechanisms that utilise emotions for motivational purposes:

- *Emotion rehearsal.* Because mental imagery evokes emotional responses, it can enable people to 'try out' the emotional consequences of certain behaviours (see Ji et al., 2016), which in turn allows them to carry out some emotional 'cost-benefit calculations.' The results of these virtual appraisals will, in turn, influence motivation and future actions; indeed, as Baumeister et al. (2007, p. 190) submit, "*anticipated* emotion may be more important in guiding behaviour than actual, felt emotion" (emphasis added).
- *Creating positive emotional associations.* Based on the correspondence of emotional impulses in real and imaged situations, carefully crafted visual stimuli can be utilised to link positive emotional responses to achievement situations, thereby increasing the learner's psychological willingness to expose themselves to such stimuli. This is in fact the same principle by which systematic desensitisation works in psychotherapy: people with phobias are incrementally exposed to a phobic target in a visionary mode that counterbalances the negative impact with additional positive imagery (e.g. Thomas, 2016). In this way, avoidance tendencies can be reversed and transformed into approach tendencies.
- *Emotional monitoring.* Emotions can also be instrumental in monitoring the flow of ongoing action: negative emotions can signal that action is slowing down or diverting from its appropriate course, while deep-seated satisfaction is experienced when aligned with the guiding vision (a point we shall revisit in the next chapter). In other words, an emotion-laden vision may act as a behavioural standard to reconcile one's actions with and also as a barometer to indicate any misalignment (see Hoyle & Sherrill, 2006).

In summary, the above discussion offers strong support to the claim that emotions are involved in the broad motivational set-up that undergirds human behaviour, and past research in the area of SLA has affirmed that the study of languages is no exception to this assertion (see e.g. Dewaele, 2010; Dewaele & Alfawzan, 2018; Prior, 2019). This has been verified in a compelling manner by MacIntyre and Vincze (2017), who examined the relationship of 19 positive and negative emotions with a list of well-established motivational variables concerning language learning. The researchers found that the vast majority of the emotions (97% of the positive ones and 74% of the negative ones) displayed a significant correlation with the motivational factors. This highly consistent pattern of meaningful associations leaves no doubt that positive emotions make a significant contribution to a variety of L2 motivational processes, which in turn points to the conclusion that some of the motivational power of vision is indeed mediated to motivated behaviour by the emotions that visionary experiences evoke.

Vision and unconscious motivation

We saw in the previous chapter that the topic of unconscious motivation has only recently gathered sufficient momentum to reach the psychological mainstream, but even during this short period this paradigm has already offered some important insights into the mechanisms underlying the motivational capacity of vision. Chapter 4 provided several illustrations of the fact that pictures are useful priming tools because they lend themselves to generating unconscious motives, and Rawolle et al. (2017) submit that mental pictures have a similar capability; as they argue, "A motive-domains-specific visionary image (i.e. a visionary image tailored to one particular motive domain) will arouse the targeted implicit motive and thereby elicit motivation indicated by changes in motive imagery, affect, behaviour, and performance" (p. 771). Thus, this proposal states in effect that some of the motivational impact of envisaged future scenarios is derived from the fact that they act as *de facto* primes for generating unconscious motivation to reach the envisaged target.

Veltkamp, Aarts and Custers (2009) explain the mechanism of vision-based priming as follows: by envisaging scenes in which the target behaviour is associated with positive emotions, one can attach a 'rosy' emotional aura to the target action, not unlike operant conditioning creates an association between a particular behaviour and a (positive or negative) consequence. This 'rosy tint' in turn may evoke motivation to pursue the target action outside conscious awareness, because the positive affect associated with the behaviour will function as a reward value; in other words, the vision turns the goal into a "reward signal that can directly mobilize effort" (Custers & Aarts, 2014, p. 388). Berridge (2018) confirms that reward cues do not necessarily have to be physical, and vivid imagery about the reward may be enough to trigger brain activations of incentive salience; that is, "Imagination lets humans manufacture our own vivid mental temptation-provoking cues" (p. 14). It will be argued in the next chapter that such unconscious processes assume particular significance with regard to long-term motivation, as the re-triggering mechanism that is necessary for sustained action is partly fuelled by unconscious motives associated with 'chronic goals.'

Vision and L2 motivation

Vision-based motivational effects were first introduced into L2 motivation research through the L2 Motivation Self System (Dörnyei, 2005, 2009). In this construct two components, the *ideal L2 self* (representing a desired 'best-case' scenario, i.e. the best that one can conceivably be) and the *ought-to L2 self* (representing attributes that one believes one ought to possess to meet other people's expectations and to avoid possible negative outcomes) have specific visionary components: following Markus and Nurius's (1986) original conception of possible selves (discussed earlier), both self-guides include a prominent *self-image* component, with the 'image' aspect taken literally and operationalised as mental imagery that the L2 learner has of him/herself projected in the future. There has been extensive research regarding various aspects of the L2 Motivational Self System over the past decade (for reviews, see Csizér, 2020; Henry, 2020), including its practical, education-centred implications (see Dörnyei & Kubanyiova, 2014), and some studies have specifically examined the vision/imagery component (see e.g. Dörnyei, 2014; You, Dörnyei & Csizér, 2016). In accordance with the objective of the current volume to describe challenges and outline forward-pointing directions, the following discussion will focus on a number of outstanding issues.

The undertheorised nature of the L2 learning experience. The three core dimensions of the L2 Motivational Self System are conceptualised in theoretically different ways, with the most obvious distinction being between the two future self-guides (discussed above) and the third component, the *L2 learning experience*: while future self-images concern *imagined* experiences of using the L2 and are rooted in possible selves theory, the third component was intended to offer an index of *actual* experiences (Dörnyei, 2014). However, in the original versions of the model, this 'actual' experience was only rather superficially described as a broad component concerning the attitudes towards L2 learning; in a recent article discussing the undertheorised nature of this factor (Dörnyei, 2019), I suggested that the 'actual experience' aspect should be anchored in the notion of *student engagement* (see CHALLENGE$_{10}$/INNOVATION$_2$), defined as the perceived quality of the learners' engagement with various aspects of the language learning process. This proposal has not been tested yet.

The theoretical distinction between the ideal and the ought-to L2 selves. The ideal L2 self concerns a self-image that is consistent with the earlier discussions of mental imagery in that it involves an internal image of a desired future state. However, the ought-to L2 self concerns *someone else's* vision for a person's future, that is, an *externally* sourced, 'imported' vision. It is currently not clear yet what the process of 'importing' a vision entails, that is, how external imagery is internalised. Understanding the underlying mechanisms would be important because this would also shed light on the process of translating physical images (e.g. colour photos) into mental imagery, which has potential relevance to priming issues as well as to the conscious generation of goal-specific vision. In addition, past empirical research has shown that the energising force of vision associated with the ought-to L2 self tends to fall short of the power of ideal self-images, but it has not been established yet why these images function in such a 'secondary,' watered-down manner.

The changing nature and accessibility of future self-images. You et al. (2016) have provided evidence that even when one has experienced a future self-image, this image does not remain constant but changes over time, and this is consistent with Henry's (2015) argument that "an ideal L2 self is likely to be subtly reformulated and revised every time it is activated" (p. 86). The default process in this respect would be for the image to become more vivid and accessible through repeatedly revisiting the scene in the mind's eye. In an insightful study, Hessel (2015) demonstrated that the motivational power of an ideal L2 self-image is indeed a function of the frequency with which it is constructed in the mind: in her study, the accessibility of the students' ideal L2 selves that is thus gained has emerged as the strongest predictor of self-motivated engagement in L2 learning. However, Hessel rightly points out that this accessibility aspect has virtually never been assessed or discussed in empirical studies.

The transformation of future self-images. Research with L2 learners has also identified a different kind of dynamics associated with visionary targets that does not so much strengthen the ideal self-image as *alters* it, for example by upwardly or downwardly revising it as a result of the perceived likelihood of its achievement in order to make it more feasible (Henry, 2015; You & Chan, 2015). Furthermore, in an intervention study, Sato and Lara (2017) have found that the increase of their students' ideal L2 self went hand in hand with a decrease in their ought-to L2 self, suggesting the operation of an internalisation process (which has also been documented by You and Chan). In their recent analysis of the relationship between current and future self-guides, Thorsen et al. (in press) conclude that processes of self-revision have not been adequately addressed in L2 motivation research, and the same holds for other kinds of vision transformations. The reason why such alterations have remained unaccounted for in most studies may partly be explained by the research methodology used: because of the typical employment of cross-sectional designs (i.e. one-off surveys), the reported self-images have most often been treated as *fixed targets* whose strength determines their pulling power. This practice could be likened to focusing only on the strength of a static magnet without considering, for example, variation caused by changing the magnet's position (e.g. how close it is to the target of the attraction).

The dynamics of self-images in multilingual contexts. The dynamics inherent to the L2 Motivational Self System are further amplified when people have studied more than one language, because these learners' motivational set-up is likely to be affected by the *multilingual experience* (see e.g. Henry, 2010, 2017, who first raised this issue, and also Busse, 2017; Ushioda, 2017). As Henry and Thorsen (2018) explain, in situations of multiple L2 learning/acquisition, the self-guides of the different language systems come into contact and interact with each other, for example in conjunction with processes of crosslinguistic influence. Indeed, in an examination of this question amongst Hong Kong students learning both English and Mandarin, Dörnyei and Chan (2013) found evidence of distinct language-specific self-images, and we have argued accordingly that these images may interfere with each other both in a positive way (e.g. transferable linguistic confidence from one language experience to another) and in a negative, demotivating manner (e.g. making unfavourable comparisons between the two languages). When interactions are complementary, Henry and Thorsen propose that an *ideal multilingual self* can develop. This will operate together with the ideal L2-specific selves in generating motivation, and it will also function to create system-level cohesion and stability. This is obviously a highly promising future research direction.

Learning languages other than English (LOTEs). Multilingual interferences are particularly likely when people learn languages other than English (LOTEs): LOTE learning almost always occurs in conjunction with the learning of Global English, and therefore, as Dörnyei and Al-Hoorie (2017) conclude, one of the unique characteristics of the motivation to learn LOTEs is that it is overshadowed by one's dispositions towards Global English. A special issue in the *Modern Language Journal* on this subject (Ushioda & Dörnyei, 2017) has provided initial evidence that LOTE learning differs in several motivational aspects from the learning of Global English, and therefore in order to do its research justice it may require a different approach. Global English is associated with "a non-specific global community of English language users" (Ushioda & Dörnyei, 2009, p. 3) and therefore integrative motivation (Gardner, 1985, 2010; see CHALLENGE$_5$/INNOVATION$_4$), whose centrepiece involves the learner's identification with an external reference group such as the L2 community, was not directly relevant to English-specific motivational constructs such as the L2 Motivational Self System (which has grown out of studying EFL learners). This L2-community-independent perspective taken by the L2 Motivational Self System, then, does not favour LOTEs, since the latter *can* usually be associated with a specific target community that speaks (or esteems) the L2 and can thus be considered the reference group for that language (see Dörnyei & Al-Hoorie, 2017).

The relationship between the ideal L2 self and integrativeness. The unique aspect of motivational constructs focusing on LOTEs discussed above brings to the fore a more general theoretical issue regarding the relationship between integrativeness and the ideal L2 self. It was mentioned above that the notion of integrativeness was based on the psychological process of identification with the L2 community; as Gardner (2020, p. 6) explains:

> Our focus on social psychological variables was influenced by Mowrer's (1950) model of first language learning that attributed the motivation to identification with the parents. … We proposed that a similar process might apply to second language acquisition which would require a social psychological link between the learning process and the language learning context.

This identification aspect forms a link with the ideal L2 self, which is also based on a process of identification with a projected future image within the person's self-concept, a relationship succinctly summarised by Claro (2020, p. 253) as follows:

> Integrativeness (Gardner) and the ideal L2 self (Dörnyei) are complementary forms of identification that differ in locus of identification. Integrativeness represents identification with an external locus (role models and reference groups), while the ideal L2 self represents identification with an internal locus.

In other words, in their seminal paper Gardner and Lambert (1959) put their finger on one of the core aspects of L2 motivation, the process of identification. Integrativeness and the ideal L2 self represent two fundamental types of this process, with both having a complementary role in future theory-building.

The viability of visionary training. It has been widely observed that although vision-based future self-guides have the capacity to motivate action, this does not always happen automatically but depends on a number of conditions. To list only the main requirements, a motivating future self-image needs to be elaborate, vivid and plausible; it needs to be activated regularly and must be accompanied by an action plan; and for maximum motivational impact, people also need to have a vivid image about the negative consequences of failing to achieve the desired end state (see e.g. Dörnyei, 2014). These conditions form an integral part of the theory in two respects: first, without them the three primary motivational dimensions of the L2 Motivational Self System lose their motivational capacity; second, they also carry considerable practical significance in that it is assumed that satisfying these conditions will result in automatic motivational enhancement, thereby turning the various methods of ensuring that these conditions are met into *de facto* vision-enhancing motivational strategies. However, Hessel (2015) rightly points out that the proposed conditions have remained largely unexplored in empirical studies over the past decade and therefore "they still have strongly hypothetical character. Thus, little is known about what kind of ideal L2 selves are likely to translate into self-motivated engagement in L2 learning" (p. 104).

The dilemma about negative imagery. One of the key vision-enhancement strategies involves evoking some kind of a 'feared self,' because vivid imagery related to failing to achieve the desired end state can be an effective 'scare tactic' to push people to act. This, however, raises an ethical dilemma: one may argue that the negative effects of visualising personal failure on the self-esteem of some, particularly vulnerable people, can be too damaging. It has been an age-old question of how 'positive' an intervention should be to reach maximum effectiveness: should it rely primarily on the pulling power of positive incentives or also on the pushing power of negative consequences that someone wants to avoid (i.e. the carrot and the stick)? Motivational psychology has recognised this contrast by distinguishing between *approach* versus *avoidance* motivation (see e.g. Elliot, 2008). In terms of the role of these two types of motivation, psychological considerations may go somewhat against the contemporary 'focus-on-the-positive' zeitgeist, because profound conceptual change often requires some degree of 'rocking the boat' to dislodge people from their comfort zones (see e.g. Kubanyiova, 2012). However, some caution is in order concerning priming the negative consequences of not succeeding even if it is fully within the spirit of being 'cruel to be kind': not everybody responds well to negativity and people differ greatly in the extent to which they thrive under pressure. Accordingly, after an analysis of this issue, Dörnyei and Kubanyiova (2014, pp. 118–121) have concluded that it might be sensible to err on the side of caution regarding the encouragement of mental visualisations of feared selves.

Summary

The essence of this chapter is captured by a quotation from renowned Yale psychologists Jerome and Dorothy Singer (2013), who have played a leading role in demonstrating to the scholarly community the significance and potentials of vision: "Our human capacity for mental imagery representations, reenactments, and anticipatory constructions, all elaborations of our direct sensory experiences, may well be a defining characteristic of our species" (p. 11). Vision is indeed one of the most remarkable human faculties: our brains are hard-wired from birth to perceive mental imagery through a built-in set of internal senses, and the ability to generate and behold vision has been found to form an integral part of higher-order mental functioning in general, from information processing to memory functions (both long-term and working memory).

Currently, the study of mental simulation and rehearsal enjoys high academic status in a number of disciplines within the social sciences, from psychology to business management, with its applications utilised in areas as diverse as leadership studies, sport enhancement and psychotherapy. Accordingly, research on vision has been wide-ranging, with one of the most notable findings being that the act of conjuring up mental pictures, particularly scenes of imagined future realities, can be highly effective in motivating people across a broad spectrum of life activities. In exploring the concrete mechanisms by which vision exerts its motivating power, the chapter surveyed several channels through which the human faculty to imagine future events can impact human behaviour, from ideal self-images to positive emotions. The chapter concluded by surveying the applications of vision in SLA, particularly within the framework of the L2 Motivational Self System, with a special focus on outstanding and challenging issues related to the theory.

References

Baddeley, A. D. (2003). Working memory and language: An overview. *Journal of Communication Disorders, 36,* 189–208.

Baddeley, A. D., & Andrade, J. (2000). Working memory and the vividness of imagery. *Journal of Experimental Psychology: General, 129*(1), 126–145.

Baumeister, R. F., Vohs, K. D., DeWall, C. N., & Zhang, L. (2007). How emotion shapes behavior: Feedback, anticipation, and reflection, rather than direct causation. *Personality and Social Psychology Review, 11*(2), 167–203.

Berg, J. L. (2015). The role of personal purpose and personal goals in symbiotic visions. *Frontiers in Psychology, 6*(443), 1–13.

Berridge, K. C. (2018). Evolving concepts of emotion and motivation. *Frontiers in Psychology, 9*(1647), 1–20.

Bértolo, H. (2005). Visual imagery without visual perception? *Psicológica, 26,* 173–188.

Boo, Z., Dörnyei, Z., & Ryan, S. (2015). L2 Motivation research 2005–2014: Understanding a publication surge and a changing landscape. *System, 55,* 147–157.

Brogaard, B., & Gatzia, D. E. (2017). Unconscious imagination and the mental imagery debate. *Frontiers in Psychology, 8*(799), 1–14.

Busse, V. (2017). Plurilingualism in Europe: Exploring attitudes toward English and other European languages among adolescents in Bulgaria, Germany, the Netherlands, and Spain. *Modern Language Journal, 101*(3), 566–582.

Cattaneo, Z., & Silvanto, J. (2015). Mental imagery, psychology of. In J. Wright (Ed.), *International encyclopedia of the social and behavioral sciences* (2nd ed., Vol. 15, pp. 220–227). Oxford: Elsevier.

Cattaneo, Z., Fastame, M. C., Vecchi, T., & Cornoldi, C. (2006). Working memory, imagery and visuo-spatial mechanisms. In T. Vecchi & G. Bottini (Eds.), *Imagery and spatial cognition: Methods, models and cognitive assessment* (pp. 101–137). Amsterdam: John Benjamins.

Chiew, K. S., & Braver, T. S. (2011). Positive affect versus reward: Emotional and motivational influences on cognitive control. *Frontiers in Psychology, 2*(279), 1–10.

Clark, B. C., Mahato, N. K., Nakazawa, M., Law, T. D., & Thomas, J. S. (2014). The power of the mind: The cortex as a critical determinant of muscle strength/weakness. *Journal of Neurophysiology, 112*, 3219–3226.

Claro, J. (2020). Identification with external and internal referents: Integrativeness and the ideal L2 self. In A. H. Al-Hoorie & P. D. MacIntyre (Eds.), *Contemporary language motivation theory: 60 years since Gardner and Lambert (1959)* (pp. 233–261). Bristol: Multilingual Matters.

Csizér, K. (2020). The L2 Motivational Self System. In M. Lamb, K. Csizér, A. Henry & S. Ryan (Eds.), *Palgrave Macmillan handbook of motivation for language learning* (pp. 71–93). Basingstoke: Palgrave.

Cumming, J. L., & Ste-Marie, D. M. (2001). The cognitive and motivational effects of imagery training: A matter of perspective. *The Sport Psychologist, 15*, 276–288.

Curtis, R. (2016). The use of imagery in psychoanalysis and psychotherapy. *Psychoanalytic Inquiry, 36*(8), 593–602.

Custers, R., & Aarts, H. (2014). Conscious and unconscious goal pursuit: Similar functions, different processes? In J. W. Sherman, B. Gawronski & Y. Trope (Eds.), *Dual-process theories of the social mind* (pp. 386–399). New York: Guilford Press.

D'Argembeau, A., & Van der Linden, M. (2006). Individual differences in the phenomenology of mental time travel: The effect of vivid visual imagery and emotion regulation strategies. *Consciousness and Cognition, 15*, 342–350.

D'Argembeau, A., Renaud, O., & Van der Linden, M. (2011). Frequency, characteristics and functions of future-oriented thoughts in daily life. *Applied Cognitive Psychology, 25*, 96–103.

Decety, J., & Grèzes, J. (2006). The power of simulation: Imagining one's own and other's behavior. *Brain Research, 1079*, 1–14.

Dewaele, J.-M. (2010). *Emotions in multiple languages* (2nd ed.). Basingstoke: Palgrave Macmillan.

Dewaele, J.-M., & Alfawzan, M. (2018). Does the effect of enjoyment outweigh that of anxiety in foreign language performance? *Studies in Second Language Learning and Teaching, 8*(1), 21–45.

Dörnyei, Z. (2005). *The psychology of the language learner: Individual differences in second language acquisition*. Mahwah, NJ: Lawrence Erlbaum.

Dörnyei, Z. (2009). The L2 Motivational Self System. In Z. Dörnyei & E. Ushioda (Eds.), *Motivation, language identity and the L2 self* (pp. 9–42). Bristol: Multilingual Matters.

Dörnyei, Z. (2014). Future self-guides and vision. In K. Csizér & M. Magid (Eds.), *The impact of self-concept on language learning* (pp. 7–18). Bristol: Multilingual Matters.

Dörnyei, Z. (2019). Towards a better understanding of the L2 learning experience, the Cinderella of the L2 Motivational Self System. *Studies in Second Language Learning and Teaching, 9*(1), 19–30.

Dörnyei, Z., & Al-Hoorie, A. H. (2017). The motivational foundation of learning languages other than global English: Theoretical issues and research directions. *Modern Language Journal*, *101*(3), 455–468.

Dörnyei, Z., & Chan, L. (2013). Motivation and vision: An analysis of future L2 self images, sensory styles, and imagery capacity across two target languages. *Language Learning*, *63*(3), 437–462.

Dörnyei, Z., & Kubanyiova, M. (2014). *Motivating learners, motivating teachers: Building vision in the language classroom*. Cambridge: Cambridge University Press.

Elliot, A. J. (2008). Approach and avoidance motivation and achievement goals. In A. J. Elliot (Ed.), *Handbook of approach and avoidance motivation* (pp. 3–14). New York: Psychology Press.

Epstein, S. (2014). *Cognitive-experiential theory: An integrative theory of personality*. New York: Oxford University Press.

Feltz, D. L., & Landers, D. M. (1983). The effects of mental practice on motor skill learning and performance: A meta-analysis. *Journal of Sport Psychology*, *5*, 25–57.

Fried, I., Rutishauser, U., Cerf, M., & Kreiman, G. (2014). *Single neuron studies of the human brain: Probing cognition*. Cambridge, MA: MIT Press.

Frijda, N. H. (2007). *The laws of emotion*. Mahwah, NJ: Lawrence Erlbaum.

Galton, F. (1880). Statistics of mental imagery. *Mind: A Quarterly Review of Psychology and Philosophy*, *19*(8), 301–318.

Galton, F. (1892/1907). *Inquiries into human faculty and its development* (2nd ed.). London: J. M. Dent & Co.

Gardner, R. C. (1985). *Social psychology and second language learning: The role of attitudes and motivation*. London: Edward Arnold.

Gardner, R. C. (2010). *Motivation and second language acquisition: The socio-educational mode*. New York: Peter Lang.

Gardner, R. C. (2020). Looking back and looking forward. In A. H. Al-Hoorie & P. D. MacIntyre (Eds.), *Contemporary language motivation theory: 60 years since Gardner and Lambert (1959)* (pp. 21–37). Bristol: Multilingual Matters.

Gardner, R. C., & Lambert, W. E. (1959). Motivational variables in second language acquisition. *Canadian Journal of Psychology*, *13*, 266–272.

Gazzaniga, M. S., Ivry, R. B., & Mangun, G. R. (2002). *Cognitive neuroscience: The biology of the mind*. New York: W. W. Norton.

Gilbert, D. T., & Wilson, T. D. (2007). Prospection: Experiencing the future. *Science*, *317*, 1351–1354.

Gollwitzer, P. M. (1999). Implementation intentions: Strong effects of simple plans. *American Psychologist*, *54*(7), 493–503.

Goodman, F. R., Disabato, D. J., Kashdan, T. B., & Machell, K. A. (2017). Personality strengths as resilience: A one-year multiwave study. *Journal of Personality*, *85*(3), 423–434.

Gregg, M., & Hall, C. (2006). Measurement of motivational imagery abilities in sport. *Journal of Sports Sciences*, *24*(9), 961–971.

Hadamard, J. (1945). *An essay on the psychology of invention in the mathematical field*. Princeton, NJ: Princeton University Press.

Hall, C. R., Mack, D. E., Paivio, A., & Hausenblas, H. A. (1998). Imagery use by athletes: Development of the sport imagery questionnaire. *International Journal of Sport Psychology*, *29*, 73–89.

Hall, E., Hall, C., Stradling, P., & Young, D. (2006). *Guided imagery: Creative interventions in counselling and psychotherapy*. London: Sage.

Henry, A. (2010). Contexts of possibility in simultaneous language learning: Using the L2 Motivational Self System to assess the impact of global English. *Journal of Multilingual and Multicultural Development*, *31*(2), 149–162.

Henry, A. (2015). The dynamics of possible selves. In Z. Dörnyei, P. D. MacIntyre & A. Henry (Eds.), *Motivational dynamics in language learning* (pp. 83–94). Bristol: Multilingual Matters.

Henry, A. (2017). L2 motivation and multilingual identities. *Modern Language Journal, 101*(3), 548–565.

Henry, A. (2020). Directed motivational currents: Extending the theory of L2 vision. In M. Lamb, K. Csizér, A. Henry & S. Ryan (Eds.), *Palgrave Macmillan handbook of motivation for language learning* (pp. 139–161). Basingstoke: Palgrave.

Henry, A., & Thorsen, C. (2018). The ideal multilingual self: Validity, influences on motivation, and role in a multilingual education. *International Journal of Multilingualism, 15*(4), 349–364.

Hessel, G. (2015). From vision to action: Inquiring into the conditions for the motivational capacity of ideal second language selves. *System, 52*, 103–114.

Higgins, E. T. (1987). Self-discrepancy: A theory relating self and affect. *Psychological Review, 94*, 319–340.

Holmes, E. A., & Matthews, A. (2010). Mental imagery in emotion and emotional disorders. *Clinical Psychology Review, 30*, 349–362.

Holt, R. R. (1964). Imagery: The return of the ostracized. *American Psychologist, 19*(4), 254–264.

Horikawa, T., Tamaki, M., Miyawaki, Y., & Kamitani, Y. (2013). Neural decoding of visual imagery during sleep. *Science, 340*(6132), 639–642.

Hoyle, R. H., & Sherrill, M. R. (2006). Future orientation in the self-system: Possible selves, self-regulation, and behavior. *Journal of Personality, 74*(6), 1673–1696.

Izard, C. E. (2007). Basic emotions, natural kinds, emotion schemas, and a new paradigm. *Perspectives on Psychological Science, 2*(3), 260–280.

Jacobs, C., Schwarzkopf, D. S., & Silvanto, J. (2018). Visual working memory performance in aphantasia. *Cortex, 105*, 61–73.

Ji, J. L. J., Heyes, S. B., MacLeod, C., & Holmes, E. A. (2016). Emotional mental imagery as simulation of reality: Fear and beyond—A tribute to Peter Lang. *Behavior Therapy, 47*, 702–719.

Kappes, A., Singmann, H., & Oettingen, G. (2012). Mental contrasting instigates goal pursuit by linking obstacles of reality with instrumental behavior. *Journal of Experimental Social Psychology, 48*, 811–818.

Kappes, H. B., & Oettingen, G. (2011). Positive fantasies about idealized futures sap energy. *Journal of Experimental Social Psychology, 47*, 719–729.

Klinger, E. (2009). Daydreaming and fantasizing: Thought flow and motivation. In K. D. Markman, W. M. P. Klein & J. A. Suhr (Eds.), *Handbook of imagination and mental simulation* (pp. 225–239). New York: Psychology Press.

Knäuper, B., Roseman, M., Johnson, P. J., & Krantz, L. H. (2009). Using mental imagery to enhance the effectiveness of implementation intentions. *Current Psychology, 28*, 181–186.

Kosslyn, S. M., & Moulton, S. T. (2009). Mental imagery and implicit memory. In K. Markman, W. M. P. Klein & J. A. Suhr (Eds.), *The handbook of imagination and mental simulation* (pp. 35–51). New York: Psychology Press.

Kosslyn, S. M., Thompson, W. L., & Ganis, G. (2006). *The case for mental imagery*. New York: Oxford University Press.

Kouzes, J. M., & Posner, B. Z. (2017). *The leadership challenge: How to make extraordinary things happen in organisations* (6th ed.). Hoboken, NJ: Wiley.

Kreiman, G., Koch, C., & Fried, I. (2000). Imagery neurons in the human brain. *Nature, 408*(6810), 357–361.

Kubanyiova, M. (2012). *Teacher development in action: Understanding language teachers' conceptual change*. Basingstoke: Palgrave Macmillan.

Kurland, H., Peretz, H., & Hertz-Lazarowitz, R. (2010). Leadership style and organizational learning: The mediate effect of school vision. *Journal of Educational Administration*, 48(1), 7–30.

Lebon, F., Collet, C., & Guillot, A. (2010). Benefits of motor imagery training on muscle strength. *Journal of Strength and Conditioning Research*, 24(6), 1680–1687.

Leondari, A., Syngollitou, E., & Kiosseoglou, G. (1998). Academic achievement, motivation and future selves. *Educational Studies*, 24(2), 153–163.

Levin, I. M. (2000). Vision revisited: Telling the story of the future. *Journal of Applied Behavioral Science*, 36(1), 91–107.

Locke, E. A. (2018). Long-range thinking and goal-directed action. In G. Oettingen, A. T. Sevincer & P. M. Gollwitzer (Eds.), *The psychology of thinking about the future* (pp. 377–391). New York: Guilford Press.

MacIntyre, P. D., & Vincze, L. (2017). Positive and negative emotions underlie motivation for L2 learning. *Studies in Second Language Learning and Teaching*, 7(1), 61–88.

MacIntyre, P. D., Ross, J., & Clément, R. (2020). Emotions are motivating. In M. Lamb, K. Csizér, A. Henry & S. Ryan (Eds.), *Palgrave Macmillan handbook of motivation for language learning* (pp. 183–202). Basingstoke: Palgrave.

Manian, N., Papadakis, A. A., Strauman, T. J., & Essex, M. J. (2006). The development of children's ideal and ought self-guides: Parenting, temperament, and individual differences in guide strength. *Journal of Personality*, 74(6), 1619–1645.

Markus, H., & Nurius, P. (1986). Possible selves. *American Psychologist*, 41, 954–969.

Markus, H., & Nurius, P. (1987). Possible selves: The interface between motivation and the self-concept In K. Yardley & T. Honess (Eds.), *Self and identity: Psychosocial perspectives* (pp. 157–172). Chichester: John Wiley & Sons.

Maslow, A. H. (1968). *Toward a psychology of being* (2nd ed.). New York: D. Van Nostrand.

Meister, I. G., Krings, T., Foltys, H., Boroojerdi, B., Müller, M., Töpper, R., & Thron, A. (2004). Playing piano in the mind: An fMRI study on music imagery and performance in pianists. *Cognitive Brain Research*, 19, 219–228.

Michaelian, K., Klein, S. B., & Szpunar, K. K. (2016). The past, the present and the future of future-oriented time travel. In K. Michaelian, S. B. Klein & K. K. Szpunar (Eds.), *Seeing the future: Theoretical perspectives on future-oriented mental time travel: Editors' introduction* (pp. 1–18). New York: Oxford University Press.

Miloyan, B., McFarlane, K. A., & Suddendorf, T. (2019). Measuring mental time travel: Is the hippocampus really critical for episodic memory and episodic foresight? *Cortex*, August, 371–384.

Modell, A. H. (2003). *Imagination and the meaningful brain*. Cambridge, MA: MIT Press.

Morris, T. (2010). Imagery. In S. J. Hanrahan & M. B. Andersen (Eds.), *Routledge handbook of applied sport psychology: A comprehensive guide for students and practitioners* (pp. 481–489). Abingdon: Routledge.

Moulton, S. T., & Kosslyn, S. M. (2009). Imagining predictions: Mental imagery as mental emulation. *Philosophical Transactions of the Royal Society B*, 364, 1273–1280.

Munroe-Chandler, K. J., & Guerrero, M. D. (2017). Psychological imagery in sport and performance. In O. Braddick (Ed.), *Oxford research encyclopedia of psychology* (Online) (pp. 1–27). Oxford: Oxford University Press.

Nelissen, R. M. A. (2017). The motivational properties of hope in goal striving. *Cognition and Emotion*, 31(2), 225–237.

Norton, J. D. (2013). Chasing the light: Einstein's most famous thought experiment. In M. Frappier, L. Meynell & J. R. Brown (Eds.), *Thought experiments in science, philosophy, and the arts* (pp. 123–140). London: Routledge.

Oettingen, G., & Sevincer, A. T. (2018). Fantasy about the future as friend and foe. In G. Oettingen, A. T. Sevincer & P. M. Gollwitzer (Eds.), *The psychology of thinking about the future* (pp. 127–149). New York: Guilford Press.

Oettingen, G., Pak, H.-j., & Schnetter, K. (2001). Self-regulation of goal-setting: Turning free fantasies about the future into binding goals. *Journal of Personality and Social Psychology, 80*(5), 736–753.

Oettingen, G., Sevincer, A. T., & Gollwitzer, P. M. (2018). Introduction. In G. Oettingen, A. T. Sevincer & P. M. Gollwitzer (Eds.), *The psychology of thinking about the future* (pp. 1–11). New York: Guilford Press.

Oyserman, D., & James, L. (2009). Possible selves: From content to process. In K. Markman, W. M. P. Klein & J. A. Suhr (Eds.), *The handbook of imagination and mental simulation* (pp. 373–394). New York: Psychology Press.

Oyserman, D., & Markus, H. R. (1990). Possible selves and delinquency. *Journal of Personality and Social Psychology, 59*, 112–125.

Paivio, A. (1985). Cognitive and motivational functions of imagery in human performance. *Canadian Journal of Applied Sport Sciences, 10*, 228–288.

Paivio, A. (1986). *Mental representations: A dual coding approach*. New York: Oxford University Press.

Palombo, D. J., Alain, C., Söderlund, H., Khuu, W., & Levine, B. (2015). Severely deficient autobiographical memory (SDAM) in healthy adults: A new mnemonic syndrome. *Neuropsychologia, 72*, 105–118.

Palombo, D. J., Sheldon, S., & Levine, B. (2018). Individual differences in autobiographical memory. *Trends in Cognitive Sciences, 22*(7), 583–597.

Pearson, D. G., Deeprose, C., Wallace-Hadrill, S. M. A., Heyes, S. B., & Holmes, E. A. (2013). Assessing mental imagery in clinical psychology: A review of imagery measures and a guiding framework. *Clinical Psychology Review, 33*, 1–23.

Pearson, J., & Kosslyn, S. M. (2015). The heterogeneity of mental representation: Ending the imagery debate. *PNAS, 112*(33), 0089–10092.

Pearson, J., Naselaris, T., Holmes, E. A., & Kosslyn, S. M. (2015). Mental imagery: Functional mechanisms and clinical applications. *Trends in Cognitive Sciences, 19*(10), 590–602.

Prior, M. T. (2019). Elephants in the room: An "affective turn," or just feeling our way? *Modern Language Journal, 103*(2), 516–527.

Ranganathan, V. K., Siemionow, V., Liu, J. Z., Sahgal, V., & Yue, G. H. (2004). From mental power to muscle power—gaining strength by using the mind. *Neuropsychologia, 42*, 944–956.

Rasmussen, K. W., & Berntsen, D. (2014). "I can see clearly now": The effect of cue imageability on mental time travel. *Memory & Cognition, 42*, 1063–1075.

Rawolle, M., Schultheiss, O. C., Strasser, A., & Kehr, H. M. (2017). The motivating power of visionary images: Effects on motivation, affect, and behavior. *Journal of Personality, 85*(6), 769–781.

Reeve, J. (2015). *Understanding motivation and emotion* (6th ed.). Hoboken, NJ: Wiley.

Richardson, J. T. E. (1999). *Imagery*. Hove, East Sussex: Psychology Press.

Robertson, I. (2002). *The mind's eye: An essential guide to boosting your mental power*. London: Bantam Books.

Rogers, C. R. (1965). *Client-centered therapy: Its current practice, implications, and theory*. Boston, MA: Houghton Mifflin.

Samuels, M., & Samuels, N. (1975). *Seeing with the mind's eye: The history, techniques and uses of visualization*. New York: Random House.

Sato, M., & Lara, P. (2017). Interaction vision intervention to increase second language motivation. In M. Sato & S. Loewen (Eds.), *Evidence-based second language pedagogy* (pp. 287–313). New York: Routledge.

Schacter, D. L., Addis, D. R., & Buckner, R. L. (2008). Episodic simulation of future events: Concepts, data, and applications. *Annals of the New York Academy of Sciences*, *1124*, 39–60.

Schacter, D. L., Benoit, R. G., & Szpunar, K. K. (2017). Episodic future thinking: mechanisms and functions. *Current Opinion in Behavioral Sciences*, *17*, 41–50.

Singer, J. L. (2006). *Imagery in psychotherapy*. Washington, DC: American Psychological Association.

Singer, J. L., & Singer, D. G. (2013). Historical overview of research on imagination in children. In M. Taylor (Ed.), *The Oxford handbook of the development of imagination* (pp. 11–27). Oxford: Oxford University Press.

Slimani, M., Tod, D., Chaabene, H., Miarka, B., & Chamari, K. (2016). Effects of mental imagery on muscular strength in healthy and patient participants: A systematic review. *Journal of Sports Science and Medicine*, *15*, 434–450.

Snyder, C. R. (2002). Hope theory: Rainbows in the mind. *Psychological Inquiry*, *13*(4), 249–275.

Strange, J. M., & Mumford, M. D. (2002). The origins of vision: Charismatic versus ideological leadership. *Leadership Quarterly*, *13*, 343–377.

Suddendorf, T., & Corballis, M. C. (2007). The evolution of foresight: What is mental time travel, and is it unique to humans? *Behavioral and Brain Sciences*, *30*, 299–351.

Szpunar, K. K. (2010). Episodic future thought: An emerging concept. *Perspectives on Psychological Science*, *5*(2), 142–162.

Taylor, S. E., Pham, L. B., Rivkin, I. D., & Armor, D. A. (1998). Harnessing the imagination: Mental simulation, self-regulation, and coping. *American Psychologist*, *53*(4), 429–439.

Thomas, V. (2016). *Using mental imaging in counselling and psychotherapy: A guide to more inclusive theory and practice*. Abingdon: Routledge.

Thorsen, C., Henry, A., & Cliffordson, C. (in press). The case of a missing person? The current L2 self and the L2 Motivational Self System. *International Journal of Bilingual Education and Bilingualism*.

Tomkins, S. S. (2008). *Affect, imagery, consciousness: The complete edition*. New York: Springer.

Ushioda, E. (2017). The impact of Global English on motivation to learn other languages: Toward an ideal multilingual self. *Modern Language Journal*, *101*(3), 469–482.

Ushioda, E., & Dörnyei, Z. (2009). Motivation, language identities and the L2 self: A theoretical overview. In Z. Dörnyei & E. Ushioda (Eds.), *Motivation, language identity and the L2 self* (pp. 1–8). Bristol: Multilingual Matters.

Ushioda, E., & Dörnyei, Z. (Eds.). (2017). Beyond Global English: Motivation to learn languages in a multicultural world (Special issue). *Modern Language Journal*, *101*(3).

van der Helm, R. (2009). The vision phenomenon: Towards a theoretical underpinning of visions of the future and the process of envisioning. *Futures*, *41*, 96–104.

Veltkamp, M., Aarts, H., & Custers, R. (2009). Unravelling the motivational yarn: A framework for understanding the instigation of implicitly motivated behaviour resulting from deprivation and positive affect. *European Review of Social Psychology*, *20*, 345–381.

Watkins, N. W. (2018). (A)phantasia and severely deficient autobiographical memory: Scientific and personal perspectives. *Cortex*, *105*, 41–52.

Weinberg, R. S., & Gould, D. (2015). *Foundations of sport and exercise psychology* (6th ed.). Champaign, IL: Human Kinetics.

Weiner, B. (2019). My journey to the attribution fields. In A. J. Elliot (Ed.), *Advances in motivation science* (Vol. 6, pp. 185–211). Cambridge, MA: Academic Press.

Wigfield, A., & Eccles, J. S. (2000). Expectancy value theory of achievement motivation. *Contemporary Educational Psychology, 25,* 68–81.
Woolfolk, R. L., Parrish, M. W., & Murphy, S. M. (1985). The effects of positive and negative imagery on motor skill performance. *Cognitive Therapy and Research, 9*(3), 335–341.
Yao, W. X., Ranganathan, V. K., Allexandre, D., Siemionow, V., & Yue, G. H. (2013). Kinesthetic imagery training of forceful muscle contractions increases brain signal and muscle strength. *Frontiers in Human Neuroscience, 7*(561), 1–6.
You, C. J., & Chan, L. (2015). The dynamics of L2 imagery in future motivational self-guides. In Z. Dörnyei, P. D. MacIntyre & A. Henry (Eds.), *Motivational dynamics in language learning* (pp. 397–418). Bristol: Multilingual Matters.
You, C. J., Dörnyei, Z., & Csizér, K. (2016). Motivation, vision, and gender: A survey of learners of English in China. *Language Learning, 66*(1), 94–123.
Zeman, A., Della Sala, S., Torrens, L. A., Gountouna, V.-E., McGonigle, D. J., & Logie, R. H. (2010). Loss of imagery phenomenology with intact visuo-spatial task performance: A case of 'blind imagination'. *Neuropsychologia, 48,* 145–155.
Zeman, A., Dewar, M., & Della Sala, S. (2015). Lives without imagery: Congenital aphantasia. *Cortex, 73,* 378–380.
Zeman, A., MacKisack, M., & Onians, J. (2018). The Eye's mind: Visual imagination, neuroscience and the humanities. *Cortex, 105,* 1–3.

6
RESEARCH FRONTIERS III
Long-term motivation and persistence

We saw in Chapter 1 that because the scope of the notion of motivation is very broad – after all, it is responsible for *any* kind of human behaviour – it has posed scholars considerable difficulty over the past century to produce a precise scientific definition of the term. Perhaps the only thing about motivation that most researchers would agree on is that it determines both the *direction* and the *magnitude* of human behaviour, that is, the *choice* of a particular action, the *effort* expended on it and the *persistence* with it. This being the case, motivation theories in general try to answer three fundamental questions: *why* do people decide to do something, *how hard* are they going to pursue the activity and *how long* are they willing to sustain it? The curious fact is, however, that the third of these motivational dimensions – persistence – has received far less attention in past research than the other components; for example, in the *Oxford Handbook of Human Motivation* Grant and Shin (2012, p. 514) conclude, "Compared to research on the direction and intensity of effort, few theoretical models and empirical studies have focused on the maintenance or persistence of effort." In a similar vein, Beltman and Volet (2007, p. 315) submit, "Overall, there is a paucity of research on sustained motivation in complex, real-life activities." There are various historical and conceptual reasons for this imbalance, of which two are particularly relevant for the current discussion:

- As we have seen earlier (CHALLENGE$_2$), psychology has traditionally displayed a certain amount of *unease* about relating motivation to time, as a result of which the *temporal aspect* of motivation – and thus long-term motivation – has been rather overlooked in theorising. Indeed, there have been few process-oriented conceptualisations (CHALLENGE$_2$/INNOVATION$_1$) and the sustained nature of motivation has rarely been discussed.
- Psychological theories have traditionally separated motivation from the subsequent motivated behaviour it causes, that is, the initial energy source from its

actional consequence. As Dörnyei et al. (2016) have explained, the standard way of thinking in this vein has been to assume that the more powerful someone's initial motive, the more persistent the person's subsequent behaviour. While this view is not incorrect, it does not take into consideration the possibility that the outworking of the initial motive can itself become *part of the energy source*, that is, that motivated behaviour can generate *further* motivation. In motoring terms, the standard view of motivation research can be likened to traditional car engines which consume fuel, whereas we know now that it is also possible to construct *hybrid* engines, which will *generate* further energy while the car moves (a topic we shall discuss in more detail below).

The imbalanced treatment of the three dimensions of motivation is in stark contrast with the perception of classroom practitioners, who know all too well that persistence is a key aspect of a student's disposition: student motivation is not constant but displays continuous ebbs and flows, and it is also characterised by a steady 'leak,' that is, a tendency to decrease and even peter out with time. Accordingly, a better understanding of the nature of student perseverance is crucial in areas such as SLA where sustained learning behaviours that last sometimes for years are required. In this sense, therefore, the exploration of L2 learning persistence is a debt that motivation research – both in mainstream psychology and in the field of applied linguistics – still owes to the teaching profession.

In the light of the above considerations, how can we redress the balance? Again using motoring language, if we want to undertake a long car journey, the following will contribute to achieving an extended range: an efficient car (e.g. with low fuel consumption and a hybrid engine), a full tank of good-quality fuel, regular opportunities to refuel and a breakdown cover to deal with any mishaps. Translated into motivational terms, one would need a strong initial goal/vision with an effective action plan that includes energy-saving, energy-regenerating and energy-amplifying features, as well as sufficient self-control to draw on when encountering difficulties and setbacks. The following discussion will elaborate on each of these components, starting with the initial goal/vision that guides the whole process.

High-octane motivational fuel: 'Self-concordant vision'

If we survey the psychological literature to identify potent motivational fuel that can energise long-lasting journeys, two concepts stand out in this respect, *self-concordance* and *vision*; because the latter was the subject of the previous chapter, most of the discussion in this section will concern the notion of self-concordance and its fusion with vision. Self-concordance refers to the degree to which one's actions are autonomous and congruent with one's personality and identity (see e.g. Ehrlich, in press); as Sheldon et al. (2015, p. 575) summarise, "'self-concordant' individuals are those who have managed to select personal goals that are congruent with their implicit personalities and growth potentials." In other words, a self-concordant goal is self-appropriate in a deep sense, representing a person's enduring interests and passions, as well as his/her central values and beliefs (Sheldon & Elliot, 1999). Self-concordance therefore concerns a deep-seated personal meaning that is in alignment with strongly held convictions. This quality was linked to persistence right from the introduction of the notion, as evidenced for example by Sheldon and Elliot's assertion that "because the developing interests and deep-seated values that such goals express are relatively enduring facets of personality, self-concordant goals are likely to receive sustained effort over time" (p. 483). Recently, Sheldon et al. (2019, p. 120) have confirmed that "self-concordance has been shown to predict more sustained effort, and thus greater goal-attainment, over time."

We saw in the previous chapter that the faculty of vision is involved in a range of mental functions, from remembering to daydreaming and planning ahead, and that it also has considerable motivational power. For the purpose of the current discussion of long-term motivation, vision becomes particularly relevant when future self-images are fused with self-concordance. When one visualises scenarios that are closely aligned with one's deepest feelings, values and aspirations, these identity-relevant visionary images – or 'self-concordant visions' – have long-lasting motivational capacity; for example, as Markus and Nurius (1987) have argued:

> The unique behavioural power of certain positive possible selves is suggested by the impressive ability of some people to *endure* years of gruelling training for a future occupation, or to scrimp and save for *an equally long time* for a certain house or a special vacation. The resolve to deploy enormous effort or to suffer deprivation now for a goal that may not be attained for years must be sustained by *enduring elements*. These enduring elements that prompt people to *persevere* in pursuit of their aims and that remain as significant aspects of consciousness are their possible selves.
>
> *p. 160; emphases added*

In a similar way, Pizzolato (2006, p. 58) has also submitted that when possible selves are linked to identity goals, they become "representations of *long-term goals*, because they ... compel us to act in ways that will either keep us from becoming a particularly feared self or on the road toward becoming a particularly desired self" (emphasis added). So, how does self-concordant vision 'keep us on the road'?

One important function of self-concordant vision concerns continually 're-triggering' action. Long-term motivated behaviour inevitably means *intermittent* action, because it has to fit in with various aspects of daily life. The inevitable pauses foreground the significance of smooth and regular re-starts in order to be able to carry on from where one left before taking a break. At the heart of this re-triggering mechanism are *chronic goals*, which were introduced in Chapter 4 when discussing automatised, unconscious goal pursuit. It was explained there that a 'chronic state' in motivation research refers to permanent accessibility, and goals can acquire this state through consistent and habitual pursuit that automatises them (see e.g. Stajkovic & Sergent, 2019). Such habit formation, however, is not the only avenue for a goal to become chronically accessible. It was also argued that powerful visions – such as self-concordant vision – can also acquire enduring salience because of their significance in defining the self, and can thus become automatic regulators of behaviour. The resulting chronic state of the visionary goal, then, is capable of *reigniting* the motivational stream repeatedly after action has temporarily been overridden by the distractions of various life situations. This is not unlike how a combustion engine produces smooth motion in cars even though it works through a rapid succession of individual explosions (usually around 10–100 per second).

We shall see later in this chapter that self-concordant vision is further linked to the generation of the kind of positive emotional loading that serves as an effective lubricant for long-term action, and that visualising future scenarios also facilitates persistence by helping to combat short-term temptations. Here, let me finish with some challenging questions: with self-concordance playing a central role in the visionary support of long-term motivation, how effective are people at identifying what is self-concordant for them, that is, what is congruent with their innermost feelings and values? Do they know what is best for them? Can we assume the existence of sufficient wisdom and self-awareness for making such a wise choice? After all, Sheldon et al. (2015) themselves underline the fact that "people do not always have the insight or wherewithal to identify and pursue self-concordant goals" (p. 575), and this may, according to these authors, lead to negative consequences regarding motivational longevity: non-concordant strivers often drop off over time, and even if they manage to attain their goals, they may not benefit from those as much in terms of their well-being.

Of course, objectively speaking, it might be unrealistic to expect everybody to know exactly which course of action would best fit his/her personality and growth potentials, particularly in view of the discussion of unconscious/implicit motivation in Chapter 4. And yet, Sheldon, Prentice and Osin (2019) express their conviction that people can know "how they feel about what they think they want" (p. 120; note the double-hedging: "... *feel* ... *think*..."); this personal feeling in turn can serve as a signal of the goodness of fit of a particular goal. In many cases, however, such a subjective test turns out to be a rather crude indicator, and Sheldon (2014) acknowledges that there is a fair bit of evidence pointing to the prominence of "motivational cluelessness" (p. 352). Indeed, one may wonder to what extent subjective personal feelings can be taken at face value, given that, as we have seen earlier, conscious desires can be influenced at an unconscious level. Having said that, it was also argued in Chapter 4 that in-depth deliberation, particularly when accompanied by discussion and brainstorming with others, does have the capacity to offer fairly accurate conscious self-insight, and we have also seen that human agency can be effective in monitoring events. As a result, the task of identifying self-concordant goals is not outright unrealistic.

Limiting energy depletion through energy saving

Self-concordant vision can be likened to a full tank of fuel, yet even such high-octane initial motivation will gradually diminish over time. For example, Thorsen,

Henry and Cliffordson's (in press) summary of findings in SLA show that motivation has a tendency to wane: "Generally, the picture emerging is of an initial enthusiasm at the start of language programs which thereafter diminishes, sometimes rapidly." Similar observations have also been made in other educational contexts as well as in work environments, leading to the introduction of an enigmatic and somewhat controversial term in the motivation literature to account for this decrease, 'ego depletion' (e.g. Muraven, 2012). Let us look at this phenomenon more closely.

Ego depletion

We know that exerting physical energy leads to fatigue, but recent research has found that exhaustion is not limited to the physical domain, because effortful cognitive engagement would equally lead to mental fatigue (see e.g. Müller & Apps, 2019). Similar to its physical counterpart, mental fatigue also results in a temporary reduction in performance in a subsequent task, and only some rest will restore one's effectiveness (e.g. Moskowitz, 2014). The phenomenon whereby one's mental resource pool has been drained is referred to as *ego depletion*, which has been defined by Baumeister and Vohs (2007, p. 116) as follows:

> *Ego depletion* refers to a state in which the self does not have all the resources it has normally. We shall suggest that self's executive function, which includes self-regulation as well as effortful choice and active initiative, depends on a limited resource that is consumed during such activities. Ego depletion renders the self temporarily less able and less willing to function normally or optimally.

Although this scenario makes intuitive sense, it is not at all clear what substance is actually depleted by mental engagement, and this uncertainty about the nature of the mental pool that is drained has caused controversy and debate regarding the notion of ego depletion. There have been suggestions that ego depletion is related to the glucose in the bloodstream (Baumeister & Vohs, 2007), but Muraven (2012) points out that even if there is some biological mediation, the process is "psychologically driven, as … the process of depletion can be moderated by individuals' mood, feelings toward the self-control activity, and ability to recover lost resources" (p. 122). We should also note Muraven, Tice and Baumeister's point (1998) that an indirect confirmation of the notion of ego depletion is that the existence of a limited pool of ego strength has also been implicit in the traditional concept of *willpower*.

In sum, it has been widely observed that applying mental effort drains one's mental strength, and an area where ego depletion has a specific bearing on long-term motivation is *self-control*. As we shall see later in more detail, this notion involves the capability to resist temptation, combat distractive or counterproductive urges and in general, consciously controlling one's behaviour. As Muraven (2012) summarises, after a period of exerting self-control, subsequent attempts at self-control appear to suffer, thereby undermining long-term motivation. This also seems to apply to other volitional aspects such as making choices, and Peterson and Seligman (2004, p. 510) therefore conclude that "regulating the self or making a decision temporarily depletes some crucial resource of the self, so that the self is less able to perform another act of self-regulation or volition."

Conserving motivational energy through habits and behavioural routines

With motivation being a limited volitional resource that gets depleted over time, one way of lengthening the duration of motivated action is limiting the exertion of energy. In motoring terms this would be analogous to driving a car with low fuel consumption. Does fuel efficiency have an analogue in the motivational domain? That is, are there any ways of engaging in behaviours with no or limited volitional costs? The answer is yes, and the key concept in this respect is *habit*. A habit is a behaviour pattern that has become (semi-)automatic in the sense that it is performed with little or no awareness, almost involuntarily. Habits are a necessary part of human life, because, as Robertson (2002) rightly points out, if we were to consciously ponder and decide about everything we do, "our brains would collapse from information overload in seconds. Habits of speech, of thought, of emotion and of perception are our saviour" (p. 84). Accordingly, many if not most daily activities are patterned into repeated sequences, associated with specific times and/or places, and as a result, a great deal of everyday life can be seen as habitual (see e.g. Wood & Neal, 2007).

From a motivational point of view, the significance of habits lies in the fact that they are not initiated by volitional decisions but are triggered by environmental cues, that is, as Wood and Neal (2007) explain, by certain features of one's context such as performance locations, preceding actions in a sequence or particular people. For example, during a typical evening routine someone does not conduct cost-benefit calculations before brushing their teeth but simply does it because it is part of the evening routine. If we therefore set up constructive, goal-specific habits – for example by repeatedly pairing behaviours with specific situations such as going for a run every morning – we can, in effect, outsource the behavioural control of certain behaviours to context cues, and consequently the execution of these actions will not incur any significant volitional costs. In other words, performing goal-promoting habits and behavioural routines can greatly reduce ego depletion.

It follows from the above that being strategic about utilising habits may offer considerable rewards. Putting in place some habitual 'if-then' implementation plans will constitute a powerful tool to control one's behaviour (e.g. in combating distractions and temptations), thereby "taking the effort out of effortful control" (Mischel, 2014, p. 258). Hofer (2010) argues along these lines that the *temporal structuring* of daily routines with fixed slots for different activities during the day can achieve a positive outcome. Indeed, Dörnyei et al. (2016) have described several L2 learning cases when establishing and then adhering to set 'behavioural routines' (the term we used for habitual actions) helped students to achieve their learning targets, as these routines became an integral part of an entrenched pattern of goal-directed behaviour. Consistent with the theoretical considerations outlined above, we observed that the routines created a type of 'motivational autopilot' in the learners, which allowed the initiation and execution of learning activities to become a semi-automatic process; this autopilot, we argued,

> rules out the necessity for motivational processing each and every time a step within the sequence is to be carried out. That is, one gets down to learning not because of any conscious decision to do so, but because these routines become a smooth, self-evident, and unreflected-upon part of the process. We see such routines as a key element of self-renewing currents of motivation in all areas of life.
>
> p. 83

Regenerating energy 1: Lessons from 'directed motivational currents'

It was mentioned briefly at the beginning of this chapter that virtually all past theorising in motivational psychology has separated motivation from subsequent behaviour. The traditional argument has been that motivation concerns the antecedents of behaviour, and therefore a motive is an entity that fuels action towards a particular outcome. The standard way of thinking about L2 motivation has been to assume that if a language learner has a powerful motive to do well in a school subject – stemming, for example, from curiosity, interest, need, obligation or incentive – this motive will energise his/her motivated learning, and the stronger the student's motivation, the longer-lasting his/her commitment. While this view is in most cases correct, one may still wonder whether a scenario exists whereby motivated behaviour does not gradually deplete the initial energy source but rather generates some further power. Before we dismiss this idea as wishful thinking, we should remember what an innovation hybrid car engines have been in the automobile industry exactly by demonstrating that some energy can be regenerated during driving (through producing electric power during braking, which is, in turn, reinvested in fuelling the drive further). Can a similar principle work in the domain of motivation? A new theoretical concept in L2 motivation research, 'directed motivational currents' (DMCs), has evidenced that the answer can be affirmative.

Directed motivational currents

The notion of directed motivational currents (DMCs) was first introduced by Dörnyei, Muir and Ibrahim (2014) and was then fully developed by Dörnyei, Henry and Muir (2016; for a recent review, see Henry, 2020; Muir, in press). DMCs involve powerful motivational drives that unfold over time, impacting their participants in a significant way. They represent a particularly intensive state of focused productivity which allows people to achieve a great deal, often much more than they would have believed possible at the outset. A DMC can be likened to a motivational surge that, while it lasts, dominates a person's life like an all-consuming preoccupation around which all other activities are somehow accommodated. In everyday parlance it is often referred to as being 'totally absorbed in a project' or 'getting in the zone.' The term 'directed motivational current' comes from the phenomenon's similarity with ocean currents such as the Gulf Stream, as both motivational and ocean currents represent a formidable flow of energy that carries the life-forms caught up within them unimaginable distances.

Although most people will have some direct or indirect experience of a DMC (see Muir, in press), these surges are admittedly not very frequent, which begs the question of why they are relevant to the understanding of long-term motivation in general. We have argued (Dörnyei et al., 2016) that the broader theoretical significance of DMCs is that they can be seen as the *optimal form* of long-term motivated behaviour; that is, the factors that drive DMCs are potentially at work in all long-term motivational sequences, and the special intensity of a DMC occurs when all the necessary conditions and components are present and act as a harmonious whole. To use a science fiction analogy, in such cases a fast-moving spacecraft will shift from normal drive into 'hyperdrive' (Star Wars) or 'warp drive' (Star Trek). Thus, an understanding of how and why a DMC occurs can help us to identify the principal building blocks of the construct of sustained motivation in general.

What makes a DMC unique is that the outworking of the initial motive becomes *part of the energy source* itself: once a person is caught up in the midst of a whirlwind of factors which somehow 'sweep us off our feet,' the motivated behaviour *does not use up* energy but, conversely, actively *generates* energy, resulting in self-propelling and seemingly effortless action. Accordingly, in a DMC, the motive and subsequent behaviour form a *unified construct* and are inseparable from one another. Dörnyei et al. (2016) describe four main components of a DMC: (a) goal/vision-orientedness, (b) triggering factor, (c) facilitative action structure and (d) positive emotionality. The first of these, vision, has already been covered, while triggering mechanisms and positive emotionality will be addressed in separate sections below. Here we shall look at the facilitative action structure of a DMC, which is responsible for the unique energy renewal capacity of the process. The structural properties of a DMC that create a prolonged flow of self-propelling motivational impetus are centred around three key structural elements: *automatised behavioural routines* (already discussed above under the rubric of 'habits'), *subgoals* and *progress checks*, and *affirmative feedback*.

Subgoals and progress checks

It is a well-established fact in motivational psychology that setting short-term, incremental goals – or *proximal subgoals*, as they are often referred to – tends to be more energising than having only long-term, distal goals. For example, as already discussed in Chapter 2 (CHALLENGE₆/INNOVATION₃), in their seminal paper, Bandura and Simon (1977) found that dieters who set for themselves several daily targets lost significantly more weight than those who set only weekly targets. In another oft-cited study, Bandura and Schunk (1981) showed that students who were given specific, short-term learning goals achieved more than 20% more work than those with vague or distant goals. The explanation for this advantage is relatively straightforward: distal goals are too far off – or too general – to motivate specific actions in immediate situations; for this to happen, people have to create for themselves proximal subgoals to guide a detailed course of action which then leads to distal outcomes. Moreover, proximal subgoals also present the task in smaller and shorter chunks, which makes it appear more doable, and this in turn increases a person's self-efficacy/confidence. We may conclude therefore that long-term, sustained motivation is facilitated by breaking down larger, more distal goals into a series of more manageable targets.

While the motivational value of structuring an action sequence along specific subgoals is considerable, from our current perspective there is an even greater benefit of such a structure: subgoals also function as standards against which performance can be evaluated, and this being the case, they provide ideal opportunities for *progress checks*. The significance of these checks is that they make progress towards the desired target visible, and the satisfaction gained from the tangible sense of progress has a potent energy-yielding capacity (e.g. when the dieter steps on the bathroom scales and registers a weight loss). Indeed, in their book on *The Progress Principle: Using Small Wins to Ignite Joy, Engagement, and Creativity at Work*, Amabile and Kramer (2011, p. 7) argue that "of all the positive events that influence inner work life, the single most powerful is progress in meaningful work." Phrased more generally, the satisfaction one feels when perceiving that concrete steps have been taken towards the fulfilment of a self-concordant vision can become a main driver of long-term motivation. This is in accordance with what we found in Chapter 1 (CHALLENGE₂/INNOVATION₂) about the link between satisfaction and the motivational velocity of goal pursuit (i.e. the rate at which people perceive that they are approaching their goal).

Mercer and Dörnyei (2020) point out that the principle of making progress visible so that learners can draw energy from the perception is well illustrated in sports and recreation by the popularity of pedometers tracking one's steps, or in weight-loss systems by plotting the calories consumed on one's smart phone; the power of the various metrics acting as progress criteria lies in the fact that they make personal development more tangible, thereby causing a sense of accomplishment. Monitoring progress closely also helps people to make ongoing, dynamic adjustments, which, according to Beltman and Volet (2007), is a prerequisite of long-term motivation; these researchers found in their study that "sustained motivation was being constantly revised as the result of ongoing changes in personal and contextual circumstances over time" (p. 321).

Affirmative feedback and social support

There is one further source of constructive progress information besides proximal subgoals, namely the *feedback* one receives. Feedback in general is nothing more than "information provided by an agent (e.g. teacher, peer, book, parent, self, experience) regarding aspects of one's performance or understanding" (Hattie & Timperley, 2007, p. 81), but the type of information provided makes all the difference when it comes to long-term motivation. We may distinguish two main categories of feedback – *progress feedback* and *discrepancy feedback* – based on their reference points: as Voerman et al. (2012) explain, progress feedback concerns the difference between the initial and the current levels of performance (thus emphasising what has *already* been achieved), whereas discrepancy feedback focuses on the difference between the current and the desired levels of performance (thus emphasising what is *yet to be* achieved). Unfortunately, the most common type of feedback in SLA – corrective feedback – falls under the latter category, whereas motivation is mainly enhanced by positive progress feedback – or *affirmative* feedback – as it constitutes a powerful type of progress check.

There is a further aspect of affirmative feedback that sets it apart from other progress check methods, its *social character*, since this kind of feedback is received from someone who, by definition, is familiar with and supportive of the person's endeavour. This is an important point, because available research suggests that *social support* is a valuable aid for encouraging persistence (see e.g. Peterson & Seligman, 2004). For example, in a recent study, Székely and Michael (2018) have found that persistence in a joint action was enhanced by the perception of a partner's striving, pointing to the conclusion that the perception of a partner's effort elicits a sense of commitment to remain engaged in the joint project. The researchers demonstrated that participants persisted longer in a task that was made intentionally increasingly boring when they perceived cues of their partner's effortful contribution. These findings affirm the ample anecdotal evidence that social concerns of this kind shape people's behaviour, including their persistence, which underlines the teacher's role and responsibility in providing regular affirmative feedback.

Regenerating energy 2: Lessons from 'psychological momentum'

The word 'momentum' is used in physics as a property of a moving object, related to its mass and velocity, but it is also used frequently in everyday parlance to refer to a metaphorical force that is gained by movement or by a series of events (e.g. *"the quest for the understanding of long-term motivation is gathering momentum each day"*). In a discussion of the emergence of DMCs, Dörnyei et al. (2016) have reported the use of the term by an informant when describing his increased motivation as a result of investing some initial time and effort in a project, and as we argued, linking a significant initial investment to the increase of one's personal commitment towards a group goal is consistent with the principles of group dynamics (see Dörnyei & Murphey, 2003). These considerations are also fully in line with a growing body of research in the social sciences examining the properties of 'psychological momentum.' Although the genesis of this notion was in the early 1980s when American sociologist Peter Adler published a monograph on *Momentum: A theory of social action*, this pioneering work turned out to be decades ahead of its time, and even Adler himself did not pursue it any further. As we shall see below, the concept has started to gain real traction in the research community only during the past decade. Let us begin the exploration of the notion by looking at Adler's initial conceptualisation.

Adler's original conception of momentum

Adler's (1981) initial conceptualisation of momentum bears a strong resemblance to the notion of a DMC; he defines the phenomenon as "a state of dynamic intensity marked by an elevated ... rate of motion, grace, and success" (p. 29) and then offers the following description:

> The term momentum describes a type of movement that is noticeable as unique among the many ordinary types of motion. Occurrences that capture this rare quality flow with an accelerated rhythm and intensity, whether they carry their participants soaring exuberantly onward or plunging despairingly backward.
>
> *p. 13*

Adler proposed both a positive and a negative momentum, but most of his discussion concerns the positive, forward-moving aspect of the phenomenon. This is reflected in his linking momentum to future goals, explaining that momentum "results from a purposeful striving for accomplishment. Attention becomes centrally focused on a specific goal or end state, ranging in nature from the short-term or frivolous to the long-term crux of identity and existence" (p. 30). He further underlines the goal-directed – and in fact, *vision*-directed – nature of momentum when he submits that

> goal-oriented behaviour is key to momentum. The vision of a goal, arising from any of several spheres, serves as the central inspiration that binds and impels the entire vortex of subsequent behaviour. Goals also perform the vital function of defining the direction toward which people strive. Holding constant as ideal stimulations to creative activity, goals identify the relative progress, stagnation, and/or negative slippage that has been attained throughout the entire quest and serve as partial performance yardsticks.
>
> *p. 53*

These ideas are reminiscent of some key tenets of DMCs, and another important parallel between momentum and a DMC is the enhanced productivity they both entail: "Perhaps the most recognizable aspect of momentum is the elevated performance it yields, raising the quality and/or quantity of achievement to a plane often 'over the heads' of those possessing it" (p. 32). Moreover, according to Adler, momentum is also energised partly by the satisfaction gained from perceived progress: "once motion toward the goal gets under way, the sense of making clear progress yields a feeling of power and ability that is inherently pleasurable. People recognize that they are acting closer to peak potential and achieve inner satisfaction" (p. 31). Quite remarkably, Adler then specifically highlights the self-propelling nature of momentum:

> we note the universal presence of an internally self-generating mechanism in operation. With individuals, groups, and social institutions alike, a circular feedback system develops through which accomplishments already achieved are instrumental in aiding further propulsion. As people developing momentum react to the sense of satisfaction (or frustration) generated by coworkers and responsive outside others, a recycled source of impetus is made available to fuel further motion. Energy already spent can thus be partially recaptured and coupled with the continuing output of fresh effort, making subsequent progress toward the goal easier. As each new wave of productive energy becomes converted into tangible achievement and then tapped to be fed back for reuse, another spiral of the burgeoning momentum process is forged. A dynamic, internally circular process is thus envisioned, whereby input and output are continually reutilized to maintain a high level of velocity.
>
> p. 33

Thus, a central aspect of Adler's conception of momentum is a regenerative mechanism, and later he characterises this as "a sophisticated carry-through process encompassing the circular return (feedback) of expended energy through the satisfaction obtained from previous efforts and the anticipation of future gratification; an internally self-generating feature combining continuing fresh impulses with this recycled derivative impulse" (p. 178). These quotations show without any doubt that despite the differences in disciplinary background and approach, the phenomenon Adler described under the rubric of momentum is akin to a directed motivational current.

Modern conceptualisations of momentum

Looking back, we can see why Adler's proposal was not picked up by the research community of his time: in the early 1980s, motivational psychology had just embarked on its cognitive renewal (championing issues such as attributions, self-determination and expectations and values), and it simply had not been ready to accommodate a construct with a prominent temporal axis and a behavioural dimension. It did not help either that Adler framed the concept in largely sociological terms (although he does use 'motivation' in several places in his book), trying to reach a largely non-psychologist audience. This latter aspect changed markedly at the resurrection of the concept in the new millennium, as manifested by the fact that a paper that has played a crucial role in turning the tide, by Markman and Guenther (2007), was published in the *Personality and Social Psychology Bulletin*, referring to the phenomenon as 'psychological momentum' (PM). In fact, the authors did not even appear to be aware of Adler's (1981) book – as it is not cited et all – but justified their interest in the subject with the growing popularity of the term in the sports literature as well as in a range of lay and professional contexts; their introduction captures the zeitgeist so well that it is worth citing it at some length:

> There is a common perception among individuals that a psychological force called momentum exists that can powerfully influence performance. In athletic contexts, the belief in psychological momentum (PM) is so pervasive that one can hardly read about or view a sporting event without being exposed to references from commentators, coaches, and players regarding how "turning points" and "momentum-shifting" plays influenced the progression and outcome of a game. In kind, the belief exists that winning a hard-fought and important contest against a strong opponent can help build momentum and thereby increase one's chances for success in a subsequent contest. It is important to note, however, that the PM concept extends beyond athletic domains. Individuals believe that they can experience momentum while they are designing a computer program, writing a paper, or cleaning an apartment, and political campaigns and celebrity careers are often described as gaining (or losing) momentum.
>
> *Markman and Guenther, 2007, p. 800*

The rising appeal of 'momentum' is also illustrated by concrete figures indicating how deeply the notion has come to be ingrained in the public mind: according to Iso-Ahola and Dotson's (2014) review, over 90% of sports fans, 92% of coaches and 76% of NBA basketball players believe that their performance is crucially determined by momentum.

The new understanding of psychological momentum has displayed two marked shifts from Adler's original proposal. First, some scholars intended to undergird the notion through explicitly linking it to its scientific counterpart in Newtonian physics by trying to find social equivalents to 'mass' and 'velocity': while velocity has been used in motivation research before (see CHALLENGE$_2$/INNOVATION$_2$), mass had to be more creatively defined, for example as "the strength of contextual variables that connote value, immediacy, and importance" (Markman & Guenther, 2007, p. 801; for other analogues, see Hubbard, 2017, which offers the most developed discussion in this vein). Second, instead of emphasising the self-propelling character of the phenomenon, scholars tended to highlight its sequential, gradually increasing nature (which is closer to how the word 'momentum' is used in everyday parlance); this is exemplified well by Markman and Guenther's (2007) description: "Following a precipitating event, PM takes on a life of its own and snowballs, much like a boulder gathers momentum as it rolls down an incline, and builds in intensity over time if uninterrupted" (p. 802). It is this second approach that is particularly relevant to the understanding of long-term motivation, because, as we shall see below, it incorporates the notion of *success*, which is a powerful motivational factor that has curiously been rather undertheorised in motivational psychology in general. Let us have a closer look at this approach.

The 'success-breeds-success spiral'

At the heart of virtually all discussions of psychological momentum is some variation of a 'success-breeds-success spiral.' It is well known that an experience of success can promote motivation, but the theory of psychological momentum goes one step beyond this principle and suggests that if a person experiences success in a task within an action sequence, this will influence the likelihood of success on a similar subsequent task (see e.g. Guenther & Kokotajlo, 2017; Hubbard, 2017). In such a conception the notion of 'psychological momentum' refers to the force that mediates the elevating impact over time (i.e. between early and subsequent success). We should note here that because such sequences are common in sport – competitions, for example, are often entirely made up of such repetitive action blocks – sport settings have become the natural laboratory for most contemporary momentum research (Briki & Markman, 2018). Psychological momentum therefore concerns a kind of 'dependency structure' between consecutive performances in terms of the extent of success (Iso-Ahola & Dotson, 2017), and so the colloquial phrase for it would not be 'getting in the zone' – which was relevant to a DMC and also to a large extent to Adler's conception – but rather 'getting on a roll.' And once on a roll, people can experience remarkable achievement, sometimes beyond their expectations, which makes psychological momentum similar to DMSs.

How does psychological momentum mediate success? This is the point where theoretical accounts often become rather vague. Scholars agree that momentum has a definite *phenomenological validity*, because when it happens, people are not only acutely aware of it themselves but outside observers can also sense that someone, or even a whole sport team, has the momentum on their side (with things going unstoppably their way). Most of the theoretical explanations have tried to locate this momentum in the actors' mindset, as a combination of increased confidence and self-efficacy, a sense of control and optimism, perceived competence and superiority (in contests), accompanied by a focus of energy and concentration (e.g. Iso-Ahola & Dotson, 2014; Vallerand, Colavecchio & Pelletier, 1988). This is therefore a heightened state of consciousness associated with an increased subjective belief in success, and as Vallerand et al. (1988) point out, it also involves the highly motivating perception of progression towards the goal (which is of course also a hallmark of a DMC). The resulting winning mindset, in turn, is likely to precipitate the occurrence of further success, contributing to an upward spiral.

With regard to how the experience of psychological momentum is mediated to actual performance, it is assumed that it causes optimal psychological conditions for engaging with the task at hand. Iso-Ahola and Dotson (2016) propose that when people sense that they can succeed, this increased perceived likelihood of success is instrumental in expanding their mental and physical effort. Several authors also mention the initiation of automatic, unconscious processing and execution of necessary behaviours (e.g. Briki, 2017; Iso-Ahola & Dotson, 2016), without specifying the details. This might sound like a cop-out (in the sense that it is easy to say that something occurs unconsciously if we do not know how it takes place), but in the light of the discussion in Chapter 4 of unconscious motivation and goal pursuit, such an explanation may not be that farfetched.

Lessons offered by momentum research for the understanding of long-term motivation

The previous overview has shown that momentum is a popular concept that "commentators, observers, and pundits have used to describe a variety of situations, ranging from football games, to gambling, to political campaigns" (Jansen, 2004, p. 276). The important aspect of this, Jansen argues, is that all these situations exhibit a certain energy pattern and a rhythm that is recognisable both by participants and observers. So, how does this phenomenon inform the understanding of long-term motivation? Two broad lessons emerge in this respect: first, although its roots are different to those of DMCs, the principles established about momentum offer compelling confirmation of the notion of a DMC, and thus affirm the feasibility of drawing analogies between DMCs and sustained motivated action (as we have done earlier); second, momentum research has foregrounded the *building-up* aspect of long-term motivation. As explained by Dörnyei et al. (2016), DMCs have been largely understood to be launched in a different way, by a powerful trigger (like a rocket launch), and Adler's original conception did include this DMC-like type:

> Several distinct forms emerge that represent typical patterns of momentum's occurrence. Toward one extreme we have *explosive* momentum, a fast-moving, excitable state that is less marked by synchrony than intensity. Often launched rapidly, a fragility surrounds this plateau that enables it to come crashing down just as impetuously as it arose. In these instances the empowered body moves with great vigour and strength, hurdling barriers with ease and flair. Momentum spirals upward into a state of frenzy, continuing in this highly charged condition …
>
> *p. 34*

However, Adler (1981) also talks about another version of momentum, 'placid momentum,' which gains energy gradually; he characterises it as a "a performative state that displays a calm, unhurried grace. Often slipped into gradually and in a less noticeable fashion than its explosive counterpart, it enables its possessor to glide through obstacles with a settled but steady surety" (p. 34). Later he describes this sequence using a motoring metaphor: "Like a car, people approach an endeavour in low gear, eventually shifting into higher ratios as they warm up and accelerate their velocity" (p. 50). This more steady acceleration process is highly relevant to sustained motivation, because the great intensity of a DMC is unsustainable in the long run. Also, in accordance with Adler's proposal of a 'placid momentum,' it has been a recurring observation that "Persistence tends to produce further persistence, insofar as people will stay with a course of action because they have already invested some time, energy, money, or other resources in it" (Peterson & Seligman, 2004, p. 240).

Augmenting energy with positive emotionality

A prominent feature of a DMC is that it offers an absorbing and fully satisfying emotional state – "a thrilling experience" (Dörnyei et al., 2016, p. 99) – against which the emotional state of everyday life does not compare. Adler (1981) also observed this feature regarding momentum:

> The ascendance of a motivational drive and its accompanying vision of the goal spark an abundance of feelings centering on both the perception and internalization already accomplished, and on the visualization of potential future developments. Strong responses are often evoked, which well up inside people, filling them with voluminous but sometimes conflicting irrational and impulsive sentiments that will soon spill over into propulsion.
>
> *pp. 54–55*

Where does this highly positive tenor originate from and how is it sustained during the overall course of a DMC/momentum? These are relevant questions from the perspective of long-term motivation, because we have seen in the previous chapter that emotions have the capability to sustain and amplify existing motivation, and thus a steady positive emotional loading would be an ideal foundation for sustaining energy during lasting action.

Dörnyei et al. (2016) argued that the pervading sense of pleasure and satisfaction in a DMC is rooted in the perception of progressing closer and closer to the ultimate, highly desired and personally meaningful goal. Progress thus evokes a feeling of being in a state of harmonious advancement, successfully participating in something that is personally rewarding. This joyful satisfaction is in fact at the heart of Waterman's (1993) famous notion of 'eudaimonic well-being and happiness' (see Henry, 2020), which is generated by the successful pursuit of an authentic, self-concordant goal. A particularly important aspect of this heightened state of emotion is that in a DMC each step along the way to the envisaged goal reproduces – or becomes permeated with – some of the overall passion linked to the realisation of the ultimate target. As Dörnyei et al. (2016) have argued,

> the emotional power of the satisfaction of moving ever closer toward an ultimate goal can be such that it is able to override potentially energy-sapping

factors – such as exhaustion or continual interruptions from mindless distractions – and can generate renewed energy from unrealized reserves.

p. 109

In summary, having a clear and ongoing perception that one is on track towards reaching a vision can be the source of ongoing positive emotional loading, which in turn acts as effective fuel for the ongoing motivated action. This emotionality can be seen as the projection of the overall passion associated with the vision onto the constituent steps leading to the vision; the actor perceives – almost in a 'fractal' manner – the same fulfilment after completing each forward-pointing task as after completing the overall mission. The experience of this zealous joy has also been captured by psychological theories of 'passion,' most notably by Vallerand et al.'s (2003) 'Dualistic Model of Passion.' Let us have a closer look at the lessons this theory can offer.

The notion of passion in psychology

Passion in everyday speech refers to a very intense feeling, with a hint of it being barely controllable. It is used in different connotations, from sexual desire to an enthusiasm for doing something. It is this second, non-romantic aspect of passion that is relevant to the current discussion of long-term motivation. The important point to realise about this aspect is that it is not merely a synonym for strong emotion but is rather a step above it, signalling something qualitatively new that takes hold of a person and drives him/her to do things beyond normal expectations. This drive is a salient psychological phenomenon and therefore one would expect to find an extensive body of literature on it, but this is unexpectedly not the case; when I investigated the subject, I soon shared Vallerand's (2012, p. 47) experience:

> When we started our research on passion in the late 1990s, we expected to find a lot of research on the subject. Yet, surprisingly, very little if any psychological research had been conducted on this concept (there was research on romantic passion, but not for passion for activities). So we found ourselves in the unique position to open up a new field of psychological inquiry. This has led us to formulate the first, and as of now the only, psychological theory on passion for activities.

Before we have a closer look at Vallerand et al.'s (2003) Dualistic Model of Passion, we should note that while it is indeed the only fully developed theoretical construct in this area to date, this does not mean that passion has not been implied in other psychological theories, and some of these are relevant to the current discussion. The most notable example is the personality characteristic 'grit' (to be discussed in the next section), which has been defined by Duckworth et al. (2007) as "perseverance and passion for long-term goals" (p. 1087), thereby linking passion specifically to motivational persistence. However, we shall also see that most research on grit focuses on the perseverance aspect, without adequately capturing the critical role of passion (see Jachimowicz et al., 2018). Other scholars describe passion as a special aspect of emotions; Frijda (2007) for example, equates passion with the "core characteristic of emotions" (p. 26), arguing that although most everyday emotions are not very passionate, they can be viewed "as the thin trail of smoke arising above a volcano. They betray the stirrings below. Truly passionate emotions show those stirrings in full" (p. 25). What is remarkable about her conception is that passion is seen to have specific motivational qualities, as it is associated with "states of action readiness" and being "set towards completing the aim in the face of delays and difficulties, and to seek precedence over ongoing behaviour or interference from other sources" (p. 4).

Vallerand et al.'s (2003) Dualistic Model of Passion is similar to Frijda's understanding in that it is also *action-specific*: passion is defined in it as "a strong inclination toward an activity that people like, that they find important, and in which they invest time and energy" (p. 756). The model is 'dualistic' because it proposes two main types of passion, *obsessive* and *harmonious*, depending on how the passionate activity is internalised into one's core self. Harmonious passion is fully autonomous, with the person engaging with a project for the intrinsic pleasure gained from it. The target activity occupies a significant space in the person's life without being overpowering, and it is in harmony with other aspects of the person's identity. In contrast, obsessively passionate people participate in their beloved activity because of some internal or external pressure/obligation. As Vallerand (2008) further explains, this kind of passion can control the person in the sense that he/she cannot help but to participate; as such, it can result in rigid persistence, even leading the person to eventually become dependent on the activity. This is, however, still passion in that people enjoy pursuing the activity in question, but this pursuit will conflict with other activities or other aspects of the person's life.

The main lesson emerging from research on passion is that it can indeed be seen to contribute to the fuel that creates long-term engagement with a treasured activity, and Vallerand (2012) also reports that (just like DMCs) passion helps people to carry out tasks that are not necessarily enjoyable themselves, for example the sometimes relentless, deliberate practice that is indispensable in sport or music training. Of the two types of passion, the ideal background for persistence has been found to be harmonious rather than obsessive passion. This makes sense, because for motivated behaviour to be sustainable in the long run, it needs to be harmonised with – and sometimes to take the back seat to – the events and obligations of everyday life, and harmonious passion offers the flexibility to do so.

Motivational breakdown cover: Persistence and self-control

We have seen earlier (CHALLENGE$_{10}$/INNOVATION$_4$) that motivated action can be frustrated, and even halted, by demotivating influences. These can involve a wide range of factors, from internal temptation to external humiliation, and as such, they constitute a major impediment to long-term motivation. This means that even when someone is energised by solid, passionate, long-term motivation, unexpected setbacks can occur and cancel it out; indeed, Beltman and Volet (2007) report that past longitudinal examinations of sustained motivation showed that "Even the most motivated students experienced self-doubt and periods of reduced interest which required the external support of parents and teachers to overcome" (p. 315). Accordingly, the ability to withstand the diverting pulls of various motivational obstructions can be seen as a key ingredient of the ability to pursue sustained action.

When we start exploring the educational psychological literature with a focus on what can help people to stand firm and stick to their plans, the overwhelming impression we are likely to have is that (a) there has been a *lot* written recently on the various facets of personality strength and self-control, using a *wide range of labels* such as grit, resilience, coping capacity, hardiness, buoyancy, conscientiousness, mental toughness, perceived control, self-efficacy, self-regulation and even optimism; but (b) the many persistence-related constructs appear to *overlap* greatly. They all concern in one way or another individual agency exercising self-discipline and willpower in the face of distractions and setbacks, that is, the capacity to overcome "the natural tendency to quit" (Peterson & Seligman, 2004, p. 234) in the face of discouraging or disrupting impulses. As Peterson and Seligman further explain, most acts of such self-regulation involve "stopping the self from having a response, such as when a dieter refrains from eating a tempting but fattening food" (p. 500). Currently the concept of 'grit' (mentioned briefly in the previous section) appears to be a particularly popular persistence-related notion (see e.g. Duckworth & Eskreis-Winkler, 2015; for an SLA application, see Teimouri, Plonsky & Tabandeh, in press), but as we shall see below, this may well be due to the saleability of the catchy term (especially in educational circles) as well as the charismatic personality of the main champion of the concept, Angela Duckworth, and her high-profile promotion work in the media (e.g. a TED talk). Let us examine more closely two challenging aspects of the various self-control dimensions: the *overlapping nature* of the different conceptualisations and *assessment* issues.

Overlapping theoretical constructs

There are numerous variations of human functioning in the face of adversity, and in many cases it may not be a straightforward task to unambiguously match them with theoretically defined categories. What complicates the matter further is that many of the terms introduced are also used in everyday communication with somewhat different or flexible meanings. These factors have resulted in the introduction of a number of overlapping persistence-related terms in the psychological literature; for example, Peterson and Seligman (2004) submit that 'self-control' is

> sometimes used as a synonym for self-regulation, but other writers use it more narrowly to refer specifically to controlling one's impulses so as to behave in

a moral fashion. The term self-discipline is also related to self-regulation and usually is used in a somewhat narrower sense, such as to refer to making oneself do things that one does not want to do and resisting temptation.

p. 500

In comparing self-control with the concept of grit, Vazsonyi et al. (2019) explain that whereas self-control is more concerned with sustaining an *ongoing* task with a focus on *desisting* from distractions (i.e. placing the emphasis on an avoidance system in the present), grit tends to be used in relation to doggedly pursuing *longer-term* goals and is thus more linked to an *approach* motivation system. Although this distinction may sound convincing, in actual practice the two aspects often go hand in hand: the determined, 'gritty' pursuit of a long-term goal would be expected to subsume self-control over one's everyday temptations and, similarly, resisting temptation in the present is often best energised by one's determination to pursue future goals. Indeed, Duckworth and Gross (2014, p. 320) admit that "It is perhaps no wonder that self-control and grit are often used interchangeably by laypeople and scientists alike. These two determinants of success are highly correlated" (p. 320). Grit has also been found to correlate highly with one of the Big Five dimensions (CHALLENGE$_i$/INNOVATION$_i$), 'conscientiousness' (Rimfield et al., 2016), and Duckworth et al.'s (2007) interpretation of this relationship further illuminates the complexity of the issue:

> Conscientious individuals are characteristically thorough, careful, reliable, organized, industrious, and self-controlled. Whereas all of these qualities bear a plausible contribution to achievement, their relative importance likely varies depending upon the type of achievement considered … Grit overlaps with achievement aspects of conscientiousness but differs in its emphasis on long-term stamina rather than short-term intensity.

p. 1089

Let us also consider briefly another well-known persistence factor, 'resilience.' As Chmitorza et al. (2018, p. 79) summarise, this has been understood by some scholars as the capacity to bounce back after a traumatic event – that is, as a "trajectory of recovery" – and as such, it has been distinguished from another construct, 'stress resistance,' which involves "maintaining homeostasis and a stable adaptive functioning when faced with adversity" (ibid). Other scholars, however, consider these two factors merely two facets of the same phenomenon, and one may also wonder how different these facets are from another high-profile persistence factor, 'hardiness,' which has been defined as "a pattern of attitudes and strategies that together facilitate turning stressful circumstances from potential disasters into growth opportunities" (Maddi, 2013, p. 8) – indeed, Maddi submits that "Hardiness has been put forward as the pathway to resilience under stress" (p. 9). Furthermore, resilience has also been compared with another well-known concept in the literature, 'academic buoyancy' (Martin & Marsh, 2009; see also Yu, Hiver & Al-Hoorie,

2018, for an SLA application). Fong and Kim's (in press) summary expresses well the overlapping nature of the two terms as they appear to differ only in degree, concerning 'chronic' versus 'mild' adversities: "In contrast to academic resilience, which refers to students' ability to successfully deal with chronic and acute academic adversities in their school settings, academic buoyancy primarily focuses on bouncing back from daily and mild adversities" (p. 3).

These examples suffice to illustrate that the differences between the various persistence-specific constructs largely lie in how broadly or narrowly they are defined, what timescale they occupy, which facet of adversity they are concerned with and how they are assumed to navigate the difficulty in question. In the end, the distinctions often boil down to a matter of emphases, which explains why the scholarly community has been rather inconsistent in the use of the various monikers to refer to the different types of persistence (for insightful discussions of the proliferation of persistence-related terms, see for example Duckworth et al., 2019; Fong & Kim, in press; Howard & Crayne, 2019; Sheldon et al., 2015; Vazsonyi et al., 2019).

Assessment issues

The issue of the absence of firm defining boundaries for the various persistence-related factors comes to a head in empirical research where the assessed variables need to be precisely operationalised. Leys et al.'s (in press) conclusion about resilience can be seen as typical of the whole domain:

> "Since resilience is a term which alludes to a complex process, it becomes not only difficult to define but also difficult to measure ... This variety of measurements highlights the imprecision of the theoretical framework."
>
> *p. 2*

Over the past 15 years, a sizeable research industry has emerged in educational psychology examining various persistence-related factors and their interrelationships, partly because the protection of goal pursuit in the face of adversity has considerable practical implications, and partly because such studies are fairly easy to design, quick to run and straightforward to analyse. Most of these investigations operationalise persistence-related personal qualities as self-report measures, assessed by means of questionnaires. It is, however, an established principle in survey theory that questionnaires are rather crude measurement instruments, because respondents tend to exert little cognitive energy interpreting and rating questionnaire items; rather, they rely on quick, gut-level evaluations, and any attempt to get respondents to rate other than simple and robust item content usually leads to low reliability (Dörnyei, 2010). This feature of survey instruments simply does not allow for focusing on nuanced theoretical dissimilarities and subtle content differences at the actual measurement level; consequently, as will be illustrated below, many of the empirical results reported in the persistence literature may be merely artefacts of *item wording* rather than conceptual distinctions (see e.g. Vazsonyi et al., 2019).

We have already seen briefly that the definition of grit includes both perseverance and passion for long-term goals, but that the actual items used in established grit-instruments almost entirely focus only on the perseverance dimension (Jachimowicz et al., 2018). Muenks et al. (2017, p. 600) further scrutinised the grit construct, and point out that although the definition of the notion explicitly states *long-term* goals, this longevity aspect is not reflected at the item level (e.g. "I finish whatever I begin"; "Setbacks don't discourage me"; "I am diligent"; "I am a hard worker"). This is particularly problematic in view of the fact that, as seen above, the primary conceptual distinction between grit and self-control concerns the former's emphasis on long-term goals (Duckworth & Gross, 2014). Taking a different angle, Fong and Kim (in press) address the potential overlap between the assessment of grit and academic buoyancy (Martin & Marsh, 2009), with the former including the item "Setbacks don't discourage me" and the latter "I am good at dealing with setbacks in class." While one could argue that the two items represent slightly different perspectives, an average student responding to these two items with little deliberation is likely to rate them on the basis of the same internal belief. Muenks et al.'s review concurs with Fong and Kim's point when they state: "The broad point here … is that each proposed component of grit overlaps to a degree with constructs already in the literature" (p. 601). As these scholars conclude, "Grit, effort regulation, cognitive self-regulation, and engagement overlap greatly conceptually and empirically, and so it is not surprising that each explain about the same amount of variance in an important achievement outcome" (p. 616).

Lessons emerging from the persistence literature

Much of the burgeoning literature on persistence-related issues is taken up by comparing the different constructs against each other or validating them against real-life measures such as perseverance and performance in education and other achievement situations (e.g. the military). While these studies generally confirm that persistence matters, we have seen above that the various constructs are intercorrelated and that no particular conceptualisation of persistence appears to stand out. There have also been, however, some other, generalisable lessons emerging from the extensive research efforts. In the following I will summarise four issues relevant to the understanding of long-term motivation: the question as to whether the capacity to persist is a trait; lessons offered by the famous 'Marshmallow test'; practical strategies to promote self-control; and the relationship between vision and persistence.

Is the capacity to persist a trait?

Some people appear to be more persistent than others, with their demonstrated self-control manifested across a variety of goals and situations. This observation has led researchers to propose that the capacity to persist is a relatively stable personality trait that functions as a predictor of perseverance and personal success (see e.g. Howard & Crayne, 2019). This domain-general, trait-level conceptualisation has been, however, questioned by scholars who highlight the significance of situational factors, and regard persistence as a kind of coping capacity that is centred around the ongoing appraisal of stressors and obstacles as well as the application of appropriate resources to work through them (e.g. Beltman & Volet, 2007). Coping research has indeed identified several adaptive and maladaptive patterns in dealing with difficulties and, as a result, recent scholarship has conceptualised coping as part of a "complex adaptive system that includes stress, resilience, and competence. Although no consensus exists about the specifics of such a perspective, it seems clear that coping operates at multiple levels and across several different time scales" (Skinner & Zimmer-Gembeck, 2007, p. 137). We have thus two, seemingly conflicting, approaches to the understanding of the human capacity to resist diverting temptations and to deal with setbacks, but the discussion in Chapter 1 of MacAdams's New Big Five model suggests that there does not have to be a conflict between trait-level and situation-specific conceptions of personal qualities, as they can be conceived at different levels of situatedness at the same time. We can illustrate this point further by taking a look at the concept of 'resilience.'

Broadly speaking, the psychological definition of *resilience* concerns positive functioning in the face of adversity (e.g. King & Trent, 2013). As Masten (2018) summarises, the buffering of the individual from the effects of difficulties has been attributed to a variety of factors, such as "a trait, a process, an outcome or pattern of the life course, or a broad conceptual domain that encompasses all these ideas" (p. 14). Indeed, thriving in adverse conditions can involve a bit of all these elements, ranging from a trait-like capability to bounce back from setbacks (as some people do seem to exhibit better levels of functioning than others who experience the same adversity) to strategic adaptation to respond to challenges in a flexible and inventive way, which would thus involve an interaction of the individual's unique resources with specific situational factors (see e.g. Goodman et al., 2017; Rutter, 2012; Windle, 2011). There is therefore widespread agreement that resilience-boosting, goal-protective factors operate across a number of levels, and in a recent overview entitled "Perspectives on resilience: Personality trait or skill?" Leys et al. (in press) conclude that "It is currently impossible to determine with certainty the nature of the trait or skill of resilience" (p. 5). The following description of the 'Marshmallow test' will offer further insights into this matter.

The Marshmallow test

No discussion of the nature of persistence would be complete without describing one of the most famous experiments in psychology, the 'Marshmallow test,' which sheds unique light on both the trait-like and the strategic aspects of self-control. The test involved a series of studies in the late 1960s and early 1970s at Stanford University, led by Walter Mischel (e.g. 2014) on 'delayed gratification,' which is the ability to persevere and resist temptation of an immediate reward in preference for a later reward. Accordingly, participating preschool children were offered a simple choice: they could receive one small reward *immediately* or two small rewards if they waited for a short period, approximately *15 minutes*. The children varied in their choices and also in how long they were able to persist if they chose to wait, and the astonishing subsequent discovery came when follow-up studies unambiguously showed that children who were able to wait longer tended to have better life outcomes as adults; as Mischel recounts:

> Around age twenty-five to thirty, those who had delayed longer in preschool self-reported that they were more able to pursue and reach long-term goals, used risky drugs less, had reached higher educational levels, and had a significantly lower body mass index. They were also more resilient and adaptive in coping with interpersonal problems and better at maintaining close relationships.
>
> *Mischel, 2014, pp. 24–25*

The remarkable finding that effective self-control at an early age can predict positive outcomes in adulthood – including the ability to pursue and reach long-term goals – was replicated in many studies, pointing to the stable and situation-neutral (i.e. trait-like) nature of self-control. However, in analysing the strategies that the children applied to help them to wait successfully, the researchers also identified three common features: (a) the children kept actively reminding themselves of their chosen goal; (b) they monitored their progress towards their goal and made the necessary corrections by shifting their attention and cognitions flexibly between goal-oriented thoughts and temptation-reducing techniques; and (c) they inhibited impulsive responses like thinking about how appealing the temptation was. These observations led Mischel (2014) to assert that "Self-control involves more than determination; it requires strategies and insights, as well as goals and motivation" (p. 230). Reassuringly, he also concluded that the ability to delay immediate gratification for the sake of future consequences is an acquirable cognitive skill: "self-control skills, both cognitive and emotional, can be learned, enhanced, and harnessed so that they become automatically activated when you need them" (ibid).

A further important lesson that Mischel and his colleagues have arrived at (see Mischel, 2014) is that even some people who had done well on the Marshmallow test were later found to fail in exercising self-control, which made Mischel ask a more general question: "Why then do smart people so often act stupidly, managing to unravel the lives they diligently constructed? What trips them up?" (p. 98). He suggests that the answer is related to a host of considerations, including, most notably, how one perceives the specific situation and how the specific issue in question is related to the person's overall motivation: "To be able to delay gratification and exert self-control is an ability, a set of cognitive skills, that, like any ability, can be used or not used depending primarily on the motivation to use it" (p. 198). In other words, even trait-like characteristics are not consistent across all situations and conditions, a point we already addressed in Chapter 1 (CHALLENGE$_1$). Let us continue the examination by looking at the strategic aspects of self-control.

Strategies to reduce the fallibility of self-control

The above discussion showed that no matter how much a person is naturally inclined to persist and exercise self-control, there will be times and situations when he/she may falter. Duckworth et al. (2019) come to the same conclusion when they assert that "the capacity to effortfully enact or inhibit responses is quite fallible" (p. 388). Is it possible to consciously limit this inherent weakness? Mischel's (2014) lifelong research suggests that it is if one applies appropriate strategies. This, of course requires familiarity with relevant strategies, and indeed, Mischel has demonstrated that the knowledge of strategies that can help people against being controlled by temptations and pressures makes a considerable difference in their ability to resist and persist. What is more, he found that "enhancing such understanding ... might be fairly easy to achieve" (p. 40). One useful approach in this respect is devising 'if-then' implementation plans (discussed earlier in this chapter) that can then be automatised through practice, and research over the past decades has also identified several other relevant self-control strategies, from removing distractions from one's environment and seeking support to psychologically distancing oneself from the temptation by inventing fun distractions (e.g. creating games, body movements) (see e.g. Duckworth et al., 2019; Mischel, 2014; Skinner & Zimmer-Gembeck, 2007). Significantly, these strategies may include the use of mental imagery (see Chapter 5): for example, when asked how to make easy the waiting for the marshmallows, Simon (age nine) told Mischel, "I have at least a thousand imaginary characters in my head, like those little toy figures I have in my room, and in my imagination I just take them out and play with them – I make up stories, adventures" (p. 39). Let us conclude this section by examining the relationship between visualisation and self-control more closely.

Visualisation and self-control

In a fascinating study that has even reached TV news bulletins, Hershfield et al. (2011) used visual stimuli to increase people's pension saving intentions, that is, to shift their mindsets from short-term rewards (spending money now) to prioritising long-term benefits. The researchers designed an instrument that, by means of virtual reality hardware and 'ageing' software, allowed the participants to see an image of their old-age appearance, thereby making their pensioner persona more realistic. This visual short-circuiting of present and future had a dramatic effect on the participants' financial disposition as they all exhibited an increased tendency to allocate more resources towards their future retirement funds. Baumeister and Bargh (2014) also report findings that showed that simulating the future outcome in the mind's eye helped people to overcome more immediately tempting stimuli; as these researchers explain, "A vivid conscious thought of these desired outcomes can bolster the otherwise feeble wish to do the right thing" (p. 45). The mental time travel literature (see Chapter 5) offers further evidence that episodic future thinking can help to maintain the value of future goals that would otherwise be discounted because of their distance in time: Peters and Büchel (2010) found that high-imagery participants significantly outperformed their low-imagery counterparts in this respect, and O'Donnell, Daniel and Epstein (2017) explain that by letting people imagine themselves in the future accomplishing their goal, episodic future thinking helps them to resist the immediate gratification of giving in to temptation, because taking a longer-term view allows them to consider the value of future rewards fully. Consistent with these findings, Peterson and Seligman (2004) make the following general point in this regard:

> Most acts of self-control involve overcoming some incipient response to the immediate situation in order to pursue some greater, long-term benefit. Hence the ability to transcend the immediate situation is crucial. People who live only in the present moment are unlikely to exhibit good self-control, whereas future-mindedness will facilitate self-regulation.
>
> *pp. 510–511*

Summary

We began this chapter by pointing out that for various reasons the study of long-term motivation has remained an undertheorised topic in motivational psychology. The discussion, then, outlined a broad framework of motivational processes and factors that together can sustain motivation in the long run. The resulting construct accommodates a number of components whose joint operation can be meaningfully elucidated by using an extended motoring metaphor:

- In order to undertake a long car journey, we need high-octane fuel (self-concordant vision) that not only provides the initial energy but which is also capable of reigniting the engine after each stop during the intermittent ride.
- To make the fuel last longer, we can turn the car into being as fuel-economic as possible (through conserving energy through habits and behavioural routines).
- To make the fuel last even longer, we can regenerate some of the used-up fuel by organising the journey in a strategic way (by including regular subgoals, progress checks, affirmative feedback and social support, as well as by building up momentum).
- We may add some extra fuel (through building up positive emotionality around the project, approximating passion).
- Finally, we can obtain an effective breakdown cover that will enable us to deal with any hindrances (through strategic self-control and gritty resilience).

All of the components involved in this construct lend themselves to some degree of training and strategic improvement, thereby opening up various avenues to fostering long-term motivation consciously.

References

Adler, P. (1981). *Momentum: A theory of social action*. Beverly Hills, CA: Sage.

Amabile, T., & Kramer, S. (2011). *The progress principle: Using small wins to ignite joy, engagement, and creativity at work*. Boston, MA: Harvard Business Review Press.

Bandura, A., & Schunk, D. (1981). Cultivating competence, self-efficacy and intrinsic interest through proximal self-motivation. *Journal of Personality and Social Psychology, 41*, 586–598.

Bandura, A., & Simon, K. M. (1977). The role of proximal intentions in self-regulation of refractory behavior. *Cognitive Therapy and Research, 1*(3), 177–193.

Baumeister, R. F., & Bargh, J. A. (2014). Conscious and unconscious: Toward an integrative understanding of human mental life and action. In J. W. Sherman, B. Gawronski & Y. Trope (Eds.), *Dual-process theories of the social mind* (pp. 35–49). New York: Guilford Press.

Baumeister, R. F., & Vohs, K. D. (2007). Self-regulation, ego depletion, and motivation. *Social and Personality Psychology Compass, 1*(1), 115–128.

Beltman, S., & Volet, S. (2007). Exploring the complex and dynamic nature of sustained motivation. *European Psychologist, 12*(4), 314–323.

Briki, W. (2017). Rethinking the relationship between momentum and sport performance: Toward an integrative perspective. *Psychology of Sport and Exercise, 30*, 38–44.

Briki, W., & Markman, K. D. (2018). Psychological momentum: The phenomenology of goal pursuit. *Social and Personality Psychology Compass, 12*(e12412), 1–14.

Chmitorza, A., Kunzlera, A., Helmreicha, I., Tüschera, O., Kalischa, R., Kubiaka, T., Wessaa, M. & Lieb, K. (2018). Intervention studies to foster resilience: A systematic review and proposal for a resilience framework in future intervention studies. *Clinical Psychology Review, 59*, 78–100.

Dörnyei, Z. (2010). *Questionnaires in second language research: Construction, administration, and processing* (2nd ed.). New York: Routledge.

Dörnyei, Z., & Murphey, T. (2003). *Group dynamics in the language classroom*. Cambridge: Cambridge University Press.

Dörnyei, Z., Henry, A., & Muir, C. (2016). *Motivational currents in language learning: Frameworks for focused interventions*. New York: Routledge.

Dörnyei, Z., Muir, C., & Ibrahim, Z. (2014). Directed motivational currents: Energising language learning through creating intense motivational pathways. In D. Lasagabaster, A. Doiz & J. M. Sierra (Eds.), *Motivation and foreign language learning: From theory to practice* (pp. 9–29). Amsterdam: John Benjamins.

Duckworth, A. L., & Eskreis-Winkler, L. (2015). Grit. In J. D. Wright (Ed.), *International encyclopedia of the social & behavioral sciences* (2nd ed., Vol. 10, pp. 397–401). Amsterdam: Elsevier.

Duckworth, A. L., & Gross, J. J. (2014). Self-control and grit: Related but separable determinants of success. *Current Directions in Psychological Science, 23*(5), 319–325.

Duckworth, A. L., Peterson, C., Matthews, M. D., & Kelly, D. R. (2007). Grit: Perseverance and passion for long-term goals. *Journal of Personality and Social Psychology, 92*(6), 1087–1101.

Duckworth, A. L., Taxer, J. L., Eskreis-Winkler, L., Galla, B. M., & Gross, J. J. (2019). Self-control and academic achievement. *Annual Review of Psychology, 70*, 373–399.

Ehrlich, C. (in press). The goal-striving reasons framework: Further evidence for its predictive power for subjective well-being on a sub-dimensional level and on an individual goal-striving reasons level as well as evidence for its theoretical difference to self-concordance. *Current Psychology*, 1–14.

Fong, C. J., & Kim, Y. W. (in press). A clash of constructs? Re-examining grit in light of academic buoyancy and future time perspective. *Current Psychology*, 1–14.

Frijda, N. H. (2007). *The laws of emotion*. Mahwah, NJ: Lawrence Erlbaum.

Goodman, F. R., Disabato, D. J., Kashdan, T. B., & Machell, K. A. (2017). Personality strengths as resilience: A one-year multiwave study. *Journal of Personality*, *85*(3), 423–434.
Grant, A. M., & Shin, J. (2012). Work motivation: Directing, energizing, and maintaining effort (and research) In R. M. Ryan (Ed.), *The Oxford handbook of human motivation* (pp. 505–519). New York: Oxford University Press.
Guenther, C. L., & Kokotajlo, C. (2017). Psychological momentum and risky decision-making. *Journal of Theoretical Social Psychology*, *1*, 43–51.
Hattie, J., & Timperley, H. (2007). The power of feedback. *Review of Educational Research*, *77*(1), 81–112.
Henry, A. (2020). Directed motivational currents: Extending the theory of L2 vision. In M. Lamb, K. Csizér, A. Henry & S. Ryan (Eds.), *Palgrave Macmillan handbook of motivation for language learning* (pp. 139–161). Basingstoke: Palgrave.
Hershfield, H. E., Goldstein, D. G., Sharpe, W. F., Fox, J., Yeykelis, L., Carstensen, L. L., & Bailenson, J. N. (2011). Increasing saving behavior through age-progressed renderings of the future self. *Journal of Marketing Research*, *48*, 823–837.
Hofer, M. (2010). Adolescents' development of individual interests: A product of multiple goal regulation? *Educational Psychologist*, *45*(3), 149–166.
Howard, M. C., & Crayne, M. P. (2019). Persistence: Defining the multidimensional construct and creating a measure. *Personality and Individual Differences*, *139*, 77–89.
Hubbard, T. L. (2017). Toward a general theory of momentum-like effects. *Behavioural Processes*, *141*, 50–66.
Iso-Ahola, S. E., & Dotson, C. O. (2014). Psychological momentum: Why success breeds success. *Review of General Psychology*, *18*(1), 19–33.
Iso-Ahola, S. E., & Dotson, C. O. (2016). Psychological momentum: A key to continued success. *Frontiers in Psychology*, *7*(1328), 1–7.
Iso-Ahola, S. E., & Dotson, C. O. (2017). Momentum and elite performance. *Journal of Nature and Science*, *3*(3:e325), 1–10.
Jachimowicz, J. M., Wihler, A., Bailey, E. R., & Galinsky, A. D. (2018). Why grit requires perseverance and passion to positively predict performance. *PNAS*, *115*(40), 9980–9985.
Jansen, K. J. (2004). From persistence to pursuit: A longitudinal examination of momentum during the early stages of strategic change. *Organization Science*, *15*(3), 276–294.
King, L. A., & Trent, J. (2013). Personality strength. In H. A. Tennen, J. I. Suls & I. B. Weiner (Eds.), *Handbook of psychology, Vol. 5: Personality and social psychology* (2nd ed., pp. 197–222). New York: Wiley.
Leys, C., Arnal, C., Wollast, R., Rolin, H., Kotsoua, I., & Fossion, P. (in press). Perspectives on resilience: Personality trait or skill? *European Journal of Trauma & Dissociation*, 1–6.
Maddi, S. R. (2013). *Hardiness: Turning stressful circumstances into resilient growth*. Dordrecht, the Netherlands: Springer.
Markman, K. D., & Guenther, C. L. (2007). Psychological momentum: Intuitive physics and naive beliefs. *Personality and Social Psychology Bulletin*, *33*(6), 800–812.
Markus, H., & Nurius, P. (1987). Possible selves: The interface between motivation and the self-concept. In K. Yardley & T. Honess (Eds.), *Self and identity: Psychosocial perspectives* (pp. 157–172). Chichester: John Wiley & Sons.
Martin, A. J., & Marsh, H. W. (2009). Academic resilience and academic buoyancy: Multidimensional and hierarchical conceptual framing of causes, correlates and cognate constructs. *Oxford Review of Education*, *35*(3), 353–370.
Masten, A. S. (2018). Resilience theory and research on children and families: Past, present, and promise. *Journal of Family Theory & Review*, *10*, 12–31.

Mercer, S., & Dörnyei, Z. (2020). *Engaging language learners in contemporary classrooms*. Cambridge: Cambridge University Press.

Mischel, W. (2014). *The marshmallow test: Understanding self-control and how to master it*. London: Corgi.

Moskowitz, G. B. (2014). The implicit volition model: The unconscious nature of goal pursuit. In J. W. Sherman, B. Gawronski & Y. Trope (Eds.), *Dual-process theories of the social mind* (pp. 400–422). New York: Guilford Press.

Muenks, K., Wigfield, A., Yang, J. S., & O'Neal, C. R. (2017). How true is grit? Assessing its relations to high school and college students' personality characteristics, self-regulation, engagement, and achievement. *Journal of Educational Psychology, 109*(5), 599–620.

Muir, C. (in press). *Directed motivational currents and language education: Exploring implications for pedagogy*. Bristol: Multilingual Matters.

Müller, T., & Apps, M. A. J. (2019). Motivational fatigue: A neurocognitive framework for the impact of effortful exertion on subsequent motivation. *Neuropsychologia, 123*, 141–151.

Muraven, M. (2012). Ego depletion: Theory and evidence. In R. M. Ryan (Ed.), *The Oxford handbook of human motivation* (pp. 111–126). New York: Oxford University Press.

Muraven, M., Tice, D. M., & Baumeister, R. F. (1998). Self-control as limited resource: Regulatory depletion patterns. *Journal of Personality and Social Psychology, 74*(3), 774–789.

O'Donnell, S., Daniel, T. O., & Epstein, L. H. (2017). Does goal relevant episodic future thinking amplify the effect on delay discounting? *Consciousness and Cognition, 51*, 10–16.

Peters, J., & Büchel, C. (2010). Episodic future thinking reduces reward delay discounting through an enhancement of prefrontal-mediotemporal interactions. *Neuron, 66*, 138–148.

Peterson, C., & Seligman, M. E. P. (2004). *Character strengths and virtues: A handbook and classification*. Washington, DC: American Psychological Association.

Pizzolato, J. E. (2006). Achieving college student possible selves: Navigating the space between commitment and achievement of long-term identity goals. *Cultural Diversity and Ethnic Minority Psychology, 12*(1), 57–69.

Rimfield, K., Kovas, Y., Dale, P. S., & Plomin, R. (2016). True grit and genetics: Predicting academic achievement from personality. *Journal of Personality and Social Psychology, 11*(5), 780–789.

Robertson, I. (2002). *The mind's eye: An essential guide to boosting your mental power*. London: Bantam Books.

Rutter, M. (2012). Resilience as a dynamic concept. *Development and Psychopathology, 24*, 335–344.

Sheldon, K. M. (2014). Becoming oneself: The central role of self-concordant goal selection. *Personality and Social Psychology Review, 18*(4), 349–365.

Sheldon, K. M., & Elliot, A. J. (1999). Goal striving, need satisfaction, and longitudinal well-being: The self-concordance model. *Journal of Personality and Social Psychology, 76*(3), 482–497.

Sheldon, K. M., Jose, P. E., Kashdan, T. B., & Jarden, A. (2015). Personality, effective goal-striving, and enhanced well-being: Comparing 10 candidate personality strengths. *Personality and Social Psychology Bulletin, 41*(4), 575–585.

Sheldon, K. M., Prentice, M., & Osin, E. (2019). Rightly crossing the Rubicon: Evaluating goal self-concordance prior to selection helps people choose more intrinsic goals. *Journal of Research in Personality, 79*, 119–129.

Skinner, E. A., & Zimmer-Gembeck, M. J. (2007). The development of coping. *Annual Review of Psychology, 58*, 119–144.

Stajkovic, A. D., & Sergent, K. (2019). *Cognitive automation and organizational psychology: Priming goals as a new source of competitive advantage*. New York: Routledge.

Székely, M., & Michael, J. (2018). Investing in commitment: Persistence in a joint action is enhanced by the perception of a partner's effort. *Cognition, 174*, 37–42.

Teimouri, Y., Plonsky, L., & Tabandeh. (in press). L2 grit: Passion and perseverance for second language learning. *Language Teaching Research*.

Thorsen, C., Henry, A., & Cliffordson, C. (in press). The case of a missing person? The current L2 self and the L2 Motivational Self System. *International Journal of Bilingual Education and Bilingualism*.

Vallerand, R. J. (2008). On the psychology of passion: In search of what makes people's lives most worth living. *Canadian Psychology, 49*(1), 1–13.

Vallerand, R. J. (2012). From motivation to passion: In search of the motivational processes involved in a meaningful life. *Canadian Psychology, 53*(1), 42–52.

Vallerand, R. J., Blanchard, C., Mageau, G. A., Koestner, R., Ratelle, C., Léonard, M., Gagné, M., & Marsolais, J. (2003). Les pde l'âme: On obsessive and harmonious passion. *Journal of Personality and Social Psychology, 85*(4), 756–767.

Vallerand, R. J., Colavecchio, P. G., & Pelletier, L. G. (1988). Psychological momentum and performance inferences: A preliminary test of the antecedents-consequences psychological momentum model. *Journal of Sport & Exercise Psychology, 10*, 92–108.

Vazsonyi, A. T., Ksinan, A. J., Jiskrova, G. K., Mikuška, J., Javakhishvili, M., & Cui, G. (2019). To grit or not to grit, that is the question! *Journal of Research in Personality, 78*, 215–226.

Voerman, L., Meijer, P. C., Korthagen, F. A. J., & Simons, R. J. (2012). Types and frequencies of feedback interventions in classroom interaction in secondary education. *Teaching and Teacher Education, 28*, 1107–1115.

Waterman, A. S. (1993). Two conceptions of happiness: Contrast of personal expressiveness (eudaimonia) and hedonic enjoyment. *Journal of Personality and Social Psychology, 64*(4), 678–691.

Windle, G. (2011). What is resilience? A review and concept analysis. *Reviews in Clinical Gerontology, 21*, 152–169.

Wood, W., & Neal, D. T. (2007). A new look at habits and the habit–goal interface. *Psychological Review, 114*(4), 843–863.

Yu, S., Hiver, P., & Al-Hoorie, A. H. (2018). Academic buoyancy: Exploring learners' everyday resilience in the language classroom. *Studies in Second Language Acquisition, 40*, 805–830.

CONCLUSION

There is no 'one-size-fits-all' conclusion for a book like the current one that covers such a wide range of issues, because too many of the lines of inquiry addressed are ongoing and would therefore require their own individual summaries. While reviewing the recent developments in motivation research during the preparation of this book, I experienced again the same feeling of wonder about the vast intricacy of the field that initially drew me to this domain; I was genuinely impressed that after 35 years of active research on motivation I still came across completely new areas with exciting and unexpected potential. This, of course, merely confirms what we have long known, namely that a complex question such as why human beings behave and think as they do cannot have a simple answer. In fact, the real question is whether we should expect any straightforward answers at all. That is, with motivation involving so many dimensions and conditions, and with all of the components interacting with each other in both linear and nonlinear ways, is it indeed realistic to expect some generalisable regularities to emerge?

Personally, I lean towards an affirmative response. Without question, we are unlikely to ever be able to completely fine-tune our predictions about how human beings will behave, but this is something that every social scientist has to come to terms with. Unlike in the natural sciences, where the molecules of a cell, if treated identically, will respond identically, in the social sciences where the units of analysis are human beings, behaviour – even that of identical twins – will show variation in response to any given stimulus. However, the very fact that the social sciences have thrived as a field is proof that even amongst the diversity of humanity we can identify robust trends that are meaningful for scientific research. For the past century, motivation research has been seeking to uncover such enduring human tendencies and has achieved reasonable success in this search. While questions will always remain, there are some motivational areas which, on balance, scholars have mapped out reasonably well. Perhaps the most relevant of these to the current book is short-term student motivation: notwithstanding contextual and cultural variations, past research has successfully documented the main relevant factors and has accumulated a fair amount of knowledge of what motivates students to engage in learning activities. The first three chapters of this book highlighted some problematic aspects in this area, offering a number of constructive solutions and innovations.

However, research over the past century has also demonstrated that the field will always move on once a box has been ticked, and the last three chapters of the current book outlined three as yet 'unticked boxes,' the issues of unconscious motivation, vision and long-term motivation. The reason why these topics have remained relatively unexplored for so long is that the big issues they concern required special, dedicated theoretical frameworks, research strategies and workable methodologies, which had not until recently been in place:

- Academic psychology in general has had an ambivalent relationship with the unconscious mind, hence the ambivalent treatment of unconscious motivation.
- Academic psychology has had a turbulent relationship with the notions of internal sensation and visionary imagination, hence the ambivalent treatment of vision.
- Finally, academic psychology has had an ambivalent relationship with the notion of time, hence the ambivalent treatment of long-term motivation.

And yet, it seems that the ice has finally been broken in all three areas, as a number of fruitful research avenues have been initiated and successfully pursued over the past two decades. Research on these subjects promises a considerable pay-off for our understanding of language learning motivation:

- Because of the complex role that language plays in our lives at multiple levels – personal, social and societal – unconscious L2 attitudes and motives are an inevitable corollary of SLA. These implicit psychological undercurrents can undermine even the best-laid plans and efforts, but if we learn to harness their power, they can also become assets.
- Because developing language competence is a holistic, whole-person enterprise, the utilisation of one of the most powerful and remarkable human faculties – the faculty of vision/mental imagery – can become a hugely profitable learning strategy. L2 motivation research has opened the door into this direction and the outcome, the L2 Motivational Self System, has proved to be successful. However, vision/mental imagery has even more to offer to the field of SLA as a whole, from memory enhancement to the teaching of various language skills. Indeed, the central tenet of the Pedagogic Creed of eminent American philosopher and educational reformer John Dewey (1897) was that one of the most important aspects of education in general is vision-building, or as he termed it, 'image-formation.'

- Because second language acquisition is one of those educational strands that require long and sustained learning histories in order to achieve any usable working knowledge, the success of learning an L2 ultimately depends on whether we can inspire sufficient long-lasting learning commitment in our students. In order to build up a repertoire of strategies to promote such long-term motivation, we have to identify its key constituents and their interrelationships as a prerequisite.

It is thus safe to predict that these three themes will remain ongoing emphases for the L2 motivation research community. There will undoubtedly be other new issues arising, but it is difficult to imagine that our field will move on without first making considerable strides in these domains. So, as the material in this book shows, we have ample to be getting on with!

Reference

Dewey, J. (1897). My pedagogic creed. *School Journal, 54*(3), 77–80.

AUTHOR INDEX

Aarts, H. 79, 83–84, 86, 89, 97, 123, 129, 134
Abel, E. 73
Achtziger, A. 11, 17
Addis, D. R. 108, 134
Adler, P. 146–151, 162
Adolphs, S. 58, 62, 70, 73
Ajzen, I. 30, 45
Alfawzan, M. 122, 129
Al-Hoorie, A. H. 36, 44–45, 47–48, 66–67, 69, 72, 74, 81–82, 91–92, 95–97, 126, 129–130, 155, 165
Allexandre, D. 135
Amabile, T. 144, 162
Ames, C. 26, 45
Ames, R. 26, 45
Anderson, J. R. 85, 96
Andrade, J. 106, 110, 128
Anyidoho, N. A. 19
Apps, M. A. J. 140, 164
Arano, K. 24, 49
Arao, H. 58, 73
Araújo, A. M. 19
Arisandy, F. E. 62, 65, 72
Armor, D. A. 111, 134
Arnal, C. 163
Asendorpf, J. B. 92, 99
Ash, S. R. 18
Atkinson, J. W. 7, 12, 17, 20

Baars, B. J. 76, 96
Baba, K. 69, 73
Baddeley, A. D. 104–106, 110, 128

Bailenson, J. N. 163
Bailey, E. R. 163
Ballard, T. 36–37, 40, 45, 47
Ballhausen, N. 19
Bandura, A. 36, 45, 58, 70, 144, 162
Bargh, J. A. 16–17, 20, 76–77, 82–83, 85–87, 96–98, 160, 162
Baumeister, R. F. 16–18, 20, 77–78, 82–83, 87, 97, 121–122, 128, 140, 160, 162, 164
Beck, J. 38, 48
Becker, M. 99
Bell, B. S. 89, 99
Beltman, S. 23–24, 49, 136, 144, 154, 158, 162
Benoit, R. G. 107, 134
Berg, J. L. 114, 128
Berntsen, D. 108, 133
Berridge, K. C. 15, 18, 120–121, 123, 128
Bértolo, H. 104, 128
Blanchard, C. 165
Boo, Z. 29, 45, 51, 54, 69–70, 95, 97, 101, 128
Boroojerdi, B. 132
Boudreau, C. 34, 46
Bowles, A. R. 72
Boyd, J. N. 13, 20
Brass, M. 99
Braver, T. S. 51–52, 70, 121, 129
Briki, W. 149–150, 162
Brogaard, B. 104, 128
Bronfenbrenner, U. 24–25, 46
Browman, A. S. 8–9, 18
Brown, C. 19

Author index

Brown, J. D. 68, 70
Büchel, C. 161, 164
Buck, R. 14, 18
Buckner, R. L. 108, 134
Busse, V. 125, 129

Cameron, L. 67, 73
Carlsmith, K. M. 14, 19
Carstensen, L. L. 163
Carver, C. C. 13, 18, 19, 45–46
Cattaneo, Z. 103, 106, 129
Cerf, M. 97, 130
Chaabene, H. 134
Chabot, H. F. 14, 19
Chamari, K. 134
Chan, H. 73
Chan, L. 69–71, 75, 125, 130, 135
Chang, C.-H. D. 13, 18
Chapelle, C. A. 61, 72
Cheng, C. M. 99
Chiew, K. S. 121, 129
Chiu, C.-J. 27, 48
Chmitorza, A. 155, 162
Clark, B. C. 113, 129
Clark, L. 70
Claro, J. 126, 129
Clément, R. 31, 34, 44, 46–49, 73, 132
Cliffordson, C. 115, 134, 140, 165
Cohen, A. D. 56, 71
Colavecchio, P. G. 149, 165
Collet, C. 113, 132
Corballis, M. C. 108, 134
Cornoldi, C. 129
Costa, P. T. Jr. 5, 18
Covington, M. 54, 71
Crayne, M. P. 156–157, 163
Crocker, L. D. 14, 18
Crookes, G. 52, 71
Csizér, K. 69, 74, 124, 129, 135
Cui, G. 165
Cumming, J. L. 102, 129
Curtis, R. 110, 129
Custers, R. 79, 83–84, 86, 89, 97, 123, 129, 134

D'Argembeau, A. 107–109, 129
Dale, P. S. 164
Daniel, T. O. 161, 164
Danziger, K. 2–3, 54–55, 71
de Bot, K. 32–33, 35, 46, 49, 66, 75
De Houwer, J. 91–92, 97
de Jong, P. J. 92, 98
De Volder, M. L. 13, 18
Decety, J. 103, 129

Deci, E. L. 26, 46
Deeprose, C. 133
Della Sala, S. 106, 135
Dembo, M. H. 31, 48
Destin, M. 8, 18
Dewaele, J.-M. 34, 46, 122, 129
DeWall, C. N. 128
Dewar, M. 106, 135
Dewey, J. 167–168
Disabato, D. J. 130, 163
Dominik, T. 80, 97
Dostál, D. 97
Dotson, C. O. 148–150, 163
Douglas Fir Group 23, 25, 43, 46
Duarte, A. M. 19
Duckworth, A. L. 56–57, 71, 152, 154–157, 160, 162
Dunton, B. C. 97
Dweck, C. S. 8, 18, 27, 59–61, 71, 74

Eccles, J. S. 16, 18, 119, 135
Ehrlich, C. 137, 162
Eichstaedt, J. 92, 99
Elicker, J. D. 13, 18
Elliot, A. J. 127, 130, 138, 164
Ellis, N. C. 83, 97
Engelmann, J. B. 52, 74
Entin, E. E. 12, 20
Epstein, L. H. 121, 130
Epstein, S. 161, 164
Eskreis-Winkler, L. 71, 154, 162
Essex, M. J. 132

Falout, J. 59–60, 71
Fastame, M. C. 129
Fazio, R. H. 91, 93, 97
Feltz, D. L. 111, 130
Ferguson, M. J. 76, 97
Fillenbaum, S. 98
Fishbein, M. 30, 45
Foltys, H. 132
Fong, C. J. 13, 19, 156–157, 162
Forstmeier, S. 19
Fossion, P. 163
Fox, J. 163
Frank, V. M. 72
Freud, S. 16, 78, 97, 110
Freynik, S. 72
Fried, I. 80–81, 97, 103, 130–131
Frijda, N. H. 121, 130, 153, 162
Funder, D. C. 24–25, 48

Gagné, M. 165
Galinsky, A. D. 163

Galla, B. M. 71, 162
Galton, F. 105, 110, 130
Ganis, G. 103, 131
Gardner, R. C. 29–31, 46, 65, 72, 98, 126–127, 130
Gatzia, D. E. 104, 128
Gawronski, B. 87, 99
Gazzaniga, M. S. 103, 130
Genoud, P. 24, 46
Gerritsen, M. 99
Gilbert, D. T. 107–108, 116, 118, 130
Ginns, P. 57, 73
Gleason, C. A. 79, 98
Glover, T. 70
Goldberg, L. R. 5, 19
Goldstein, D. G. 163
Göllner, L. M. 13, 19
Gollwitzer, P. M. 11, 17, 19, 107, 118, 130, 133
Golonka, E. M. 62, 72
Gomes, A. I. 19
Goodman, F. R. 119, 130, 158, 163
Gould, D. 112, 134
Gountouna, V.-E. 135
Govorun, O. 99
Graham, S. 26–27, 46
Grant, A. M. 136, 163
Greenwald, A. G. 91, 97
Gregersen, T. 69, 72
Gregg, M. 112, 130
Grèzes, J. 103, 129
Grosche, M. 92, 98
Gross, J. J. 71, 155, 157, 162
Guenther, C. L. 148–149, 163
Guerrero, M. D. 112, 132
Guillot, A. 113, 132
Gurtner, J.-L. 24, 46

Hadamard, J. 100–101, 130
Hall, C. 102, 110, 130
Hall, C. R. 112, 113, 130
Hall, E. 130
Han, Y. 8, 19
Han, Z. 42, 47
Hassin, R. 76, 97
Hattie, J. 145, 163
Hausenblas, H. A. 113, 130
Haynes, J.-D. 99
Heckhausen, H. 10–11, 19, 38, 46
Heggestad, E. D. 8, 19
Heift, T. 61, 72
Heinze, H.-J. 99
Heller, W. 18
Helmreicha, I. 162

Hendriks, M. 89, 97
Henry, A. 9, 18, 53, 56–57, 62, 65, 70–73, 97, 115, 124–125, 130–131, 134, 140, 142, 151, 162–163, 165
Hershfield, H. E. 160, 163
Hertz-Lazarowitz, R. 114, 132
Hessel, G. 125, 127, 131
Heyes, S. B. 131, 133
Higgins, E. T. 115, 131
Hodgson, R. C. 98
Hofer, M. 39–41, 47, 141, 163
Hoffman, B. 88, 97
Holland, R. W. 89, 92, 97
Holmes, E. A. 119, 131, 133
Holt, R. R. 111, 131
Hong, J.-J. 27, 48
Horikawa, T. 104, 131
Horn, I. S. 28, 47
Hornstra, L. 78, 98
Howard, M. C. 156–157, 163
Hoyle, R. H. 122, 131
Hruska, B. J. 26
Huang, Y. T. 19
Hubbard, T. L. 148–149, 163
Huijding, J. 92, 98
Husman, J. 13, 19

Iberri-Shea, G. 67, 74
Ibrahim, Z. 142, 162
Infantolino, Z. P. 18
Irie, K. 69, 72
Iso-Ahola, S. E. 148–150, 163
Ivry, R. B. 103, 130
Izard, C. E. 121–122, 131

Jachimowicz, J. M. 153, 157, 163
Jackson, J. R. 97
Jacobs, C. 107, 131
James, L. 109, 133
Janeiro, I. N. 13, 19
Janiszewski, C. 89, 98
Jansen, K. J. 150, 163
Jarden, A. 164
Järvelä, S. 27, 49
Javakhishvili, M. 165
Ji, J. L. J. 122, 131
Jiskrova, G. K. 165
Johnson, P. J. 131
Johnson, R. E. 13, 18
Jose, P. E. 131
Juvonen, Y. 27, 47

Kalischa, R. 162
Kamitani, Y. 131

Kamsteega, A. 98
Kanfer, R. 8, 19
Kaplan, B. 19
Kappes, A. 117–118, 131
Karpinski, A. 92, 98
Kashdan, T. B. 130, 163–164
Kauffman, D. F. 13, 19
Kehr, H. M. 133
Kelly, D. R. 162
Kiefer, M. 93, 98
Kihlstrom, J. F. 82–83, 87, 93, 98
Kikuchi, K. 59, 68, 72, 74
Kim, T.-Y. 59–60, 72, 74
Kim, Y. W. 13, 18, 156–157, 162
Kim, Y.-K. 59, 72
King, L. A. 158, 163
King, R. B. 22, 47
Kiosseoglou, G. 116, 132
Klauer, K. C. 99
Klein, S. B. 108, 132
Kliegel, M. 19
Klinger, E. 100, 131
Knäuper, B. 118, 131
Koch, C. 103, 131
Koestner, R. 7, 19, 79, 98, 165
Kohari, N. E. 18
Kokotajlo, C. 149, 163
Kormos, J. 53, 71–72
Korthagen, F. A. J. 165
Kosslyn, S. M. 103, 105, 110, 131–133
Kotsoua, I. 163
Kouzes, J. M. 114, 131
Kovas, Y. 164
Kramer, S. 144, 162
Krantz, L. H. 131
Kreiman, G. 80, 97, 103, 130–131
Krings, T. 132
Kruglanski, A. W. 94, 99
Ksinan, A. J. 165
Kubanyiova, M. 114, 116, 124, 127, 130–131
Kubiaka, T. 162
Kuhl, J. 10–11, 19, 38, 46
Kunda, Z. 86, 98
Kunzlera, A. 162
Kurland, H. 114–115, 132

Lafford, B. A. 23, 47
Lamb, M. 56, 62, 65, 72
Lambert, C. 53, 73
Lambert, W. E. 29, 46, 65, 72, 90, 98, 127, 130
Landers, D. M. 111, 130
Lara, P. 125, 134
Larsen-Freeman, D. 23, 42–44, 47, 67, 73

Latham, G. P. 82–85, 90, 94, 96, 98–99
Law, T. D. 129
Lawrence, J. W. 13, 19
Lebon, F. 113, 132
Legate, N. 16, 20, 67, 74, 76, 99
Lens, W. 13, 18–19
Léonard, M. 165
Leondari, A. 116, 132
Levin, I. M. 114, 132
Levine, B. 107, 133
Lewthwaite, R. 52, 73
Leys, C. 156, 158, 163
Libet, B. 78–80, 82, 98
Lieb, K. 162
Liegel, N. 98
Liu, J. Z. 133
Locke, E. A. 82–83, 98, 117, 132
Logie, R. H. 135
Lord, R. G. 13, 18
Lou, N. M. 8, 19, 60–61, 73
Lowie, W. 42, 49, 66, 67, 73, 75
Lüke, T. 92, 98
Lundberg, K. 93, 99

Machado, M. A. 19
Machell, K. A. 130, 163
MacIntyre, P. D. 31, 33–34, 44–47, 49, 56, 67, 69, 71–73, 120–122, 132
Mack, D. E. 113, 130
MacKay, E. 73
MacKisack, M. 110, 135
MacLeod, C. 131
Maddi, S. R. 156, 163
Maehr, M. L. 27, 47
Mageau, G. A. 165
Mahaj, J. 97
Mahato, N. K. 129
Mangun, G. R. 103, 130
Manian, N. 116, 132
Marek, M. W. 64, 73
Markman, K. D. 148–149, 162–163
Markus, H. R. 22, 47, 86, 98, 109, 116–117, 123, 132–133, 138, 163
Marsh, H. W. 155, 157, 163
Marsolais, J. 165
Martin, A. J. 57, 73, 155, 157, 163
Masicampo, E. J. 78, 82, 97
Maslow, A. H. 26, 47, 111, 132
Masten, A. S. 158, 163
Matthews, A. 119, 131
Matthews, G. 15, 19
Matthews, M. D. 162
Mayer, J. D. 14–15, 19
McAdams, D. P. 5–9, 19

McClelland, D. C. 7–8, 19, 26, 47, 78–79, 90, 93–94, 98
McConnell, N. L. 18
McCrae, R. R. 5, 18
McDonough, K. 8, 19
McFarlane, K. A. 108, 132
McGhee, D. E. 91, 97
McGonigle, D. J. 135
McInerney, D. M. 22, 47
McLean, K. C. 9, 19
Medvedeff, M. E. 18
Meijer, P. C. 165
Meister, I. G. 103, 132
Melnikoff, D. E. 86–87, 98
Mercer, S. 8, 20, 53, 56–57, 61, 63, 73, 144, 164
Miarka, B. 134
Michael, J. 145, 165
Michaelian, K. 108, 132
Mikuška, J. 165
Miller, E. R. 23, 49
Miller, G. A. 18
Miloyan, B. 108, 132
Mischel, W. 141, 158–160, 164
Miyawaki, Y. 131
Modell, A. H. 103, 132
Molden, D. C. 8, 18
Monnard, I. 24, 46
Moors, A. 97
Morgan, W. G. 90, 98
Morris, T. 112, 132
Moskowitz, G. B. 86, 98, 140, 164
Moulton, S. T. 103, 105, 131–132
Mozgalina, A. 53, 73
Muenks, K. 157, 164
Muir, C. 9, 18, 53, 56, 58, 70–71, 73, 97, 142–143, 162, 164
Mukamel, R. 80, 97
Müller, M. 132
Müller, T. 140, 164
Mumford, M. D. 114, 134
Munroe-Chandler, K. J. 112, 132
Muraven, M. 140, 164
Murphey, T. 58, 73, 146, 162
Murphy, S. M. 112, 135

Nakamura, S. 53, 73
Nakazawa, M. 129
Naselaris, T. 133
Neal, A. 36–37, 40, 45, 47
Neal, D. T. 141, 165
Nejjari, W. 91, 99
Nelissen, R. M. A. 119, 132
Neumann, M.-L. 79, 99

Nitta, R. 69, 73
Noels, K. A. 8, 19, 31, 46–47, 60–61, 73
Nolen, S. B. 28, 31, 47
Norton, J. D. 100, 132
Nurius, P. 109, 116, 123, 132, 138, 163

O'Donnell, S. 161, 164
O'Hare, A. J. 18
O'Neal, C. R. 164
Oettingen, G. 107, 117–118, 131–133
Onians, J. 110, 135
Ortega, L. 42, 47, 67, 74
Osin, E. 139, 164
Ottó, I. 11, 18, 38, 46, 55, 71
Otto, S. E. K. 61, 74
Oyserman, D. 109, 116–117, 133

Paivio, A. 104–106, 108, 112–113, 130, 133
Pak, H.-j. 117, 133
Palombo, D. J. 106–107, 133
Pals, J. L. 6, 19
Papadakis, A. A. 132
Papi, M. 8, 20, 43, 47, 61, 75
Papworth, B. 57, 73
Paris, S. G. 31, 47
Parrish, M. W. 112, 135
Paunesku, D. 61, 74
Payne, B. K. 91–93, 99
Pearl, D. K. 98
Pearson, D. G. 105–106, 133
Pearson, J. 102, 133
Pelletier, L. G. 149, 165
Penke, L. 92, 99
Peretz, H. 114, 132
Pessoa, L. 52, 74
Peters, J. 161, 164
Peterson, C. 141, 145, 151, 154, 161, 162, 164
Peterson, S. J. 99
Pham, L. B. 111, 134
Philp, J. 53, 73
Piniel, K. 69, 74
Pintrich, P. R. 9, 20, 27, 29, 31, 47
Pizzolato, J. E. 138, 164
Planken, B. 99
Plomin, R. 164
Plonsky, L. 154, 165
Pon, G. 31, 47
Posner, B. Z. 114, 131
Pota, S. 98
Poupore, G. 53, 74
Prentice, M. 139, 164
Prior, M. T. 122, 133
Procházka, R. 97

Ranganathan, V. K. 113, 133, 135
Rasmussen, K. W. 108, 133
Ratelle, C. 165
Rauthmann, J. F. 22–24, 48
Rawolle, M. 115–116, 123, 133
Raynor, J. O. 12, 17, 20
Reeve, J. 120, 133
Reichardt, R. 99
Renaud, O. 107, 129
Riazi, A. M. 68, 74
Richardson, D. L. 72
Richardson, J. T. E. 106, 133
Rigby, C. S. 62, 74
Rimfield, K. 155, 164
Rivkin, I. D. 111, 134
Robertson, I. 102, 104, 113, 133, 141, 164
Roeder, G. P. 12, 20
Rogers, C. R. 111, 133
Rolin, H. 163
Romero, C. 74
Roseman, M. 131
Ross, J. 73, 120, 132
Rubenfeld, S. 31, 48
Rueda, R. 31, 48
Rutishauser, U. 97, 130
Rutter, M. 158, 164
Ryan, R. M. 2–3, 16, 20, 26, 41, 46, 48, 62, 66–67, 74, 76, 99
Ryan, S. 5–6, 8, 18, 20, 23, 29, 45–46, 51, 60–61, 69–73, 128

Sahgal, V. 133
Salili, F. 27, 48
Sampson, R. J. 35, 48
Samuels, M. 111, 133
Samuels, N. 111, 133
Sánchez-Lozano, E. 70
Sato, M. 125, 134
Schacter, D. L. 107–108, 116, 134
Scheier, M. F. 13, 18–19, 45–46
Scherer, K. R. 15, 20, 39, 48
Schiefele, A. 16, 18
Schmidt, R. 52, 71, 74
Schnetter, K. 117, 133
Schultheiss, O. C. 79, 99, 133
Schunk, D. H. 9, 20, 27, 29, 47, 144, 162
Schwartz, J. L. K. 91, 97
Schwarzkopf, D. S. 107, 131
Sedláčková, Z. 97
Seginer, R. 13, 19
Seligman, M. E. P. 141, 145, 151, 154, 161, 164
Sergent, K. 85, 99, 138, 165

Serroul, A. 34, 47
Sevincer, A. T. 107, 117–118, 133
Shah, J. Y. 94, 99
Shantz, A. 84–85, 99
Sharpe, W. F. 163
Sheldon, K. 5, 8, 20, 82–83, 87, 99, 137–139, 156, 164
Sheldon, S. 133
Sherman, J. W. 87, 99
Sherman, R. A. 24, 48
Sherrill, M. R. 122, 131
Shin, J. 136, 163
Siemionow, V. 133, 135
Silvanto, J. 103, 107, 129, 131
Simon, K. M. 36, 45, 144, 162
Simons, R. J. 165
Şimşek, E. 7, 20
Singer, D. G. 128, 134
Singer, J. L. 110, 115, 128, 134
Singmann, H. 118, 131
Sitzmann, T. 89, 99
Skinner, E. A. 158, 160, 164
Slimani, M. 113, 134
Smith, E. N. 74
Snyder, C. R. 119, 134
Song, B. 60, 74
Soon, C. S. 80–81, 99
Sorrentino, R. M. 16, 20
Spruyt, A. 97
Stajkovic, A. D. 82, 85, 98–99, 138, 165
Steinman, R. B. 92, 98
Ste-Marie, D. M. 102, 129
Stewart, B. D. 99
Stockwell, G. 61–65, 74
Stradling, P. 130
Strange, J. M. 114, 134
Strasser, A. 133
Strauman, T. J. 132
Suddendorf, T. 108, 132, 134
Sundqvist, P. 65, 72
Symons, C. 1, 3
Syngollitou, E. 116, 132
Székely, M. 145, 165
Szpunar, K. K. 107–108, 116, 132, 134

Tabandeh, F. 154, 165
Takahashi, S. 52, 74
Tamaki, M. 131
Taxer, J. L. 71, 162
Taylor, S. E. 102, 111–112, 118–120, 134
Teige-Mocigemba, S. 91, 93, 97, 99
Teimouri, Y. 154, 165
Thomas, J. S. 129
Thomas, V. 110–111, 122, 134

Thompson, W. L. 103, 131
Thorner, N. 59, 74
Thorsen, C. 57, 65, 72, 115, 125, 131, 134, 139, 165
Thron, A. 132
Tice, D. M. 140, 164
Timperley, H. 145, 163
Tod, D. 134
Tomkins, S. S. 120, 134
Töpper, R. 132
Torrens, L. A. 135
Trent, J. 158, 163
Trope, Y. 87, 99
Turner, J. C. 31, 47
Tüschera, O. 162

Unsworth, K. 38, 40, 48
Urdan, T. C. 27, 48
Ushioda, E. 10, 20, 28–29, 31–32, 37, 45–46, 48–49, 51–52, 64, 66, 69, 74, 125–126, 134

Vallacher, R. R. 9, 20
Vallerand, R. J. 149, 152–153, 165
Valsiner, J. 24, 49
Valstar, M. 70
van der Helm, R. 100, 115, 134
Van der Linden, M. 107–109, 129
van Dijk, M. 73
van Hout, R. 99
Vancouver, J. B. 36–37, 40, 45, 47
Vazsonyi, A. T. 155–156, 165
Vecchi, T. 129
Veltkamp, M. 123, 134
Verheija, L. 98
Verspoor, M. H. 42, 49, 66, 73, 75
Vincze, L. 122, 132
Vlaeva, D. 62, 75
Voerman, L. 145, 165
Vohs, K. D. 17–18, 20, 78, 82, 97, 128, 140, 162
Volet, S. 27, 31, 49, 136, 144, 154, 158, 162

Walker, C. J. 1, 3
Wallace-Hadrill, S. M. A. 133
Waller, L. 1, 3
Walton, G. M. 74
Waninge, F. 35, 49, 91, 99
Ward, C. J. 28, 47
Warren, S. L. 18

Waterman, A. S. 151, 165
Watkins, N. W. 106–107, 134
Weinberg, R. S. 112, 134
Weinberger, J. 8, 19, 79, 98
Weiner, B. 7, 9, 16, 20, 26–27, 49, 67, 75, 120–121, 135
Wentura, D. 98
Wentzel, K. R. 27, 47, 49
Wessaa, M. 162
Wigfield, A. 16, 18, 119, 135, 164
Wihler, A. 163
Wilby, J. 53, 72
Williams, C. J. 97
Williams, M. 30, 49
Wilson, G. M. 2–3
Wilson, H. B. 2–3
Wilson, T. D. 107–108, 116, 118, 130
Windle, G. 158, 165
Wollast, R. 163
Wong, A. E. 9, 20
Wood, W. 141, 165
Woolfolk, R. L. 112, 135
Wosnitza, M. 23–24, 49
Wright, E. W. 79, 98
Wu, W.-C. V. 64, 73
Wulf, G. 52, 73
Wyer, R. S. J. 89, 98

Yang, J. S. 164
Yanguas, Í. 53, 75
Yao, W. X. 113, 135
Yashima, T. 24, 49
Yeager, D. S. 8, 18, 60–61, 71, 74
Yeo, G. 38, 48
Yeykelis, L. 163
Yim, O. 31, 34, 44, 49
You, C. J. 69, 75, 124–125, 135
Young, D. 130
Yu, S. 155, 165
Yue, G. H. 133, 135

Zeidner, M. 15, 19
Zeman, A. 106, 110, 135
Zhang, G. 53, 73
Zhang, L. 128
Zielina, M. 97
Zimbardo, P. G. 13, 20
Zimmer-Gembeck, M. J. 158, 160, 164
Zovko, M. 98
Zuengler, J. 23, 49

SUBJECT INDEX

affect/emotion 4–5, 14–16, 39, 53, 57, 93, 108, 111, 119–123, 139, 143, 151–152, 161; emotion and velocity 13; *see also* passion
Affect Misattribution Procedure 91–92
agent/agency 43–55, 77–78, 81–82, 95, 139, 154
aphantasia 106–107, 110
attention and motivation 52
attitudes *see* language attitudes
attributions/attribution theory 9, 25, 60, 147; misattribution 88, 90–92

behavioural routine 96, 141–143, 161; *see also* habit
behaviourism 16, 78–79, 84, 89, 110–111; conditioning 79, 84, 89, 123
Big Five personality model 5–6
buoyancy 154–157

cognitive control 51
complex dynamic systems (approach/theory) 32, 38–39, 41–45, 65–70, 82, 95; dynamics of self-images 125
conglomerates *see* motivational conglomerates
conscientiousness 5, 154–155
conscious vs. unconscious motivation 15–17; *see also* unconscious motivation
context 21–32, 42; Bronfenbrenner's division of context 24–25

contingent path theory 12
coping 59, 112–113, 154, 158–159
culture 22

daydreaming 100, 110, 138
demotivation and remotivation 59–61
directed motivational current (DMC) 12, 53, 96, 142–145, 147
DMC *see* directed motivational current
dual coding theory 104–106, 112
dual-process theories 16, 87–88
dynamic systems theory *see* complex dynamic systems

Einstein's vision 100–101
emotion *see* affect/emotion
engagement 56–58
Evaluative Priming Task 91, 93

feedback 62, 119, 121, 145, 161
free will 17, 44, 77, 81–82
Freud, S. 16, 78, 110

Gardner's theory of motivation 29–31, 126–127; Attitude/Motivation Test Battery 31; integrative motivation 30, 126
goals: chronic 85–86, 96, 123, 138; goal configuration 39–40; goal prioritisation 40–41; goal setting 36, 58, 79, 83–85; proximal subgoals 36, 143–144
grades *see* rewards and grades
grit 13, 152, 154–155, 157, 161

Subject index

habit 16, 40, 85–86, 138, 141–143, 161
hardiness 154–155

IAT *see* Implicit Association Test
ideal (L2) self *see* possible selves
idiodynamic method 33–34, 69
Implicit Association Test (IAT) 91–92, 95
implicit motivation 78–79, 90–91, 93–94, 139
integrative motivation *see* Gardner's theory of motivation
intervention studies 67–68

L2 learning experience 58, 124
L2 Motivational Self System 58, 101, 109, 124–128, 167; *see also* possible selves; L2 learning experience
language attitudes 30; unconscious language attitudes 95
longitudinal research 67
long-term motivation 35–36, 43, 123, 136–161, 167–168

Marshmallow test 158–159
Martin Luther King Jr.'s vision 101
Matched-Guise Technique 90–91, 95
mental contrasting 117–118
mental imagery: definition 101–103; *see also* vision
mental time travel 107–109, 116, 160
mindsets 8, 10–11, 38, 59, 60–61, 149, 160
misattribution *see* attributions/attribution theory
mixed methods research 68–69
momentum *see* psychological momentum
motivation, definition of 1–2
motivational dynamics *see* complex dynamic systems
motivational conglomerates 70
motivational strategies 53–56

narrative identity 6–7, 9
need for achievement 7–8, 79, 94
New Big Five personality model (McAdams) 5–7

ought-to L2 self *see* possible selves

passion 151–154, 157, 161
persistence 84, 136–139, 145, 153–161
person-in-context approaches 31, 42; *see also* Person-in-Context Relational View of Motivation

Person-in-Context Relational View of Motivation (Ushioda) 31–32, 44–45
phenomenological account of motivation 14–15
Picture-Story Exercise 90
possible selves 107–109, 115–116; ideal self 61, 115, 124–125, 128; ideal L2 self 61–62, 123–127; ought-to L2 self 123–125
priming 80–81, 84–5, 88–89, 91, 93–94, 123–124, 127; cross-modal priming 89; subliminal priming 81, 88, 92; supraliminal priming 88–89
process imagery 117–118
process models of motivation 10–11, 38–39, 55
progress check 58, 143–145, 161
projective test 90, 93
prospection 107
proximal subgoal 33, 36, 143–145
psychological momentum 12, 14, 33, 62, 145–151, 123–124, 138
psychological situation 24–25

qualitative research 28–29, 31, 66–67, 69–70

remotivation *see* demotivation and remotivation
resilience 13, 119, 154–156, 158, 161
retrodictive qualitative modelling 69–70
rewards and grades 54
role models/modelling 58–59

self-control 137, 140–141, 153–161
self-discipline 154–155
self-discrepancy theory 115–118
self-efficacy 69, 144, 149, 154
self-regulation 17, 140–121, 154–155, 157, 161
social motivation 26–27, 30
student engagement *see* engagement
subliminal/supraliminal priming *see* priming

task-based motivation 52–53
TAT *see* Thematic Apperception Test
technology and motivation 61–65
testing/assessing motivation 65–70; *see also* longitudinal research; mixed methods research; qualitative research; retrodictive qualitative modelling
Thematic Apperception Test (TAT) 79, 90
time perspective 13
timescales 32–36, 67

trait vs. state motivation 4–5, 7–9; in persistence 157–158

unconscious motivation 76–99, 167; in SLA 95–96; *see also* conscious vs. unconscious motivation

velocity 13–14, 144–145, 147–148, 151
vision 36, 82, 86, 100–135, 167; in business 113–114; corporate 114; in DMCs 96, 143; and emotions *see* affect/emotion; and hope 119; and psychological momentum 146–147; self-concordant 137–139, 144, 161; and self-control 160–161; in sport 112–113

willingness to communicate 56
willpower 140, 154
working memory 51–52, 77, 104–107, 128

Made in the USA
Middletown, DE
13 February 2024